Making Leisure Provision for People with Profound Learning and Multiple Disabilities

Making Leisure Provision for People with Profound Learning and Multiple Disabilities

Edited by

J. Hogg

Director, White Top Centre and White Top Research Unit,
University of Dundee, UK

and

J. Cavet

Senior Lecturer, School of Social Sciences,
University of Staffordshire, UK

CHAPMAN & HALL

London · Glasgow · Weinheim · New York · Tokyo · Melbourne · Madras

Published by Chapman & Hall, 2–6 Boundary Row, London SE1 8HN, UK

Chapman & Hall, 2–6 Boundary Row, London SE1 8HN, UK

Blackie Academic & Professional, Wester Cleddens Road, Bishopbriggs, Glasgow G64 2NZ, UK

Chapman & Hall GmbH, Pappelallee 3, 69469 Weinheim, Germany

Chapman & Hall USA, One Penn Plaza, 41st Floor, New York NY 10119, USA

Chapman & Hall Japan, ITP-Japan, Kyowa Bulding, 3F, 2-2-1 Hirakawacho, Chiyoda-ku, Tokyo 102, Japan

Chapman & Hall Australia, Thomas Nelson Australia, 102 Dodds Street, South Melbourne, Victoria 3205, Australia

Chapman & Hall India, R. Seshadri, 32 Second Main Road, CIT East, Madras 600 035, India

Distributed in the USA and Canada by Singular Publishing Group Inc., 4284 41st Street, San Diego, California 92105

First edition 1995

© 1995 Chapman & Hall

Typeset in 10/12pt Palatino by Mews Photosetting, Beckenham, Kent
Printed in Great Britain by St Edmundsbury Press, Bury St Edmunds, Suffolk

ISBN 0 412 41150 4   1 56593 125 4 (USA)

A catalogue record for this book is available from the British Library

Library of Congress Catalog Card Number: 94-72669

♾ Printed on permanent acid-free text paper, manufactured in accordance with ANSI/NISO Z39.48–1992 and ANSI/NISO Z39.48–1984 (Permanence of Paper).

Contents

vi   *Contents*

Contributors

Freda Abbro, Parent and educator of people with learning disabilities, Banstead, Surrey

Howard Bailey, Manager, The Spastics Society Recreation Services, Nottingham

Judith Cavet, Senior Lecturer in Social Work, Dept. of Sociology, University of Staffordshire

Professor James Hogg, Director, White Top Research Unit and Centre, Dept. of Social Work, University of Dundee

Loretto Lambe, PAM15 Projects Director, White Top Research Unit, University of Dundee

Mark Leach, Pro-motion officer, The Spastics Society, London

Suzie Mitchell, Educational Psychologist, Borough of Camden, London

Helen Mount, Coordinator, Mencap PIMD Section, Manchester

Carol Ouvry, Independent Special Education Advisor, Ross-on-Wye, Herefordshire

Nick Pronger, Director, Brilliant Computing, Bradford

Helen Sanderson, Development Officer, Mancunian Community Health NHS Trust, Manchester

Foreword

Leisure has become a central preoccupation of society and the individual in the second half of the 20th century. The provision of leisure is now of paramount significance in the economy of many countries, with tourism the largest single world industry. From a past when only the privileged few had time to spare we have moved to a situation in which access to the leisure pursuits of our choice is viewed as an essential prerequisite for a good quality of life. For many of us, but by no means all, leisure time will occupy the largest single proportion of our waking life from the age of 18 years onwards.

People with disabilities, as well as many other minority groups, have in the past been disadvantaged in their opportunity to participate in this expansion in leisure provision. In part this has stemmed from assumptions about the feasibility of their accessing many types of leisure pursuit coupled with a lack of concern to eliminate the barriers that lead to exclusion.

This situation has now changed radically. There can be few, if any, activities left from which people with disabilities are excluded. Rose and Massey (1993) report not only on successful climbs up Kilimanjaro and the Alps by people with severe and profound learning disabilities, but on role reversals in these settings, in which the individuals with learning disabilities became the helpers and sustainers of their peers without disabilities. Nevertheless, even though this expansion of activities is the case, in reality barriers still remain – physical, organizational and attitudinal (Lawton, 1993).

People with profound intellectual disability and multiple physical and/or sensory impairments have, until the past decade, been particularly disadvantaged in their access to leisure. This situation reflects not only the complexity of their needs and our failure to appreciate what they require to enhance the quality of their lives, but perhaps a too exclusive concern with their therapeutic, medical and education needs, initially justifiable after decades of neglect. As noted in Chapter 2 of this book, parents' and carers' need for advice on, and access to, leisure provision remains great.

The extent to which change has come, however, is reflected in a number of initiatives with which the editors, as well as the authors, of this volume have been involved. Cavet (1989), in a European Commission supported study, has documented developments in several countries (summarized here in Chapter 3) in a wide range of service models reflecting both specialized and integrated provision. Lambe (1990) has brought together and described a variety of initiatives and activities in a distance training pack, discussed here in Chapter 14. The pack was the outcome of extensive work by Mencap's PRMH Project during the 1980s in which, through surveys, discussion with parent groups and contact with professionals, a clearer view of what was required was refined and developed in several areas, including leisure. The success of this venture has been confirmed by Mencap's setting up of its Profound Intellectual and Multiple Disabilities Section, showing a commitment to people with profound and multiple disabilities and their carers. In addition, PAMIS (Profound and Multiple Impairment Service), a new registered charity, is now engaged in an extensive national dissemination programme with parents and carers in which consideration of leisure provision plays an important part.

If these initiatives account for the editors' immediate impetus to produce this book, we nevertheless wish to acknowledge how broadly based has been the movement to provide leisure opportunities for people with profound disabilities. All the contributors to this volume and the work of others that they cite have played a key role in moving this field forward.

The impact of their work, however, is highly dependent upon wider changes in society's attitudes to profound disability and its willingness to share resources and opportunities on an equitable basis. In part this is a matter of education of public attitudes and of professionals in other fields, such as those in local authority recreation service departments. It also entails a commitment to imaginative thinking, innovation and a sensitivity to the aspirations of those with profound disabilities to realize ways of ensuring access to leisure.

The present volume focuses essentially on engagement in specific activities, rather than offering a detailed account of models of leisure provision. At present the situations in which leisure is offered are almost certainly biased towards specialist provision. However, as in other areas of disability, the trend is increasingly towards provision of leisure opportunities in integrated settings, where engagement takes place alongside and with peers. A model for such integration is clearly provided in Reed's (1991) development of the Meldreth games, and is vividly demonstrated in his recent accompanying videotape of the games.

This book sets out to offer a resource that will enable the interested reader to supplement his or her existing skills and to improve what is offered to those with whom they work or for whom they care. It also gives pointers as to how training may be given to front-line staff and volunteers, and to areas where further collection and dissemination of information, as well as research, would be beneficial. Its principal justification will be its usefulness to those who work with people with profound disabilities, and the extent to which the latter's quality of life is enhanced.

Cavet, J. (1989) *Occupational and Leisure Activities for People with Profound Retardation and Multiple Impairments: A Study of Creative Activities to Facilitate Social Integration*, Hester Adrian Research Centre, University of Manchester, Manchester.

Lambe, L. (1990) *Leisure Resource Training Pack for People with Profound and Multiple Disabilities*, Mencap, London.

Lawton, M. (1993) From Startrac to leisure choice: the first slow steps towards change, in *Disabling Barriers – Enabling Environments*, (eds J. Swain, V. Finkelstein, S. French and M. Oliver) Sage and Open University, London, pp. 178–85.

Reed, L. (1991) *Games with a New Look for All Ability Levels*, The Spastics Society, Meldreth, Herts.

Rose, S. and Massey, P. (1993) Adventurous outdoor activities: an investigation into the benefits of adventure for seven people with severe learning difficulties, *Mental Handicap Research*, **6**, 287–301.

Part One

Present Provision and Needs

Sources of information about the leisure of people with profound and multiple disabilities

Judith Cavet

'Like other people, intellectually disabled individuals need the personally developing and socially integrating influence of play to become fully participating and satisfied members of our society' (Lyons, 1986a, p. 229). By the word 'play', Lyons means to indicate the whole area of leisure and recreation. The need for the leisure of people with learning disability to be considered seriously within a philosophy which emphasizes an ordinary and valued lifestyle is well established (see, for example, Wertheimer, 1983; Shearer, 1986; Fain 1986). However, less well recognized is the need of people with profound and multiple disabilities for leisure, although attention has been paid to their education (for example, by Hogg and Sebba, 1986; Evans and Ware, 1987; Ouvry,1987; Carpenter and Lewis, 1989) and to their physical management (Golding and Goldsmith, 1986; Simon, 1986; Hogg, Sebba and Lambe, 1990). The aim of this introductory chapter is to indicate what information there is concerning the leisure time of people with profound and multiple disabilities. Information has been drawn from research and from literature produced by practitioners and is intended for a multidisciplinary readership.

WHAT IS LEISURE? A DEFINITION RELEVANT TO THE NEEDS OF PEOPLE WITH PROFOUND AND MULTIPLE DISABILITY

Research indicates that people with learning disability spend their time predominantly in passive, solitary leisure pursuits (Cheseldine and Jeffree, 1981; McConkey, Walsh and Mulcahy, 1981). This is likely to be especially the case for people with profound and multiple disabilities (Hogg and Lambe, 1988). This situation, and Lyons' point above about the value of recreation, is important to bear in mind when considering the leisure needs of people with profound and multiple disabilities.

The definition of leisure has attracted a good deal of academic attention (for one discussion, see Clarke and Critcher, 1985), but a useful starting point in this context is Robert's (1970) somewhat negative definition: 'Leisure can be defined as time that is not obligated and leisure activities can be defined as activities that are non-obligatory' (quoted in Wertheimer, 1983, p. 1). This avoids the problems that arise from those definitions which rest on an assumption that leisure is the converse of work. The view that leisure is time free from employment overlooks the fact that at any one time more than half of the population is not in paid employment, as well as being inappropriate for people with profound and multiple disabilities who are unlikely to be in paid work.

Sometimes there is a lack of clarity about what are leisure activities from the point of view of people with profound and multiple disabilities. Some activities which are labelled 'therapy' when carried out by people with severe and profound learning disability are often regarded as leisure activities when carried out by the general population. One example is the use of the term 'horticultural therapy' for gardening. In contrast to therapies such as physiotherapy, which are necessary on medical grounds, such activities should be regarded as leisure activities if their prime purpose is enjoyment and pleasure. As Tokarski (1985) writes, 'Therapeutics deals with many activities that are in fact leisure activities' (pp. 229–30).

Choice is an essential element in the experience of leisure. The danger of leisure provision being linked to a prescriptive, paternalistic attitude is a noted possibility in the general literature on leisure (see, for example, Smith, 1976; Heeley, 1986). This is an issue which is highlighted in any discussion of leisure provision for people with profound and multiple disabilities because of their dependence on other people for help in meeting their needs. While it is true that the leisure choices of the general population are made 'within the structures of constraint which order their lives' (Clarke and Critcher, 1985, p. 46), there are additional constraints which may affect the ease with which people with profound and multiple disabilities experience the freedom of choice implicit in notions of leisure. As well as being affected by factors such as resource limitations, which may be shared by other groups in society, they may lack the ability to indicate choices or the experiences which make clear what choices there are. A lack of control over their environment may lead to the passivity, depression and withdrawal associated with feelings of learned helplessness (Seligman, 1975), especially if exacerbated by placement in a deprived, unstimulating setting. For these reasons, elements important in any definition of leisure relevant to people with profound and multiple disabilities must place a heavy emphasis on choice, as well as recognizing the need to address the use of free time and provide stimulation and activity. Smith's (1976) definition of leisure for the general population encompasses these priorities: 'leisure involves a qualitative experience of freedom and choice, an experience which may be realized during one's free time and includes a variety of activities and interests' (p. 19).

A VARIETY OF ACTIVITIES AND INTERESTS

A wide range of pleasurable activities can be made available to people with profound and multiple disabilities. Important in this context is the notion of 'partial participation' (Brown *et al.*, 1979). 'Partial participation' means assisting people with severe disabilities to take part in activities they could not otherwise undertake. Such assistance has, no doubt, always been given by some care-givers of people with profound and multiple disabilities. However, its benefits as recognized in the literature are that it improves the quality of life of people with serious disabilities and allows the partial demonstration of skills which were once considered beyond the capabilities of people with profound and multiple disabilities. In addition, 'partial participation' can lead to a pattern of leisure activities which allows for integration into the wider community.

The development of activity provision and its documentation has been uneven. For some activities, no literature exists which deals with the needs of people with profound and multiple disabilities although these activities are undertaken by such people. In such instances texts that make relevant information available are indicated here, although some adaptation or the extra assistance implicit in the notion of partial participation may be necessary. Works which provide an overview of the range of activities available are dealt with before more specialized works are described.

The balance of information available reflects the resources and expertise which have been directed towards the needs of children with profound and multiple disabilities. Extensive and sophisticated coverage of the variety of ways in which sensory stimulation may be offered to such people is given by Longhorn (1988) and Brudenell (1986). Both authors draw on their experience in special education, and Longhorn's book falls clearly within the educational ambit, being an approach to curriculum planning. However, a sensory approach is relevant to adults as well as children, and many of the activities described could suitably be undertaken by adults. Another child-centred publication, *The Wheelchair Child* (Russell, 1989), contains a chapter about 'leisure, play and holiday activities', much of which is relevant to children with profound and multiple disabilities, although also written about more intellectually able children.

A number of newsletters and journals exist which are concerned with the needs of children with multiple disabilities and which contain some information relevant to leisure. From the field of special education comes a newsletter called *PMLD Link* which, as its name suggests, reports on developments in the field of profound and multiple learning difficulties. In addition, the Royal National Institute for the Blind (RNIB) produce a magazine called *Eye Contact*, the subject matter of which is the needs of children with a visual disability and a learning disability. An independent source of information about the needs of children and young people with a sensory disability and a severe learning disability is to be found in *Information Exchange*, which is produced by a group of parents and professionals.

Activities for adults with profound and multiple disabilities tend to have attracted less attention than those for children. One source of short accessible articles is a periodical called *Focus*, which is published by the RNIB and concerns adults affected by both a visual disability and a learning disability. Another source is *Talking Sense*, which is a quarterly publication by SENSE, the association representing the needs of deaf–blind people (see, for example, a discussion of the social and recreational needs of the 'less able deaf–blind person' by Brown, 1988). A videotape which presents an overview of some activities that can be engaged in by adults with profound and multiple disabilities is titled 'Wake-up, It's Daytime'. This is an unpretentious account by staff of the development of a day service for adults with profound disability.

For information about innovations in the pattern of leisure service delivery, relevant to people of all ages, see McConkey and McGinley (1990). This book is about people with all types of learning disability, and some of the chapters contain information about services which would help to meet the leisure needs of people with profound and multiple disabilities. Similarly, a resource pack produced by Play Matters in conjunction with the National Toy Libraries Association (1989) is concerned with the leisure needs of all people with learning disability, but includes descriptions of a variety of activities and many addresses relevant to people with profound and multiple disabilities. The most extensive source of information about leisure activities for people with profound and multiple disabilities is available in the Mencap leisure pack (Lambe, 1991), described in Chapter 14 of this volume. Another specialized publication about activities for people with multiple disabilities is called *Pro-motion – the Resource Guide* and is produced by Cerebral Palsy Sport with the UK Sports Association. This guide contains contributions on leisure activities for people with multiple disabilities written by a number of people with expertise in the field. One emphasis in the guide is upon physical activities, but other means of stimulation are also described.

Special environments

There has been increasing emphasis on improved access to public buildings in recent years, with the aim of enabling disabled people to enjoy leisure pursuits on the same basis as the rest of the community. In addition, some initiatives have been developed within these facilities in order to better meet the needs of disabled people. For an example, see Coles' (1984) account of a tactile exhibition designed to be appropriate for people with a visual disability.

Nevertheless, despite these moves to improve the general accessibility of leisure facilities for people with disabilities, interest remains in developing environments which have been designed especially for people with severe or profound learning disability. One well-known example of these environments is soft play rooms and there is a small amount of literature available on this subject (Lambert, 1984), primarily and appropriately with the focus on children. In a similar category is the use of large-scale inflatables (Sykes, Townsend and Deakin, 1985), although use by adults has also been described (Crisp *et al.*, 1984).

A large-scale environment specially developed for people with severe and profound learning disability which has attracted a great deal of attention in recent years is a sensory environment, developed in the Netherlands and often known under its Dutch name 'snoezelen'. 'Snoezelen' is a contraction of the Dutch words for sniffing and dozing, and is intended to imply a state of relaxation. The word is the registered trade mark of Robinsons & Sons Ltd of Chesterfield, a UK company who manufacture relevant equipment, but has often been used to denote this type of approach and all allied equipment. The Dutch originators of the approach have written a book on the subject (Hulsegge and Verheul, 1987), which is available in a less than totally satisfactory English translation. They describe how the approach was developed in a large Dutch institution and make concrete suggestions about how this type of environment can be established with the aid of modern technology. Chapter 4 of the present volume describes how both 'high-tech' and do-it-yourself 'snoezel' equipment can be made. However, Hulsegge and Verheul emphasize that snoezelen is not about equipment *per se*, but an approach, which they regard as having an emotional component. While their book contains interesting reading material, it is worth noting that the authors' advocacy of the need to 'play along' (p. 29) with the delusions of an old service user with dementia will be unacceptable to many readers. As Haggar and Hutchinson (1991) report, the emphasis in snoezelen environments is upon leisure rather than therapy. Haggar and Hutchinson's (1991) paper describes the development of a snoezelen centre in a Derbyshire hospital, as does a further collection of papers (Hutchinson, 1991). These papers contain useful and practical advice for potential purchasers of equipment, who should, of course, obtain quotations from more than one manufacturer before placing orders. A marketing videotape about snoezelen is available from Rompa, which is part of Robinsons. For a critical discussion of snoezelen, see Whittaker's (1992) brief, but vehement, article on the subject, and Orr's (1993) reflections about the need not to limit a multisensory approach to snoezelen rooms alone.

The arts

The general move to provide equal access to people with disabilities has led to information on the arts for disabled people – see, for example, Attenborough (1985), Pearson (1985) and Levete (1987). These books do not focus solely upon the needs of people with learning disability. For such an approach, see Upton (1979), Astell-Burt (1981), Wood (1983), McClintock (1984), Jennings (1987), Arts for Disabled People in Wales (1989), Segal (1990). Of these texts, McClintock focuses on drama for children, while Jennings, whose topic is also drama, includes a chapter about people with profound disability. Astell-Burt's subject is puppetry, while Wood writes about music.

In general, there is little written specifically about the arts and the needs of people with profound and multiple disabilities. Levete (1982) writes about dance for people with disabilities and generally assumes that participants will be able to follow practical demonstrations allied with verbal instructions. However, Sherborne (1990), in her book about developmental movement for children, does include consideration of the needs of people with profound and multiple disabilities. Moreover, Wood (1982) unusually focuses upon people with profound disability when describing her work as a trained musician in an institutional setting. Brief specialized articles are available concerning workshops run by artists for the residents of a Northumberland hospital for people with learning disability (Scott, 1986), and about a multisensory event on a circus theme for children with profound and multiple disabilities (Horner, 1987). Another source of material regarding a multisensory event is available in the form of a pack called Galaxies (Consortium, ILEA, 1984). Again designed for children, this pack contains slides, an audio tape and instructions as to how to mount a dramatic simulation of going into space. Examples of similar packs developed around other themes are included in Chapter 8. In addition a videotape, titled 'Sounds Like a Rainbow to Me', is available which is a recording of some drama sessions which were organized at Bleasdale school, and which included attention to sensory stimulation. For a further source of information about arts for people with profound and multiple disabilities, see Chapter 8.

Microtechnology

There have been major advances in the field of microtechnology in recent years. Microcomputers have become a feature of many homes and the popularity of their leisure-time use among the general public is borne out by the number of games available for purchase in high-street shops. As regards people with disabilities, both the literature and the available software have in the past generally reflected a situation where microtechnology has been seen either as an enabler of people with physical disabilities or as an educational tool for children with intellectual or physical disabilities. Those interested in pursuing leisure-time applications must therefore consult more general literature concerned with microtechnology when seeking guidance as to how to proceed, and will find a full treatment in relation to profound disability in Chapter 11 of this book.

The fact that microtechnology can introduce infants and young children with profound and multiple disabilities to the idea of cause and effect and encourage their learning is well recognized (Brinker and Lewis, 1982; Behrmann and Lahm, 1984). Indications that people with profound and multiple disabilities enjoy using computers can be derived from studies which focus principally upon other aspects of their use: see, for example, Rostron and Lovatt (1981) for the effects of the provision of microtechnology for children with profound and multiple disabilities, and Seale (1989) on the response of a man with multiple disabilities and displaying self-injurious behaviour. In response to a music program designed for him, the man is described as having 'smiled and giggled, opened his eyes to look at us and continued to press the switch to play the tune' (p. 8).

Useful background information can be found in general books about microtechnology for disabled users (e.g. Saunders, 1984; Heddell, 1985; Hope, 1986; Hope, 1987). However, while such books give an overview of what opportunities can be made available with the correct software and hardware, they are about the applications of technology to the needs of people with disabilities in general. Heddell and Saunders include useful addresses where information, help and advice can be sought. This is a necessary addition as the need for support systems in this context has been noted (Ager, 1985; Douglas, Reeson and Ryan, 1988). There is now a magazine called *Keynotes*, which is devoted to microtechnology for people with learning disability, which may be helpful in this respect.

Specific and detailed information about the use of computers and other microelectronics with profoundly and multiply disabled children is available from the Nottinghamshire special needs unit at Kinder School (Tait, Graham and Watts, 1990), the focus of whose work has been principally educational. Watts has also contributed a chapter specifically about the needs of children with profound and multiple disabilities in the book by Hegarty (1991). This chapter is not primarily concerned with leisure, but the author notes 'new experiences for enjoyment and sensory development' (p. 28) and the potential of microcomputers to provide 'sufficient stimulation to occupy them recreationally for relatively extended periods' (p. 30). Software and other items of equipment are for sale at cost price from Kinder School.

Another source of software developed especially for children and young people with profound and multiple disabilities is a learning package produced by Barnardo's (1991) which is called 'I CAN DO IT'. The 14 programs have been developed with an emphasis on sight, sound and touch, and the package is user friendly. Some of the programs would be suitable for use by adults as well as children. While the emphasis is on learning, enjoyment is likely to result for service users. Detailed reviews are available (e.g. *Keynotes*, 1992; Megarry, 1992; Carpenter, 1992). Like much software that is related to education, these programs are written for the BBC microcomputer. However, there are plans to publish a version for IBM and IBM-compatible computers in the near future. In addition, the British Institute of Learning Disabilities (BILD, until recently known as the British Institute of Mental Handicap or BIMH) have for sale a video tape which shows toys, switches and computers suitable for people with profound and multiple disabilities. The use of the switches, toys and computers is educational in intent, but these devices are utilized because of the rewards they offer and are only effective if service users find them pleasurable. The emphasis in the video tape is on children, but the switches and some of the software demonstrated would also be suitable for adults.

Toys, games and playgrounds

A good source of information about the general background to children's play is *Toys and Playthings* (Newson and Newson, 1979). A book which is specifically about play for children with disabilities is *Play Helps* by Lear (1986), who has experience of working with people with profound and multiple disabilities. The book offers many ideas and instructions for making simple toys, but has more than this to contribute. It is divided into chapters dealing with each sense separately, and on this basis suggests ways of providing sensory stimulation. The book raises awareness of the ways in which each sense is stimulated in an ordinary environment, and although it is directed to children, describes some activities which would be appropriate for adults. A source of instruction about how to make toys to meet the particular needs of children with multiple disabilities is available in the form of a pack of instruction sheets (Mitchell and Ouvry, 1985). These authors have also contributed a chapter to this book on the subject of play for people with multiple disabilities (see Chapter 10).

Another useful source of information about an approach especially designed for children with profound disabilities is to be found in Fuller's (1990) guide to making tactile books on a 'do-it-yourself' basis. Although this publication is clearly directed at children with profound learning disabilities, the ideas it contains, adapted as necessary, would probably appeal to some adults with profound disabilities. For a new book with practical suggestions about games and other leisure activities for people with profound disabilities, see Denziloe (1994). This includes a discussion of age appropriateness as regards play activities for adults with profound disabilities.

A different way of making play experiences available to children with disabilities is through the use of special playgrounds. The development of such playgrounds has been pioneered in the UK by the Handicapped Adventure Playground Association (HAPA). HAPA produce a pack about their work and a regular journal (for address, see end of chapter) which sometimes includes information specifically about activities for children with multiple disabilities (see, for example, Brearley, 1991). Their material is brief, practical and offers clear guidance both to those working in playgrounds for disabled children and those seeking to establish this type of resource. A free guide to play, arts and leisure activities for disabled children, their parents and carers is available for the Greater London area from Artsline (Artsline, 1992). The activities listed are coded so that those available to children with learning disability are easily identifiable.

The design and use of equipment for adults, who are often institutionalized and have either profound and multiple disabilities or are displaying difficult behaviour, is an aspect of the work of Caldwell (1990, 1991, 1992). This work, which has also been documented on video tape ('Making Progress' and 'Working with Clive'), is concerned with more than leisure time but is relevant to the provision of enjoyable and meaningful activities for people with profound and multiple disabilities. Caldwell tends to work with service users whom staff have found inaccessible when employing conventional approaches. She utilizes a stimulus liked by a service user to provide an enjoyable focus for the development of a relationship, and describes practical approaches to achieving interaction (Caldwell, 1991).

Physical activities

There is a growing awareness of the ability of people with learning disability to participate in sport, and as a result be offered opportunities for enjoyment and self-development (see, for example, Dines, 1985). The Special Olympics movement has demonstrated the ability of such people to engage in the same type of sports activities as the general population, and in regular training and competition. The movement is now taking steps to include people with profound disability within its programme, and research is being carried out into the best way of bringing this about (see, for example, Brundige, Hautala and Squires, 1990). These authors have noted the need for sufficiently small gradations in scoring skill achievements to be available within the programme to enable small but obvious improvements in skill to be noted.

Books which focus on a particular physical activity often tend to be directed towards the needs of disabled people generally, so that although they contain useful and practical advice, the requirements of those with severe, profound and multiple disabilities are not covered in detail. An example of this type of work is Britten's (1991) book about horse-riding for people with disability, which would make a good starting point for those interested in introducing people with profound and multiple disabilities to this activity.

Similarly, water-based activities are very popular with people with profound and multiple disabilities, but there is little specific information about how best to meet their needs in this area. Discussion tends to be limited to a chapter within more broadly based books, e.g. by the Amateur Swimming Association (Harrison, 1989), and in

Water Sports for the Disabled (Water Sports Division, British Sports Association for the Disabled, 1983). In neither is attention paid to people with profound and multiple disabilities. Likewise, Smedley's (1989) useful guide to canoeing for people with disability contains a section on the needs of people with learning disability but nothing about the needs of people with profound and multiple disabilities.

A smaller number of specialized articles relate to work with children. Lambe (1986) has described the organization of a hydrotherapy scheme in the summer holidays for children with profound and multiple disabilities, while Anderson (1987) and Anderson and Knight (1985) draw on their experience of special education to discuss the use of a soft play environment, a trampoline and a hydrotherapy pool.

A useful general book about physical recreation for people with learning disability is by Latto and Norrice (1989), which devotes a few pages to physical activities specifically for people with severe or profound disability, and also directs the reader to relevant activities dealt with elsewhere in the same volume. In addition it contains helpful appendices listing relevant audio tapes, films, video tapes and organizations. One appendix deals with atlantoaxial instability, which is cervical spine abnormality that affects a minority of people with Down's syndrome and can lead to serious physical injury if some especially vigorous forms of exercise are undertaken. There is evidence that people with Down's syndrome should be screened for this condition before they take part in very active sports (Collacott, 1987), and Mencap have produced an information sheet for the layperson (Mencap Medical Advisory Panel, 1992).

The adaptation of the equipment and rules for games is one important way of maximizing the potential for participation of people with profound and multiple disabilities. Detailed information is available concerning a number of adapted games which have been developed at Meldreth Manor School in order to enable participation by people with severe, profound and multiple disabilities. The games include bowls, tenpin bowling, billiards, snooker and cricket, most of which are suitable for people with profound and multiple disabilities, and were devised in order to maximize participation by service users themselves. Information is available both in a manual containing details about all of the games (Reed, 1991a) and in a series of handbooks (Reed, 1991b, c, d, e, f, g) dealing with each game separately, plus a handbook (Reed, 1990) which contains an overview of key principles and recommended practice. A video tape is also available, which is intended for those interested in running the games but which would also act as a general introduction. Another set of adapted games, some of which could be carried out by people with profound and multiple disabilities, has been devised at the (then) Nottingham Polytechnic and details are again available in the form of a manual (Smith and Williamson, 1992). All the games devised by Reed and most of those described by Smith and Williamson may be played by adults as well as children. Further ideas are available in Chapter 5 of this book.

Physical activities can be made available to people with disabilities in specialized centres. Cotton (1981) describes such a centre as 'in part a teaching establishment, in part a hotel'. This field study centre, Churchtown Farm, was designed to provide wheelchair access throughout – to bird-hides, ponds and streams, a nature reserve, etc. There are other possible venues for activity holidays for people with multiple disabilities (see, for example, Duncan, 1988). In addition, Mencap Holiday Services (1992, 1993) produce a guide to holiday accommodation which welcomes people with learning disability. All types of accommodation, including activity centres, are represented. The full guide is produced at biennial intervals and a supplement is produced in alternate years. For additional information see Chapter 9 of this volume.

Other leisure activities which are popular with the general population and enjoyed by people with profound and multiple disabilities include yoga, aromatherapy and massage. Sanderson, Harrison and Price (1991) describe what aromatherapy and massage have to offer people with learning disability and their book includes material relevant to people with profound and multiple disabilities. Sanderson has also contributed a specialized consideration of this topic in Chapter 12 of this book. Recent work about making yoga available to people with learning disability has been carried out by Gunstone, who has prepared for purchase a colour-coded instruction pack, lesson plans and a teaching video. These materials can be used as support material for training courses, which are also available.

Gardening is another area of activity which has a wide appeal and potential as a means of providing enjoyable experiences for people with profound and multiple disabilities. Service users can enjoy both the active experience of horticulture (see, for example, Abbro, 1989) and the passive enjoyment to be derived from a garden which provides sensory stimulation in a variety of ways. No one source of specific information exists, and ideas must be gleaned from more generally directed literature. Books which contain useful information include Hagedorn (1987) and Please (1990). Also useful in this respect are articles in a specialist magazine, *Growth Point*. For further information, see Chapter 7 of this volume.

INDICATIONS FROM RESEARCH

Researchers have turned their attention to some areas related to leisure for people with profound and multiple disabilities. These areas are indicated below and some examples of research studies are described. Space does not permit comprehensive coverage, but does allow an overview of relevant areas.

Choice and preference

Writing about the general population, Deem (1988) states: 'the *experience* and *meaning* of leisure are intensely personal to a given individual' (p. 78). The work of researchers reinforces the importance of this message when considering the preferences of people with profound and multiple disabilities. 'Idiosyncratic' is a word often used to describe this highly individual preference pattern (Dewson and Whiteley, 1987). Overall, the research literature highlights the need for the choices of people with profound and multiple disabilities to be assessed and attended to on an individual basis. The question that then arises is how can this pattern of preference be established? Lyons (1986a) suggests that where a service user cannot articulate their likes and dislikes, professionals have what he calls 'the usual choice of approaches:

- observation of the individual's behaviour in a variety of situations;
- asking care-givers;
- trial and error (i.e. providing the individual with experiences and watching for positive responses)' (p. 231).

Having established an appropriate activity, Lyons suggests that it is then important to highlight its enjoyable aspects by modelling appropriate behaviour or by modifying the activity in some way.

Some researchers have devised more systematic approaches to discerning the preference of service users. For example, Green *et al.* (1988) established an effective procedure for assessing the differing preferences of seven young people with profound and multiple disabilities. A number of stimuli, including a hug, verbal interaction, a vibrator, juice, pudding, rock music, soft music, etc., were presented several times to the young people participating in the study, and their reactions were noted. This process was found to be generally effective in establishing preferred stimuli, but the choices made were found to differ from care-givers' opinions about the participants' preferences. This finding that care-giver opinion is less reliable in establishing preference than systematic assessment was also the outcome of a study by Parsons and Reid (1990) into the food and drink preferences of five men with profound learning disabilities. These authors also found that routine care-givers could apply the procedure with supervision.

This type of procedure relies on service users being able to indicate preference by movement, facial expression or vocalization. Another method of establishing preference which has been accorded a lot of research attention in recent years is the use of microtechnology (e.g. Wacker *et al.*, 1985; Dewson and Whiteley, 1987; Realon, Favell and Dayvault, 1988; Wacker *et al.*, 1988; Realon, Favell and Phillips, 1989). An example of this type of study was carried out by Realon, Favell and Lowerre (1990), who employed microswitches which activated a variety of toys, a tape player and a video recorder in a study involving two people with profound and multiple disabilities. They demonstrated that the two participants were able to choose the materials with which they wanted to interact, and that if this choice was made available to them, their rates of activity rose. However, providing choice opportunities to people with profound disabilities is a complex and time-consuming undertaking, as recent work aiming to combine occupational programmes with opportunities for choice demonstrates (Lancioni *et al.*, 1993).

Increasing activity levels by altering the service user's environment

The low level of activity of people with profound and multiple disabilities who live in institutional settings is well documented. Authors note that it is difficult for such people to seek attention or request activities (e.g. Oswin, 1978), and that their interaction with staff may be very limited (e.g. Beail, 1985). Therefore, research work has been carried out aimed at enriching the environment of the recipients of institutional care.

Early work often comprised simple measures that involved making available leisure materials or an improved range of such materials in order to improve activity levels (e.g. Horner, 1980). Means of increasing accessibility gradually became more sophisticated. For example, Hamre-Nietupski *et al.* (1984) made available a modified tape recorder to some young adults, including a man who was deaf and blind with profound learning disability. Perhaps the most sophisticated way of improving leisure materials accessibility is by the use of microswitches, as already described. Another example of this approach is the work of Wacker *et al.* (1985). In this study, five students beween the ages of 13 and 18 years with profound and multiple disabilities were trained to use microswitches by raising an arm or using their head. The microswitches activated various devices, and several students demonstrated consistent preferences between devices. The authors write: ' ... the levels of responding produced by many of the students following training may constitute an active leisure skill. At the completion of the investigation, the students were actively and independently engaged in behaviours that produced desired effects for them. In this sense, the students were performing a leisure skill' (p. 178).

Before any of us engage in our chosen leisure activities, we may need to learn the necessary skills. Like the work just described, studies which improve the availability and accessibility of leisure materials also involve the training of participants so that the use of materials is demonstrated and encouraged. Teaching techniques in this field are well developed and usually utilize behavioural methods. For example, Wuerch and Voeltz (1982) outline how a number of games were taught to people with severe or profound learning disability, as a result of the games being broken down into small steps (see Schleien *et al.*, 1989, for a summary of 'best professional practices' in leisure skills programming).

A staffing technique which aims to increase the activity levels of people with severe and profound disability by putting into operation the knowledge outlined above is known as room management. This procedure involves the organization of a staff team so that one member is responsible, for short periods, for promoting activities among a number of service users. This staff member ensures the availability of attractive leisure materials and prompts and rewards their use. This room management procedure (see Jones *et al.*, 1987 and Sebba, 1988, for fuller details) has been shown to be effective in institutional and educational settings. A recent example of a study which assigned staff duties on this sort of basis and appointed a leisure activities manager has been reported by Adlem, Arco and Ngan (1990). In this case the approach was coupled with an enriched choice of leisure materials plus staff training and supervision. This resulted in increased levels of independent engagement in the manipulation of leisure materials by the six participants with profound and multiple disabilities. Activity periods, once established, have been shown to be maintained for long periods (Blunden and Evans, 1988), although these authors throw doubt on the continuing relevance of such procedures with the emergence of new community-based residential and day facilities which are delivered on an individual or small-group basis. Mansell *et al.* (1984, 1987) also question the idea of promoting the use of toys and recreational materials by adults, and suggest that involvement in domestic and household tasks is a more meaningful and socially valued way of spending time.

One frequently reported result of promoting increased active engagement by people with profound disability is a decline in problem behaviour (e.g. Horner, 1980; Murphy, Callias and Carr, 1985; Singh and Millichamp, 1987; Mace, Browder and Martin, 1988). For example, Murphy *et al.* found that a drop in stereotypical (i.e. highly repetitive) behaviour accompanied the introduction of specially designed toys which emitted stimuli (vibration, light or sound). Mace *et al.* similarly brought about a decline in stereotypical behaviour in a study involving one man with profound disability by combining ease of access to leisure materials with staff instruction. However, such gains are not completely clearcut. The participants in the studies carried out by Singh and Millichamp and by Mace were not described as having multiple disabilities, and Realon, Favell and Phillips (1989), who did work with people with multiple disabilities, found no consistent decrease in problem behaviours with any leisure material employed.

While the research studies described in this section have helped to promote an understanding of the needs and potential of people with profound and multiple disabilities, they do have a number of limitations. Frequently, age-appropriate materials are not utilized. Authors sometimes report that this is due to difficulties in finding or devising materials which are age-appropriate and attractive to all participants. In addition, although the rationale for leisure skill training may be to increase choice, difficulties do arise concerning practice. First, learning a leisure skill may not be enjoyable to a service user and researchers rationalize this dilemma by suggesting that associated pleasure is merely postponed. Certo, Schleien and Hunter (1983) write that 'a low initial level of fun may be a necessary correlate of teaching severely disabled individuals to perform leisure skills' (p. 31). Secondly, allied to this there may be a conflict between what a person prefers to do with free time and what trainers consider appropriate. For example, Nietupski *et al.* (1986) used choice charts in order to give a method of indicating preferences to people who could not talk. These were successful, especially with a young man in the severe/profound range of ability. However, the authors write ' . . . the choice charts occasionally were changed to add new materials and/or to remove those materials that students selected too frequently' (p. 261). It is a matter for debate whether one commends the trainers for their zeal in making a wide variety of activities available, or sympathizes with the students for the loss of their favourite pursuits. Lyons (1986a) highlights this difficulty for leisure providers, pointing out that fun and spontaneity may be overlooked in the effort to teach skills in activity performance. He writes: 'What is being spoken of is the difference between performance of play behaviours for their *appearance* of appropriateness and normalcy (what may essentially be a ritual for the intellectually disabled person) and the performance of play behaviours for their underlying attractiveness and gratification' (Lyons, 1986a, p. 230).

A further limitation is that many studies have tended to concentrate on working with people in institutions, overlooking the needs of service users as community and family members. This situation is beginning to be addressed. For example, Realon, Favell and Phillips (1989) noted that their study into electrically operated leisure devices had opened up numerous opportunities for positive interactions between children with disabilities in the community and their families who had been assisted to modify leisure materials for use with their children. Likewise, Schleien *et al.* (1989) pointed to the need for networking between families, professionals and agencies, as well as to the positives accruing from using parents as well as professionals to teach leisure skills to children with severe/profound and multiple disability (Schleien *et al.*, 1988).

SOCIAL INTEGRATION AND LEISURE

The literature reviewed so far has frequently referred to information collected in settings in which people with profound and multiple disabilities are to a greater or lesser extent segregated from society. This is a reflection of the past and present patterns of service delivery. However, with the recognition of the desirability of people with learning disability leading an ordinary lifestyle and adopting socially valued roles, an awareness has developed of the potential of their leisure-time pursuits as a means of social integration. In the UK, Wertheimer (1983) and Shearer (1986) have promoted this view, while North American publications have also been concerned with strategies which facilitate experiences of integrated leisure for people with severe learning disability (e.g. Hutchinson and Lord, 1979; Lord, 1981; Schleien and Tipton Ray, 1988). As patterns of service delivery alter to reflect the present emphasis on the need for a community presence for people with learning disability, so sources of information about integrated leisure for people with multiple disabilities are developing.

Some authors have described innovative ways of increasing the community presence of people with multiple disabilities. For example, Allen *et al.* (1989) describe a project in Wales which used community resources almost exclusively to provide a day service for people with multiple disabilities and challenging behaviour. Another Welsh initiative is discussed by Shuttleworth (1987) in an article about Castlefield, a day centre which placed emphasis on integration within the centre and on the use of community resources. Frank and Uditsky (1988) describe a Canadian initiative which aimed to include people with severe learning disability and/or physical disability in the life of a university campus. These authors give details of the activities of 'Roger', who was multiply disabled and had a member of staff to help him enjoy the university's facilities. Roger participated in ice-skating, went to the swimming pool and spent time at the video arcade, the greenhouse and in music concerts.

There is now an increasing focus upon community involvement and learning in community settings rather than training for leisure prior to introduction to the real leisure environment. For example, Wilcox and Bellamy (1987a, b), in *The Activities Catalog* and its accompanying guide, have produced a catalogue which is intended to be a comprehensive list of locally available activities for people with moderate and severe disabilities. The emphasis is upon learning in a natural setting and upon the complete performance of an activity. The authors claim that the catalogue is suitable for any adolescent or adult whose progress is so slow or irregular that competent daily performance seems unlikely to result in the time available. The authors suggest that the catalogue includes activities suitable for people who are profoundly and multiply disabled, although the service users described in case studies cited in the text are not of this level of functioning.

The developing debate about the value of the educational integration of children with learning disability into mainstream schools continues within the UK. A similar movement in North America has produced literature which examines ways of encouraging social play between children with profound and multiple disabilities and non-disabled children, and the effects of this on the children involved. In this context, Cole (1988) found that non-disabled children had less fun playing with children who were physically disabled as well as affected by severe learning disability. Possible strategies proposed by the author to overcome this difficulty include better preparation of the non-disabled children, social skills training for children with multiple disabilities and the provision of rewards additional to those that result directly from the relationship itself. In the same year, another study concerned with the promotion of play between non-disabled children and children who were unable to walk and were affected by severe or profound learning disability was reported by Cole, Vandercook and Rynders (1988). In this case, a group of non-disabled children who were encouraged to treat their play partners with multiple disabilities as 'special friends' found the experience more enjoyable than a group of non-disabled children who were encouraged to act as tutors to children with multiple disabilities. The children who acted as 'special friends' were prepared in accordance with a programme designed by Voeltz *et al.* (1983) to foster relationships between children with disabilities and non-disabled children. Cole, Vandercook and Rynders (1988) suggest that the 'special friends' approach promotes greater equality than a tutoring approach, and that the former type of relationship is more likely to endure as it is more rewarding to the non-disabled children involved. A study which reported positive effects for two children with multiple disabilities as a result of the promotion of social play between them and non-disabled children has been reported by Brady *et al.* (1991). One participant with multiple disabilities showed increases in arm reaching and grasping, while the other increased the amount of time he kept his head upright.

One change in the pattern of service delivery in the UK which has been commonly associated with increases in opportunities for social integration is the resettlement into the community of people from hospitals for people with learning disability. Increases in the use of community resources by such people have been noted by De Kock *et al.* (1988), Firth and Short (1987) and Rawlings (1985). A further study which focused on the changes in lifestyle of five young adults with profound and multiple disabilities who were discharged from hospital to a group home was carried out by Bratt and Johnston (1988). Again, it was found that the people concerned went out more and to a wider variety of places as a result of leaving hospital. In addition, there was an increase in active engagement and in the use of age-appropriate recreational materials. However, the authors note that there was little evidence of integration being achieved within the local community. They suggest that networking skills should have been covered in staff training sessions ('network' is used here to refer to a system of significant relationships within a local community and 'networking' refers to the facilitating of such a pattern of relationships). For a general booklet about developing and maintaining neighbourhood networks involving people with learning disability, see Atkinson and Ward (1986). A description of the social opportunities offered by residence in community-based homes to children with learning disabilities is available in a survey of 30 schemes, some of which provided care for children with profound and multiple disabilities (Leonard, 1988, 1991). The author notes that most schemes succeeded in offering residents considerable opportunities to experience holidays and excursions, as well as regular local activities and leisure pursuits. It was found that a system whereby home staff had ready access to money and transport favoured spontaneity and response to opportunities and needs as they arose. The importance of staff contact as a way of widening the young people's networks was also noted. This is consistent with the findings of Firth and Short (1987), which point to the importance of opportunities that staff bring to widen the circle of relationships of residents.

Other patterns of service delivery also have a bearing on the integrative nature of the experience of people with multiple disabilities during their leisure time. Those service users, predominantly but not exclusively children, who spend short periods in other households in order to give their care-giver a break may have their social and leisure horizons broadened as a result. Examples of these schemes have been thoroughly researched (e.g. Stalker, 1990; Robinson, 1991) and their drawbacks have been noted (Middleton, 1992). However, they do have a potential as regards social integration, which is sometimes overlooked.

The use of volunteers is another facet of service delivery which may enhance the variety of social experience available to a person with profound and multiple disabilities, especially if the volunteers are employed to support the use of community-based facilities. Literature is available about the nature of volunteers and how they can be organized to act as 'friends' to people with learning disability (e.g. Walsh, 1985a, b; Lyons, 1986b; Williams, 1986). In addition, the overall need for a paid organizer for voluntary care projects has been noted (Bulmer, 1986), as has the marked difference between volunteers and friends (e.g. Firth and Rapley, 1990). In general this literature does not focus upon people with profound and multiple disabilities and the particular care that these people may require. In this context it is perhaps worth noting Evans and Ware's (1987) comment about the extensive use of volunteers, as well as unqualified welfare assistants, for work with children with profound and multiple disabilities: 'There is an implication that special care unit children do not require qualified help to such an extent as children in the remainder of the school. ... Yet it would seem to us ... that the greater the multiplicity of handicaps, the more training is required by those who work with them' (p. 109).

TRAINING OPPORTUNITIES AND RESOURCE CENTRES

Until recently the training opportunities for staff and others seeking ways of providing enjoyable activities for people with profound and multiple disabilities were sparse. Neither leisure nor profound and multiple disabilities were seen as priority areas as far as education or training were concerned. These deficits have begun to be addressed by initiatives developing on a number of fronts, often with support from the voluntary sector. The Spastics Society carried out pioneering work in this field at their training establishment, Castle Priory, by including in their short course programmes training events that focused on developing relevant skills and knowledge in staff. Their short courses continue to be available, while others are now mounted in a variety of locations by BILD. A newer initiative, and one which is complementary to these short training events, takes the form of longer, more general courses which examine in depth the whole range of needs of people with profound and multiple disabilities. Two such courses have recently been developed, one by the RNIB and one jointly by the University of Birmingham and BILD.

Innovative work is also being carried out at a number of resource centres. In the south of England, Playtrac has operated as a regional mobile training resource concerned with play and leisure for people with learning disability. Workshops have been run by Playtrac for staff employed in a variety of settings, which included people with profound and multiple disabilities as service users. A handbook written by Playtrac staff (Save the Children Fund Playtrac Team, 1989) gives advice about setting up such a project. Also available is an evaluation of Playtrac by Garrett (1990), which gives clear insights into the benefits of training as well as into the organizational constraints and culture which can impede its effectiveness.

Further information about the contribution to the quality of service users' lives which can be made by a specialized leisure project is available in the form of an evaluation of 'Us in a Bus', a mobile service operating in four Surrey hospitals (Harris, 1992). Harris discussed the work of the 'Us in a Bus' team and notes: 'The style of UIAB has been to use a variety of materials to mediate social interactions between project staff and hospital residents' (p. 26). He introduces the notion of social engagement as a significant measure of service quality, by which he means 'making contact' or 'developing a relationship' (p. 59). Like Garrett's work on Playtrac, Harris' evaluation clearly documents the deficits arising from institutionalization in the lives of some people with profound and multiple disabilities.

In the north of England, the Profound Intellectual and Multiple Disabilities section of Mencap (formerly the Mencap Profound Retardation and Multiple Handicap Project) has organized workshops for parents, including a series about leisure, an evaluation of which is available (Prosser, 1990, 1992) (see also Chapter 13). These accounts have been supplemented by a report of a further leisure workshop which was run in Northern Ireland as a preparation for the inclusion of people with profound and multiple disabilities into a Gateway Leisure Club (Mount, 1993). The Profound Intellectual and Multiple Disabilities section also operates as a resource centre about profound and multiple

disabilities. PLANET is a national resource centre, sited in southern
England, which is concerned with play and leisure for people with learning disability. PLANET produces a series of book lists and video lists
which include coverage of profound and multiple disabilities and play
and leisure. The organization arranges open days when staff and other
carers may visit their premises and examine aids to leisure provision,
including a sensory bank. PLANET staff also undertake some training.

It is apparent that there are expanding opportunities for staff who
require training in this field. As these opportunities develop, it should
be possible for staff and other care-givers to extend their general skills
in the area of work with people with profound and multiple disabilities
by undertaking long-term courses, while also being offered the
opportunity to supplement these skills with short courses about
particular areas of activity provision. These improved opportunities
for training may well have the effect of not only expanding staff's skill
and knowledge, but are also one means of maintaining their morale
and motivation in a demanding area.

RECOMMENDATIONS

Although the needs of people with profound and multiple disabilities
are now attracting more attention than in the past, there remain significant deficits which should be addressed.

- There is insufficient information available concerning the specific
  details of how particular activities can be offered to people with
  profound and multiple disabilities. This is a lack of documentation by practitioners of the techniques and procedures they employ
  to make a particular activity in which they are skilled available to
  such people. There is evidence that particular activities have been
  engaged in by people with profound and multiple disabilities but
  the details are not made available as a model for others to follow.
  The contributions by practitioners to this book should help to
  address the situation, but efforts need to continue. The needs of
  parents, substitute parents and other informal care-givers for
  guidance in this area should be taken into account, as well the needs
  of paid staff.
- There is very little information available concerning day services
  for adults with profound and multiple disabilities. This is, no doubt,
  a reflection of the inadequate state of provision in this field, and
  an indication of the need for innovatory approaches to service
  development. Original approaches should be documented, as
  should the effects in this area of the National Health Service and

Community Care Act 1990. Specifically, evaluation will be needed to establish to what extent needs-led services for people with profound and multiple disabilities do emerge as a result of recent legislative changes. In this context it is worth noting the recent recommendation of the Social Services Inspectorate (1993) stating that explicit priority rating systems should be developed in order to ensure the targeting of services on those with the greatest needs.

- Research studies into the results of making changes in the environment of people with profound and multiple disabilities often appear too short term and not sufficiently fine grained in their estimation. This is presumably the result of external funding constraints on researchers, but does not reflect the needs and pace of people with profound and multiple disabilities.

- It is always the case that literature reflects the society that produces it, and that reviewed here is no exception. Texts and other resource material referred to in this chapter sometimes contain language that might be found offensive, although the most offensive have been excluded. Future publications should reflect best practice in this regard. The multicultural nature of British society is often not reflected in the literature available about the leisure of people with profound and multiple disabilities. A discussion about how the free-time choices of people with learning disability may be constrained by pressure to conform to prevailing 'white' norms is to be found in Baxter *et al.* (1990) which highlighted the racist aspects of UK service provision for people with learning disability. Future information about leisure for such people should take account of the needs of black people, and this perspective should be reflected in the visual images projected, as well as in the text.

- Research into the most effective ways of selecting suitable staff and of maintaining their morale needs to be carried out. Garrett's (1990) careful documentation of staff behaviour and service users' experience in some institutional settings is depressingly reminiscent at times of Oswin's (1978) classic work undertaken a decade or more earlier. Garrett is confident that positive changes have occurred, but research proposals should take into account that 'whether toys and equipment are used or not, it is relationships that generate play with these clients' (Garrett, 1990, p. 140).

REFERENCES

Abbro, F. (1989) Why horticulture? *Growth Point*, Autumn, 8–10.

Adlem, A., Arco, L. and Ngan, C. (1990) An analysis of independent engagement of persons with profound multiple handicaps. *Behavior Change*, 7, 185–95.

Ager, A. (1985) Recent developments in the use of microcomputers in the field of mental handicap: implications for psychological practice. *Bulletin of the British Psychological Society*, 38, 142–5.

Allen, D., Gillard, N., Watkins, P. and Norman, G. (1989) New directions in day activities for people with multiple handicaps and challenging behaviour. *Mental Handicap*, 7, 101–3.

Anderson, E. (1987) Physical education for children and students with special educational needs. *British Journal of Physical Education*, 18, 199–200.

Anderson, E.G. and Knight, L. (1985) Specific designs in a therapeutic environment. *Journal of the Society of Remedial Gymnastics and Recreational Therapy*, 115, 11–18.

Arts for Disabled People in Wales (1989) *Arts Matter: In Support of People with Learning Difficulties*, Arts for Disabled People in Wales, Cardiff.

Artsline (1992) *Play, Arts and Leisure for Disabled Children, Their Parents and Carers*, Artsline, London.

Astell-Burt, C. (1981) *Puppetry for Mentally Handicapped People*, Souvenir Press, London.

Atkinson, D. and Ward, L (1986) *A Part of the Community: Social Integration and Neighbourhood Networks*, Campaign for People with Mental Handicaps, London.

Attenborough, R. (1985) *Arts and Disabled People*, Bedford Square Press/NCVO, London.

Baxter, C., Poonia, K., Ward, L. and Nadirshaw, Z. (1990) *Double Discrimination*, King's Fund Centre, London.

Beail, N. (1985) The nature of interactions between nursing staff and profoundly multiply handicapped children. *Child Care, Health and Development*, 11, 113–29.

Behrmann, M.M. and Lahm, L. (1984) Babies and robots: technology to assist learning of young multiply disabled children. *Rehabilitation Literature*, 45, 194–201.

Blunden, R. and Evans, G. (1988) Long-term maintenance of staff and resident behaviour in a hospital ward for adults with mental handicap: report of a six-year follow-up. *Mental Handicap Research*, 1, 115–26.

Brady, M.P., Martin, S., Williams, R.E. and Burton, M. (1991) The effects of fifth graders' socially directed behavior on motor and social responses of children with multiple handicaps. *Research in Developmental Disabilities*, 12, 1–16.

Bratt, A. and Johnston, R. (1988) Changes in life styles for young adults with profound handicaps following discharge from hospital care into a 'second generation' housing project. *Mental Handicap Research*, 1, 49–74.

Brearley, S. (1991) Playing with children with multiple disabilities. *HAPA Journal*, 3, 11.

Brinker, R.P. and Lewis, M. (1982) Making the world work with microcomputers: a learning prosthesis for handicapped infants. *Exceptional Children*, 49, 163–70.

Britten, V. (1991) *Riding for the Disabled*, Batsford, London.

Brown, N. (1988) Social and recreational needs of the less able deaf–blind person. *Talking Sense*, 34, 14–15.

Brown, L., Branston-McClean, M.B., Baumgart, D. *et al.* (1979) Using the characteristics of current and subsequent least restrictive environments in the development of curricular content for severely handicapped students. *AAESPH Review*, **4**, 407–24.

Brudenell, P. (1986) *The Other Side of Profound Handicap*, Macmillan, Basingstoke.

Brundige, T.L., Hautala, R.M. and Squires, S. (1990) The Special Olympics Developmental Sports Program for Persons with Severe and Profound Disabilities: an assessment of its effectiveness. *Education and Training in Mental Retardation*, **25**, 376–80.

Bulmer, M. (1986) *Neighbours – The Work of Philip Abrams*, Cambridge University Press, Cambridge.

Caldwell, P. (1990) Blind people with severe learning difficulties and challenging behaviour. *Focus* (3), 4–8.

Caldwell, P. (1991) Stimulating people with profound handicaps: how can we work together? *British Journal of Mental Subnormality*, **37**, 92–100.

Caldwell, P. (1992) Establishing relationships. *Focus*, (7), 8–11.

Carpenter, B. (1992) 'I Can Do It!': A review. *PMLD Link*, Summer (13), 27–8.

Carpenter, B. and Lewis, A. (1989) Searching for solutions: approaches to planning the curriculum for integration of SLD and PMLD children, in *Making the Special Schools Ordinary, Vol I; Models for the Developing Special School*, (eds D. Baker and K. Bovair), Falmer Publications, London.

Cerebral Palsy Sport/The United Kingdom Sports Association *Pro-Motion Resource Guide*, Cerebral Palsy Sport, London.

Certo, N.J., Schleien, S.J. and Hunter, D. (1983) An ecological assessment inventory to facilitate community recreation participation by severely disabled individuals. *Therapeutic Recreation Journal*, **17**, 29–38.

Cheseldine, S.E. and Jeffree, D.M. (1981) Mentally handicapped adolescents: their use of leisure. *Journal of Mental Deficiency Research*, **25**, 49–59.

Clarke, J. and Critcher, L. (1985) *The Devil Makes Work. Leisure in Capitalist Britain*, Macmillan, Basingstoke.

Cole, D.A. (1988) Difficulties in relationships between nonhandicapped and severely mentally retarded children: the effect of physical impairment. *Research in Developmental Disabilities*, **9**, 55–72.

Cole, D.A., Vandercook, T. and Rynders, J. (1988) Comparison of two peer interaction programs: children with and without severe disabilities. *American Educational Research Journal*, **25**, 415–39.

Coles, P. (1984) *Please Touch*, Committee of Inquiry into the Arts and Disabled People, Carnegie UK Trust, Dunfermline.

Collacott, R.A. (1987) Atlantoaxial instability in Down's syndrome. *British Medical Journal (Clin. Res.)*, April 18, 988–9.

Cotton, M. (1981) *Out of Doors with Handicapped People*, Souvenir Press, London.

Crisp, A.G., Sturmey, P., Bennett, S. and Milner, S. (1984) Some evaluations of toy apparatus for severely and profoundly mentally handicapped people. *International Journal of Rehabilitation Research*, **7**, 431–4.

De Kock, U., Saxby, H., Thomas, M. and Felce, D. (1988) Community and family contact: an evaluation of small community homes for adults with severe and profound mental handicaps. *Mental Handicap Research*, **1**, 127–40.

Deem, R. (1988) *Society Now – Work, Unemployment and Leisure*, Routledge, London.

Denziloe, J. (1994) *Fun and Games. Practical Leisure Ideas for People with Profound Disabilities*, Butterworth Heinemann, London.

Dewson, M.R. and Whiteley, J.H. (1987) Sensory reinforcement of head turning with non-ambulatory, profoundly mentally retarded persons. *Research in Developmental Disabilities*, **8**, 413–26.

Dines, A. (1985) A sports club for people with mental handicaps. *Mental Handicap*, **13**, 166–8.

Douglas, J., Reeson, B. and Ryan, M. (1988) Computer microtechnology for a severely disabled preschool child. *Child Care, Health and Development*, **14**, 166–8.

Duncan, P. (1988) Special Children Welcome. *Community Outlook*, 20–23.

Evans, P. and Ware, J. (1987) *'Special Care' Provision: The Education of Children with Profound and Multiple Learning Difficulties*, NFER-Nelson, Windsor.

Fain, G.S. (1986) Leisure: A moral imperative. *Mental Retardation*, 261–3.

Firth, H. and Rapley, M. (1990) *From Acquaintance to Friendship: Issues for People With Learning Disabilities*, British Institute of Mental Handicap, Kidderminster.

Firth, H. and Short, D. (1987) A move from hospital to community: evaluation of community contacts. *Child Care, Health and Development*, **13**, 341–54.

Frank, S. and Uditsky, B. (1988) On campus: integration at university. *Entourage*, **3**, 33–40.

Fuller, C. (1990) *Tactile Stories. A Do-It-Yourself Guide to Making 6 Tactile Books*, Resources for Learning Difficulties, The Consortium, London.

Garrett, B. (1990) *Not Just Play: A Contribution to the Debate About the Play and Leisure Needs of People With Mental Handicaps. The Evaluation of Playtrac*, Save The Children, London.

Golding, R. and Goldsmith, L. (1986) *The Caring Person's Guide to Handling the Severely Multiply Handicapped*, Macmillan, Basingstoke.

Green, C.W., Reid, D.H., White, L.K. *et al.* (1988) Identifying reinforcers for persons with profound handicaps: staff opinion versus systematic assessment of preferences. *Journal of Applied Behavior Analysis*, **21**, 31–43.

Hagedorn, R. (1987) *Therapeutic Horticulture*, Nottingham Rehabilitation Ltd., Nottingham.

Haggar, L.E. and Hutchinson, R.B. (1991) Snoezelen: an approach to the provision of a leisure resource for people with profound and multiple handicaps. *Mental Handicap*, **19**, 51–5.

Hamre-Nietupski, S., Nietupski, J., Sandvig, R. *et al.* (1984) Leisure skills instruction in a community residential setting with young adults who are deaf/blind severely handicapped. *TSH Journal*, **9**, 49–54.

Harris, J. (1992) *Leisure Activities for People with Profound and Multiple Learning Difficulties: An Evaluation of the 'Us in a Bus' Project*, Spastics Society.

Harrison, J.A. (1989) *Anyone Can Swim*, Crowood Press, Marlborough.

Heddell, F. (1985) *With a Little Help from the Chip*, BBC, London.

Heeley, J. (1986) Leisure and moral reform. *Leisure Studies*, **5**, 57–67.

Hegarty, J.R. (1991) *Into the 1990s: the Present and Future of Microcomputers for People With Learning Difficulties*, Change Publications, Market Drayton.

Hogg, J. and Lambe, L. (1988) *Sons and Daughters With Profound Retardation and Multiple Handicaps Attending Schools and Social Education Centres: Final Report*, Mencap, London.

Hogg, J. and Sebba, J. (1986) *Profound Retardation and Multiple Impairment: Volume I – Development and Learning*, Croom Helm, London.

Hogg, J., Sebba, J. and Lambe, L. (1990) *Profound Retardation and Multiple Impairment: Volume III – Medical and Physical Care and Management*, Chapman & Hall, London.

Hope, M. (ed) (1986) *The Magic of the Micro: A Resource for Children With Learning Difficulties*, Council for Education Technology, London.

Hope, M. (1987) *Micros for Children with Special Needs*, Human Horizon Series, Souvenir Press, London.

Horner, J. (1987) The music circus comes to school. *British Journal of Special Education*, **14**, 14–15.

Horner, R.D. (1980) The effects of an environmental 'enrichment' program on the behaviour of institutionalized profoundly retarded children. *Journal of Applied Behavior Analysis*, **13**, 473–91.

Hulsegge, J. and Verheul, A. (1987) *Snoezelen: Another World*, Rompa, Chesterfield.

Hutchinson, R. (1991) *The Whittington Hall Snoezelen Project*, North Derbyshire Health Authority, Chesterfield.

Hutchinson, P. and Lord, J. (1979) *Recreation Integration*, Leisurability Publications, Ontario.

Jennings, S. (ed) (1987) *Dramatherapy*, Croom Helm, London.

Jones, A.A., Blunden, R., Coles, E. *et al.* (1987) Evaluating the impact of training, supervisor feedback, self-monitoring and collaborative goal setting on staff and client behaviour, in *Staff Training in Mental Handicap*, (eds J. Hogg and P.J. Mittler), Croom Helm, London.

Keynotes (1992) 'I can do it!': A review. *Keynotes*, **2**, 6.

Lambe, L. (1986) Mencap's PRMH project – hydrotherapy scheme helps handicapped children in a major way. *Parents Voice*, Summer, 10–11.

Lambe, L. (ed.) (1991) *Leisure for People with Profound and Multiple Disabilities: A Leisure Resource Pack*, Mencap, London.

Lambert, M. (1984) *Using a 'Soft Play' Environment for Pupils with Severe or Profound and Multiple Handicaps*, Victoria School, Birmingham.

Lancioni, G.E., Oliva, D., Meazzini, P. and Marconi, N. (1993) Building choice opportunities within occupational programmes for persons with profound developmental disabilities. *Journal of Intellectual Disability Research*, **37**, 23–39.

Latto, K. and Norrice, B. (1989) *Give us the Chance*, Disabled Living Foundation, London.

Lear, R. (1986) *Play Helps*, Heinemann, London.

Leonard, A. (1988) *Out of Hospital*, Department of Social Policy and Social Work, University of York, York.

Leonard, A. (1991) *Homes of Their Own*, Gower, Aldershot.

Levete, G. (1982) *No Handicap to Dance*, Souvenir Press, London.

Levete, G. (1987) *The Creative Tree*, Russell, Salisbury.

Longhorn, F. (1988) *A Sensory Curriculum for Very Special People. A Practical Approach to Curriculum Planning*, Souvenir Press, London.

Lord, J. (1981) *Participation*, National Institute on Mental Retardation, Toronto.

Lyons, M. (1986a) Unlocking closed doors to play. *Australia and New Zealand Journal of Developmental Disabilities*, **12**, 229–33.

Lyons, M. (1986b) Students as buddies: a proposal for smoothing the path towards a broader life experience through recreation. *Occupational Therapy*, April, 111–14.

McClintock, A.B. (1984) *Drama for Mentally Handicapped Children*, Souvenir Press, London.

McConkey, R. and McGinley, P. (1990) *Innovations in Leisure and Recreation for People with a Mental Handicap*, Lisieux Hall, Chorley, Lancs.

McConkey, R., Walsh, J., and Mulcahy, M. (1981) The recreational pursuits of mentally handicapped adults. *International Journal of Rehabilitation Research*, **4**, 493–9.

Mace, F.C., Browder, D.M. and Martin, D.K. (1988) Reduction of stereotypy via instruction of alternative leisure behavior. *School Psychology Review*, **17**, 156–65.

Mansell, J., Felce, D., De Kock, U. *et al.* (1987) *Developing Staffed Housing for People with Mental Handicaps*, Costello, Tunbridge Wells.

Mansell, J., Jenkins, J., Felce, D. and De Kock, U. (1984) Measuring the activity of severely and profoundly mentally handicapped adults in ordinary housing. *Behaviour Research and Therapy*, **22**, 23–9.

Megarry, J. (1992) Happy Cygnets. *Times Education Supplement*, **3693**, 12 June.

Mencap Holiday Services (1992) *Mencap Holiday Accommodation Guide 1992/1993*, Mencap, London.

Mencap Holiday Services (1993) *Mencap Supplement Holiday Accommodation Guide 1992/1993*, Mencap, London.

Mencap Medical Advisory Panel (1992) *Look Before You Leap*, Leaflet no. 12, Mencap, London.

Middleton, L. (1992) *Children First*, Venture Press, Birmingham.

Mitchell, S. and Ouvry, C. (1985) *Make it Simple*. (Available from C. Ouvry, The Old Rectory, Hope Mansell, Ross-on-Wye, Herefordshire.

Mount, H. (ed) (1993) *Planning Leisure and Recreation for People With Profound and Multiple Disabilities*, Mencap, London.

Murphy, G., Callias, M. and Carr, J. (1985) Increasing simple toy play in profoundly mentally handicapped children: I. Training to play. *Journal of Autism and Developmental Disorders*, **16**, 45–58.

Newson, J. and Newson, E. (1979) *Toys and Playthings*, George Allen and Unwin, London.

Nietupski, J., Hanmre-Nietupski, S., Green, K. *et al.* (1986) Self-initiated and sustained leisure activity participation by students with moderate/severe handicaps. *Education and Training of the Mentally Retarded*, December, 259–64.

Orr, R. (1993) Life beyond the room? *Eye Contact*, Summer, 25–6.

Oswin, M. (1978) *Children Living in Long-Stay Hospitals*, Heinemann, London.

Ouvry, C. (1987) *Educating Children with Profound Handicaps*, British Institute of Mental Handicap, Kidderminster.

Parsons, M.B. and Reid, D.H. (1990) Assessing food preferences among persons with profound mental retardation providing oportunities to make choices. *Journal of Applied Behavior Analysis*, **23**, 183–95.

Pearson, A. (1985) *Arts for Everyone*, Carnegie UK Trust, Dunfermline.

Play Matters/National Toy Libraries Association (1989) *Special Needs Resource Pack for Adults*, National Toy Libraries Association, London.

Please, P. (ed) (1990) *Able to Garden*, Batsford, London.

Prosser, H. (1990) *Evaluation of the Pilot Workshop on Evolving Approaches to Leisure: Mencap Profound Retardation and Multiple Handicap Report 15*, Mencap, London.

Prosser, H. (1992) *Evaluation of the Second Phase Workshop on Evolving Approaches* to Leisure: Mencap Profound Retardation and Multiple Handicap Report 19, Mencap, London.

Rawlings, S.A. (1985) Life-styles of severely retarded non-communicating adults in hospitals and small residential homes. *British Journal of Social Work*, **15**, 281–93.

Realon, R.E., Favell, J.E. and Dayvault, K.A. (1988) Evaluating the use of adapted leisure materials on the engagement of persons who are profoundly, multiply handicapped. *Education and Training in Mental Retardation*, **23**, 228–37.

Realon, R.E., Favell, J.E. and Lowerre, A. (1990) The effects of making choices on engagement levels with persons who are profoundly multiply handicapped. *Education and Training in Mental Retardation*, **25**, 299–305.

Realon, R.E., Favell, J.E. and Phillips, J.F. (1989) Adapted leisure materials vs. standard leisure materials; evaluating several aspects of programming for persons who are profoundly handicapped. *Education and Training of the Mentally Retarded*, **24**, 169–77.

Reed, L. (1990) *The Meldreth Series: Principle and Practice. A Look at Key Principles and Recommended Practice in the Operation of Meldreth Games*, The Spastics Society, Meldreth Manor School, Cambridgeshire.

Reed, L. (1991a) *The Meldreth Series: Old Games with a New Look for Severely Disabled People*, The Spastics Society, Meldreth Manor School, Cambridgeshire.

Reed, L. (1991b) *The Meldreth Series: Billiards. Full Rules and Equipment Guide*, The Spastics Society, Meldreth Manor School, Cambridgeshire.

Reed, L. (1991c) *The Meldreth Series: Bowls. Full Rules and Equipment Guide*, The Spastics Society, Meldreth Manor School, Cambridgeshire.

Reed, L. (1991d) *The Meldreth Series: Cricket. Full Rules and Equipment Guide*, The Spastics Society, Meldreth Manor School, Cambridgeshire.

Reed, L. (1991e) *The Meldreth Series: Roboule. Full Rules and Equipment Guide*, The Spastics Society, Meldreth Manor School, Cambridgeshire.

Reed, L. (1991f) *The Meldreth Series: Side Tennis. Full Rules and Equipment Guide*, The Spastics Society, Meldreth Manor School, Cambridgeshire.

Reed, L. (1991g) *The Meldreth Series: Tenpin Bowling. Full Rules and Equipment Guide*, The Spastics Society, Meldreth Manor School, Cambridgeshire.

Robinson, C. (1991) *Home and Away: Respite Care in the Community*, Venture Press, Birmingham.

Rostron, A. and Lovett, S. (1981) A new outlook with the computer. *Special Education: Forward Trends*, **8**, 29–31.

Russell, P. (1989) *The Wheelchair Child*, Souvenir Press, London.

Sanderson, H., Harrison, J. and Price, S. (1991) *Aromatherapy and Massage for People with Learning Difficulties*, John Abbott Printers, Lutterworth.

Saunders, P. (1984) *Micros for Handicapped Users*, Helena Press, Whitby.

Save the Children Fund Playtrac Team (1989) *Playtrac Handbook*, Save the Children, London.

Schleien, S.J. and Tipton Ray, M. (1988) *Community Recreation and Persons with Disabilities – Strategies for Integration*, Brookes, Baltimore.

Schleien, S.J., Cameron, J., Rynders, J. and Slick, C. (1988) Acquisition and generalization of leisure skills from school to the home and community by learners with severe multihandicaps. *Therapeutic Recreation Journal*, **22**, 53–71.

Schleien, S.J., Light, C.L., McAvoy, L.H. and Baldwin, C.K. (1989) Best professional practices: serving persons with severe multiple disabilities.

Therapeutic Recreation Journal. **23**, 27–40.

Scott, B. (1986) Northgate Arts project: providing hospital residents with access to the arts. *Mental Handicap,* **14**, 163–5.

Seale, J. (1989) Self-injurious behaviour – a role for the computer. *Computer Applications to Special Education, No. 9,* University of Keele, Keele.

Sebba, J. (1988) *The Education of People with Profound and Multiple Handicaps, Resource Materials for Staff Training,* Manchester University Press, Manchester.

Segal, S. (ed.) (1990) *Creative Arts and Mental Disability,* AB Academic Publishers, Bicester.

Seligman, M. (1975) *Helplessness: On Depression, Development and Death,* W.H. Freeman and Co, San Francisco.

Shearer, A. (1986) *Building Community,* Campaign for People with Mental Handicaps, London.

Sherborne, V. (1990) *Developmental Movement for Children: Mainstream, Special Needs and Pre-school,* Cambridge University Press, Cambridge.

Shuttleworth, A. (1987) Working with the community. *Community Living,* **1**, 18–19.

Simon, G. (ed) (1986) *The Step on the Ladder – Assessment and Management of Children with Multiple Handicaps,* British Institute of Mental Handicap, Kidderminster.

Singh, N.N. and Millichamp, C.J. (1987) Independent and social play training among profoundly mentally retarded adults: training, maintenance, generalization and long-term follow up. *Journal of Applied Behavior Analysis,* **20**, 23–34.

Smedley, G. (1989) *A Guide to Canoeing With Disabled Persons,* British Canoe Union, Nottingham.

Smith, M.A. (1976) Leisure: a perspective on contemporary society. *The Society of Leisure,* **1**, 13–29.

Smith, R. and Williamson, D. (1992) *Practical Innovations for Nine Adapted Activities, Games and Sports. Vol 1 Workshop Seminar Manual,* Nottingham Polytechnic, Nottinghamshire.

Social Services Inspectorate (1993) *Whose Life is it Anyway? A Report of an Inspection of Services for People With Multiple Impairments,* Department of Health, London.

Stalker, K. (1990) *'Share the Care': An Evaluation of a Family-Based Respite Care Service,* Jessica Kingsley, London.

Sykes, D., Townsend, K. and Deakin, D. (1985) Inflatable structures and their use in the education of children with profound handicaps. *Mental Handicap,* **13**, 163–5.

Tait, J., Graham, G. and Watts, T.(1990) *Computers and Other Micro-electronics in the Development of P.M.L.D. Children,* TGW Software Developments, Worksop.

Tokarski, W. (1985) Some social psychological notes on the meaning of work and leisure. *Leisure Studies,* **4**, 227–31.

Upton, G. (ed) (1979) *Physical and Creative Activities for the Mentally Handicapped,* Cambridge University Press, Cambridge.

Voeltz, L.J., Hempshill, N.J., Brown, S. *et al.* (1983) *The Special Friends Program: A Trainer's Manual for Integrated School Settings,* University of Hawaii, Department of Special Education, Honolulu.

Wacker, D.P., Berg, W.K., Wiggins, B. *et al.* (1985) Evaluation of reinforcer preferences for profoundly handicapped students. *Journal of Applied Behavior Analysis*, **18**, 173–8.

Wacker, D.P., Wiggins, B., Fowler, M. and Berg, W.K. (1988) Training students with profound or multiple handicaps to make requests via microswitches. *Journal of Applied Behavior Analysis*, **21**, 331–43.

Walsh, J. (1985a) Setting up a 'friendship scheme': Part I. *Mental Handicap*, **13**, 58–9.

Walsh, J. (1985b) Setting up a 'friendship scheme': Part II. *Mental Handicap*, **13**, 1210–11.

Water Sports Division, British Sports Association for the Disabled (1983) *Water Sports for the Disabled*, E.P. Publishing, Wakefield.

Wertheimer, A. (1983) *Leisure: A CMH Discussion Paper*, Campaign for Mentally Handicapped People, London.

Whittaker, J. (1992) Can anyone help me to understand the logic of Snoezelen? *Community Living*, October, 15.

Wilcox, B. and Bellamy, G.T. (1987a) *A Comprehensive Guide to the Activities Catalog*, Brookes, Baltimore.

Wilcox, B. and Bellamy, G.T. (1987b) *The Activities Catalog*, Brookes, Baltimore.

Williams, R.F. (1986) The values of volunteer benefactors. *Mental Retardation*, **24**, 163–8.

Wood, M. (1982) *Music for Living*, British Institute of Mental Handicap, Kidderminster.

Wood, M. (1983) *Music for Mentally Handicapped People*, Souvenir Press, London.

Wuerch, L.M. and Voeltz, L.M. (1982) *Longitudinal Leisure Skills for Severely Handicapped Learners. The Ho'onanea Curriculum Component*, Paul Brookes Publishing Co, Baltimore.

VIDEO TAPES

Making Progress (1986); Supplier: Concord Videos and Film Council, 210 Felixstowe Road, Ipswich IP3 9BJ.
Tel: 0473 726012.

Sounds Like a Rainbow to Me (1987); Supplier: Elizabeth House, 5 Cromwell Road, Lancaster LA1 5BD.
Tel: 0524 39552.

Snoezelen (1991); Supplier: Rompa, Goyt Side Road, Chesterfield S40 2PLH.
Tel: 0246 211777.

Switches, Toys, Computers Supplier: BILD, Wolverhampton Road, Kidderminster DY10 3PP.
Tel: 0562 850251.

The Meldreth Games Series; Supplier: Cerebral Palsy Sport, Sycamore Sports Centre, Hungerhill Road, St Anns, Nottingham NG3 4NG.
Tel: 0602 692314.

Wake Up It's Daytime; Supplier: Demeter Films, 30 Lambs Conduit Street, London WC1N 3LE.
Tel: 071 832 5432.

Working with Clive (1989); Supplier: Grapevine TV, Hebron House, Sion Road, Bedminster, Bristol BS3 3BD.
Tel: 0272 637973.

You and Me 'Whole-Body-Movement' Teaching Video (1993); Supplier: You and Me Yoga Centre, The Cottage, Burton-in-Kendal, Carnforth, Lancs LA6 1ND. Tel: 0524 782103.

JOURNALS, MAGAZINES AND PERIODICALS

Eye Contact; Contact address: RNIB, 224 Portland Street, London W1N 6AA. Tel: 071 388 1266.

Focus; Contact address: RNIB, 224 Portland Street, London W1N 6AA. Tel: 071 388 1266.

Growth Point; Contact address: Horticultural Therapy, Goulds Ground, Vallis Way, Frome, Somerset BA11 3DW. Tel: 0373 464782.

HAPA Journal; Contact address: HAPA, Fulham Palace, Bishop's Avenue, London SW6 6EA. Tel: 071 731 1435.

Information Exchange; Contact address: Wendy McCracken, Oakes Green, Royal Schools for the Deaf, Stanley Road, Cheadle Hulme, Cheadle, Cheshire SK8 6RF. Tel: 061 437 6744.

Keynotes: Contact address: CASE, Department of Psychology, University of Keele, Keele, Staffordshire S5 5BG. Tel: 0782 619373.

PMLD Link; Contact address: The Old Rectory, Hope Mansell, Ross-on-Wye, Herefordshire.

Talking Sense; Contact address: 11–13 Clifton Terrace, London N4 3SR. Tel: 071 272 7774.

LEARNING PACKS

A Leisure Resource Training Pack for Use with People with Profound Intellectual and Multiple Disabilities (ed. L. Lambe) (1991); Supplier: Mencap PIMD Section, Piper Hill School, 200 Yew Tree Lane, Northenden, Manchester M23 0FF.

Body Awareness, Contact and Communication Knill, M. and Knill, C. (1986); Contact address: Learning Development Aids, Duke Street, Wisbech, Cambridgeshire PE13 2AE. Tel: 0945 63441.

Galaxies The Consortium ILEA (1984); Contact address: The Resources for Learning Difficulties Consortium, Jack Tizard School, Finlay Street, London SW6 6HB. Tel: 071 736 8877.

I Can Do It! Barnardo's (1992); Contact address: Barnardo's, Tanners Lane, Barkingside, Ilford, Essex IG6 1QG.

'Whole-Body-Movement' Lessons Plans (1992) Gunstone; Contact address: You and Me Yoga Centre, The Cottage, Burton-in-Kendal, Carnforth, Lancs LA6 1ND. Tel: 0524 782103.

'Whole-Body-Movement' Colour Code Instruction pack (1993) Gunstone; Contact address: You and Me Yoga Centre, The Cottage, Burton-in-Kendal, Carnforth, Lancs LA6 1ND. Tel: 0524 782103.

ADDRESSES OF ORGANIZATIONS RELATED TO TRAINING

Spastics Society, Castle Priory College, Wallingford, Oxfordshire OX16 0HE. Tel: 0491 375511.

BILD, Wolverhampton Road, Kidderminster, Worcs DY10 3PP. (Short courses at different venues.)

Penny Lacey, School of Education, University of Birmingham, Edgbaston, Birmingham B15 2TP.
Tel: 0321 414 4878
(Part-time course, run jointly with BILD, called 'Interdisciplinary work with people with profound and multiple learning disabilities'. It is open to workers from all disciplines and takes one year to complete.)

RNIB Multiple Disability Training Service, 1 The Square, 111 Broad Street, Edgbaston, Birmingham B15 1AS. (Modular course leading to Certificate in Multiple Disability.)

PLANET, c/o Harperbury Hospital, Harper Lane, Radlett, Herts WD7 9HQ. Tel: 0923 854861, ext 4384.

Playtrac, Save the Children Fund, c/o Harperbury Hospital, Harper Lane, Radlett, Herts WD7 9HQ.
Tel: 0923 854861.

Mencap PIMD Section, Piper Hill School, 200 Yew Tree Lane, Northenden, Manchester M23 0FF.
Tel: 061 998 4161.

Profound and Multiple Impairment Service, c/o White Top Research Unit, The University, Dundee DD1 4HN.
Tel: 0382 23181.

2

The ecology of leisure provision: contexts and engagement

James Hogg

INTRODUCTION

All individuals and groups of individuals live in, and interact with, a wider world of people and places. They influence this world in varying degrees and at the same time are affected by it. With respect to leisure, this pattern of relationships may be referred to as the **ecology of leisure**. This ecology embraces the various contexts in which leisure is pursued and the activities enjoyed. With respect to people with profound and multiple disabilities, it includes their aspirations and needs as well as those of their parents, carers and the statutory and voluntary sector staff who are involved with them.

In this chapter we consider various aspects of the ecology of leisure. We begin with a brief comment on leisure for minority groups and the disadvantage they may experience. The expressed needs of parents and carers are reviewed and some of the situations and models of leisure provision that are particularly relevant to offering high-quality provision in this area are noted. Clearly, much of the detail with respect to provision is covered elsewhere in this book. Later in the chapter we address another aspect of the ecology of leisure, i.e. the interaction of the person with profound and multiple disabilities with different classes of leisure activity and the experience and benefits so gained.

LEISURE: THE WIDER CONTEXT

Although increased opportunity for leisure is seen as a significant trend in western society, many minority groups do not have equal opportunities in their access to leisure. Green, Hebron and Woodward (1990) note several groups for whom leisure in the conventional sense is not readily accessible, among them women, elderly people and those from ethnic minority groups. To those we might well add the carers of people with disabilities and those for whom they care. This is nowhere more the case than for people with profound and multiple disabilities. A survey of the needs of parents and carers of such people (Hogg and Lambe, 1988) showed that the average time spent in caring was over 7 hours per day, and in some instances extended to 16 hours. Such day-to-day and year-to-year activity inevitably curtails parents' and carers' opportunities for leisure.

Nevertheless, that people with disabilities generally should have the opportunity to participate in leisure activities has now been clearly on the agenda for some years. That people with profound and multiple disabilities should have equal access is perhaps a more recent concern, but one which is evidenced by the many initiatives described in this book.

Where does this relatively recent interest come from? Our concern with leisure for people with profound and multiple disabilities reflects in part the impact of theories of normalization and social role valorization which emphasize the importance of people having opportunities to engage in activities and live in circumstances that society values. Whatever the reality for some minority groups, leisure is a valued norm for late 20th century western society, and therefore should be extended even to those with the greatest disabilities.

THE NEEDS OF PARENTS AND CARERS

However far the developmental disabilities of people with profound and multiple disabilities claim our attention with regard to their therapeutic and educational needs, their lives are not, and should not be, one long intervention programme. As for most of us, a substantial part of their day or week offers opportunities for activities that enhance their quality of life and their development without necessarily being directed to highly specific objectives. The term 'leisure', as defined in Chapter 1, conveniently encompasses such activities. In Hogg and Lambe's (1988) national survey of the needs of parents and carers of people with profound and multiple disabilities, respondents showed clearly the extent to which they themselves recognized the need for leisure and contributed to its provision. They were asked how long they spent in organizing leisure activities for their son or daughter each day, and at weekends and during holidays. While almost half the sample spent less than an hour organizing activities during the week, a majority spent more than 1 hour each day, with nearly 15% indicating over 4 hours per day. At weekends and during holidays this pattern shifted radically, with over one-third spending more than 4 hours in organizing leisure activities. Regardless of the time spent on weekdays, all parents and carers noted a significant increase in involvement in leisure at weekends and holidays.

It should be noted that making leisure available has to be set against a background of the time-consuming care on a day-to-day basis noted above. Nevertheless, respondents indicated the need for more information on leisure activities and more facilities appropriate to their son or daughter. This theme is taken up again in Chapter 13, where Lambe and Mount describe how, in response to the demand indicated in the survey, leisure workshops were evolved for parents and carers, while Lambe, in Chapter 14, describes a distance learning pack on leisure provision for people with profound and multiple disabilities.

It should be added that, although we have taken our starting point as parents' and carers' needs, a good knowledge of leisure provision is essential for many front-line professional staff as well as volunteers. Such people provide an essential and complementary contribution to the context in which leisure provision is offered, and again, Lambe, in Chapter 14, describes the use of the distance learning pack with a group of volunteers.

The present volume, in describing specific activities, illustrates a wide range of differing contexts and models of leisure provision for people with profound and multiple disabilities. Indeed, in a very real sense any context in which members of the wider society may enjoy leisure is likely to be appropriate to such individuals. This may include clubs in which membership is totally integrated, e.g. social clubs for people generally, clubs with a special interest, clubs for people of a particular background, e.g. Irish centres, or wider community settings such as leisure centres. Such access will need to be facilitated by a friend, companion or volunteer on a one-to-one basis, either informally or through an organized scheme.

Schemes facilitating integrated leisure opportunities have been set in motion by both Social Services departments and voluntary organizations, and are now active across much of the country. Their advantage is that contact with the wider community is an inherent part of the scheme. In a recent initiative in Manchester (Sanderson, 1990), the sequence of events involved in establishing such contact is clearly described. The coordinator determines the leisure interests of the person with a learning disability through direct contact with the person or his or her family or advocate. On the basis of this information local clubs, organizations and educational establishments are approached in order to find an individual who is willing to share her or his leisure time. Introductions are made and leisure sharing begins. Leisure Together, for example, has been established as a voluntary organization outside statutory social service provision and has raised money to employ the coordinator who carries out these tasks. Other Leisure Link schemes are described elsewhere (Lees *et al.* (ND); Browne and Singh, 1990). In contrast to the club orientation, the focus here is likely to be on a specific activity, e.g. a sport, gardening, country pursuits, rather than the wider menu of the club. This approach is in no way mutually exclusive to club-based activity. Indeed, the two approaches may be seen as complementary, especially for people who may not be involved in employment or day provision.

Specialized clubs such as those supported by the National Federation of Gateway Clubs, while traditionally concerned with more able people, have increasingly turned their attention to people with profound and multiple learning disabilities, as noted in Chapter 14 of the present volume, and are actively engaged in training volunteers.

Both the fully integrated and the specialized examples of provision noted above may be accessed from the person's home or from some wider day service in which they are involved. With respect to the former, it may be anticipated from the survey findings that many individuals do enjoy a considerable range of leisure activities in their homes.

We noted earlier the substantial investment of time on the part of carers at weekends and holidays. This volume describes in detail schemes specifically aimed at providing extended leisure opportunities during such times (Chapter 9). Again, provision may be fully integrated, or involve more specialized schemes of the kind described by Lambe (1986), when facilities not normally used during holidays, such as hydrotherapy pools, can be brought into play.

In the foregoing we have focused on the overall context in which leisure needs are met. We need now to view such provision from the perspective of the person with profound and multiple disabilities. What does she or he derive from leisure activities, and indeed, what should be gained and experienced?

CHOICE AND ENGAGEMENT

One of the challenges we all confront is how we offer and understand choice for people with whom we often have great difficulty in communicating. Nash (1953) begins his book on leisure with a question that you might like to answer for yourself, and one which embodies the freedom implied by 'non-obligated time'. 'What .. ' .... he asks '. . . would you do with a year off?' And of the survey he did, he comments: 'Here they are writing poetry, building a cabin, making a piece of pottery, singing a song, playing the ukulele, painting a picture, sailing a boat, playing tennis. They are taking pictures, calling a square dance, knitting some socks, making a dress, gardening, re-doing old furniture, binding a book, writing a play. They go to the ends of the earth to see canyons, climb mountains, chase caribou, follow migratory birds, dig dinosaur eggs in the Gobi desert . . . ' and so on. The diversity of these activities is enormous, and you may be prompted to think about the different functions leisure might serve in general for us all, and in particular for people with profound and multiple disabilities. In Nash's (1953) book *Philosophy of Recreation and Leisure* are many perceptive observations and a framework in which to look at leisure. Brown, Bayer and MacFarlane (1989) have already related Nash's ideas to the field of leisure and intellectual disability. Here we will pursue this application by considering how these ideas relate specifically to profound and multiple disabilities.

Figure 2.1 shows an adaptation of an illustration in which Nash shows a progression of leisure and occupation from negative pursuits, crime and being a mere spectator, through performance of other people's creations to creative production, and beyond to Rodin's brooding thinker. The heights of athletic success and, a little lower, the ability to make things, are also acknowledged. (In Nash's original illustration this progression is almost entirely all male, whether crime or a male artist painting a fellow male. Women do appear, from behind, watching the tennis.) Nash also provides a more abstract account of his scheme which is helpful and interesting.

First, Nash's scale on the left runs from below zero, through zero up to 4 and on to infinity. He comments; 'A little of each above zero, depending on work patterns, may be good, but too many activities low on the scale are dulling, and in the end progress and development of the individual and group are retarded.'

Acts performed against society form the lowest level. The examples Nash gives are ones which relate closely to some of the events in England over past years, as he is talking about antisocial behaviour as a form of distorted leisure activity. He would certainly see the events on a number of English council estates in recent years as an appropriate example. Here, stolen cars are driven in a spectacularly dangerous fashion ('hotting'), to the delight of some and the horror of others. This may not be our idea of a leisure pursuit, but according to those who enjoy the activity, what is important is the 'buzz' it gives them

USE OF LEISURE TIME
Participation broadly interpreted

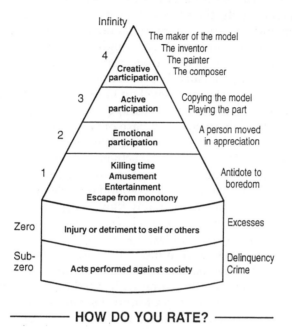

Infinity

The maker of the model
The inventor
The painter
The composer

4 Creative participation

3 Active participation — Copying the model / Playing the part

2 Emotional participation — A person moved in appreciation

1 Killing time / Amusement / Entertainment / Escape from monotony — Antidote to boredom

Zero — Injury or detriment to self or others — Excesses

Sub-zero — Acts performed against society — Delinquency / Crime

——— HOW DO YOU RATE? ———

Figure 2.1 Nash's (1953) hierarchical scheme of leisure in relation to varying degrees of participation. He noted: 'A little of each above zero, depending on work patterns, may be good, but too many activities low in the scale are dulling, and in the end progress and development of the individual and the group are retarded.'

in a life which lacks the opportunity for creative engagement in other fields, or where the opportunity for such engagement is not perceived.

If these below-zero activities are very unlikely to be undertaken by people with profound disabilities, not so Nash's zero level of 'Injury or detriment to self'. Among people with profound disabilities examples of both types of behaviour will be observed. In Hogg and Lambe's (1988) survey over 70% of parents and carers reported that their son or daughter exhibited some problematical behaviour. High on their lists were the self-stimulatory stereotyped behaviours that act as a barrier to any kind of creative engagement with the world around. Self-injurious behaviour, sometimes literally life-threatening, was also reported. There is no one simple explanation for such behaviour, though we have learnt in recent years how to go about functionally analysing its causes (Emerson, 1992). But among these analyses there can be little doubt that absence of stimulation from, and interaction with, the world plays its part. Through appropriate stimulation and encouragement to interact, some difficult behaviours can be reduced or eliminated. Although we might see such efforts as educational or therapeutic, there can be little doubt that creative occupation through leisure has a central part to play in moving individuals from Nash's zero level on to more constructive activities.

Entertainment, amusement, escape from monotony, although forming only the 'above-ground' base of Nash's pyramid, might well provide one such form of engagement. We know from several surveys that have been undertaken that it is activities at this level that constitute the primary leisure activity for so many people with intellectual disabilities, including those with profound disabilities. Watching television or listening to music invariably figure large in such reports. But such essentially passive activities also constitute a central part of use of free time for many of us. Nash has a subscale here that runs from 'killing time', to 'escape from monotony' to 'amusement' and on to entertainment. The overall aim of all of these is an antidote to boredom. There is nothing inherently wrong with avoiding boredom. Certainly, if we can assist people with profound disabilities to avoid boredom this would be a notable success, particularly if such success was reflected in some reduction or elimination of self-destructive behaviour. Recent work by Argyle at Oxford University's experimental psychology laboratory has looked at leisure in relation to people's personalities. He reports that those who watch a great deal of television emerge as a somewhat unsatisfied group of people, although those who watch soap operas seriously tend to be a much happier group. Argyle comments: 'People come to know the characters even though they are fictional. There is a tight supportive group, and people feel they belong to this. It's like having a set of secondhand friends.'

We cannot determine whether this is exactly what Nash intended when he made the distinction between what is essentially passive enjoyment of 'entertainment' and active emotional participation while listening to music, going to the theatre, or indeed watching soap operas. Nevertheless, difficult though it may be to identify, there are quite distinct experiences of being involved in leisure in situations in which we are not actively, physically taking part.

This distinction is crucially important in relation to leisure provision and creative occupation for people with profound and multiple disabilities. The last few years have seen exciting developments in the field of multisensory stimulation (see Chapter 4). What is urgently needed is a greater understanding of the **kind** of engagement in which people are involved when they enjoy such activities. There is no inherent reason why placing someone in a room which has cost tens of thousands of pounds to prepare should be any more meaningful than sitting them in front of a television set. Only by understanding intimately the personality, the sensory strengths and the way in which the person communicates emotional experiences can we begin to utilize these developments in a way which takes us from mere antidotes to boredom, to what Nash calls emotional participation. It is worth noting that psychologists have started to study in detail the behavioural and emotional states and communicative strengths of people with profound disabilities, and this research may well provide the basis for careful evaluation of the significance of leisure in the lives of individual people (e.g. Latchford, 1989; Guess *et al.*, 1991).

Such approaches are equally applicable when we move to Nash's active participation. Again, Argyll's work has shown that people who do actively participate in leisure through sports, choirs, etc. are generally happier than those for whom these are passive pursuits. There is nothing new in that finding. Particularly in the study of ageing, active involvement in leisure and social activities is one of the best predictors, along with good health and financial security, of successful ageing (Schaie, 1983). We have seen a revolution in the weight given to active involvement in leisure by people with profound disabilities; we must be clear that, in engaging in these activities, it is not only the experience the person has that is important but also their active input. This input might be, for example, the postural adjustments that a person makes to the movement of a horse. Here, the use of muscles, organs of balance, motivation to remain on the horse, albeit with support, are the contribution of the person to the activity, a contribution that would simply not have been possible without the opportunity to engage in the activity. Again I would suggest that we need to be sensitive to such contributions to the activity, and not overwhelm the person with excessive support that takes all the initiative from them. Similarly, sensitivity to their progress is called for, with our making increasing, if sometimes minutely small, demands on the person.

From such active involvement Nash moves to creative participation. Psychologists have traditionally proposed two views of creativity. One is creativity of the kind I think Nash has in mind, the creativity of Charlie Parker or Marie Curie, Virginia Woolf or Ella Fitzgerald, Charles Darwin or Benjamin Britten – original work that offers a new vision and serves as a model and influence for others. While this kind of creativity is rarely identified with leisure in the sense defined here,

Nash's model clearly places it on a continuum with the kind of creativity that can be manifest in leisure activities. The other view of creativity is not linked to the great names but suggests that each of us can be creative within a chosen sphere, doing things which for us are original and involve new perceptions. In this sense much of life can be creative, particularly perhaps in the early stages of development.

Can people with profound and multiple disabilities be creative? Certainly in the second sense, the sense in which I believe all of us can express creativity. The choice of a novel combination of colours while painting, a new expressive movement during dance, a movement personal to that individual, are all creative in personal terms.

Helpful though Nash's scheme is, it might usefully be revised to a more democratic model which is non-hierarchical, and which acknowledges that non-adaptive behaviour may in varying degrees be a consequence of any level of activity (Figure 2.2). The hierarchical

USE AND SIGNIFICANCE OF LEISURE TIME

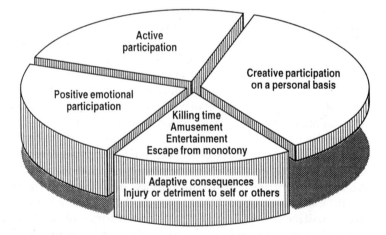

Figure 2.2 A non-hierarchical scheme derived from Nash's conception of the purpose of leisure. Here, however, movement between any two categories is possible, although the higher value placed by Nash on increasing participation and creativity is reflected in the increasing area of the segments as we move clockwise from 'killing time' to 'creative participation'. The depth from lower to upper circles indicates the degree of maladaptive consequences that are potentially associated with type of activity. This is greatest for 'killing time' and least for 'creative participation'.

structure has been removed, although Nash's four areas of activity are retained. Movement between them, however, is within a single plane, reflecting that we can move between any pair and that all areas will contribute to our overall pattern of leisure time. The area of the circle as we move around it has been increased, with creative participation given greater weight than killing time, etc. The bottom edge replaces Nash's lower depths and is intended to indicate that any of the categories of engagement can have detrimental consequences. Even creative participation is not entirely dissociated from self-destructive behaviour in this scheme, and illustrates that some creative people do engage in such activity, e.g. through excessive alcohol intake by the jazz trumpeter Chet Baker, or destruction of the nasal passages through paint fumes by the painter Paul Klee. However, the probability of such maladaptive behaviour is greatest in the 'killing time' category, as reflected in the difference between the upper and lower circles, and is least in the case of creative participation.

In assisting people to plan both their obligated and non-obligated time, I would like to suggest that such a scheme could provide a useful heuristic for professionals in a number of ways. First, in determining the availability of the leisure options we offer in such a way that the range of activities potentially provides the different levels of engagement described by Nash. Exposing people with profound learning disabilities to such a range will put them in a position to make informed choices. Secondly, evaluation of the significance of leisure activities for individuals can be undertaken on a psychologically and socially more meaningful level. In a detailed analysis of the many concepts that go to make up 'quality of life', Goode (1988) notes a variety of psychological factors, including self-esteem, frequency and intensity of positive and negative affect, as well as avoidance of negative affect, i.e. restlessness, loneliness, boredom, depression and anxiety, and optimization of positive affect, i.e. excitement and pride. Among psychosocial concepts he notes social contacts and support, stress and positive social interaction.

Whatever level of involvement we are considering, it is important to recall that normalization philosophy has emphasized that the activities in which we engage people should be seen to be appropriate to their age. However, since choice is at the heart of leisure, many will be aware that our judgement of age-appropriateness may on occasions clash with a person's choice of activity. Some professionals in this situation, whose commitment to normalization is paramount, would urge that ensuring age-appropriateness should take priority over choice, and an activity should be denied or substituted with a less preferred but age-appropriate one. The challenge, however, is to find an equivalent and equally enjoyable activity that **is** deemed age-appropriate. Often there is equipment or material that is age-appropriate, and the Mencap Leisure Pack (see Lambe 1991, and Chapter 14 of the present volume) draws attention to some of this. But as with all philosophies, we should not lose sight of what is really behind the emphasis on age-appropriateness, which is much more to do with the overall image that is conveyed to others about the people with whom we are concerned. Interior decor that lacks dignity and conveys a very demeaning image of people is not acceptable.

In terms of reconciling conflicts between choice and age-appropriateness, we should also be looking on leisure activities as the opportunity to begin to make choices and to learn about making choices. Some educational curricula for children and adults are now emphasizing the ability to make choices as part of the curriculum, something to be learnt along with and as a part of self-help skills, communication and the other familiar areas of the curriculum (e.g. Bannerman *et al.*, 1990).

It is also important to note that, while we may distinguish leisure from other activities by referring to 'non-obligated time', there is a sense in which leisure is not so readily separated from 'obligated time', such as from education, therapy or even religious worship. The experiences we have during particular leisure activities and the benefits that may be gained may not be so readily distinguishable from what goes in these other areas of life. The physical gains from swimming or horse-riding merge these activities with therapy, and indeed both activities may be viewed as therapies: 'hydro-' and 'hippo-' respectively. Many leisure activities do require education and continued learning, whether relatively cerebral like chess, or requiring great motor coordination like fencing. Even some definitions of work that see such as activity as the fulfilment of a predetermined goal do not differ in every respect from engagement in leisure.

CONCLUSION

The total context for leisure provision that we have reviewed in this chapter embraces our philosophy in relation to people in minority groups, notably those with profound and multiple disabilities and their carers, the form that provision takes, and our sensitivity

to the way in which the person with profound disabilities responds to, and contributes to, leisure activities. It is clear that we have only just begun to explore these relations, relations which constitute as worthwhile a field of study and endeavour as others already on the agenda concerned with therapy, education and management. Only by placing leisure on an equal footing to these other areas will we be able to say that we are truly addressing the whole person in a way in which they are fully respected as an individual.

REFERENCES

Bannerman, D.J., Sheldon, J.B., Sherman, J.A. and Harchik, A.E. (1990) Balancing the right to habilitation with the right to personal liberties: the rights of people with developmental disabilities to eat too many doughnuts and take a nap. *Journal of Applied Behavior Analysis*, **23**, 79–89.

Brown, R.I., Bayer, M.B. and MacFarlane, C. (1989) *Rehabilitation Programmes: Performance and Quality of Life of Adults With Developmental Handicaps*, Lugus, Toronto.

Browne, C. and Singh, R. (1990) 'Leisure Links': the way forward for community leisure. *Mental Handicap*, **18**, 35–7.

Emerson, E. (1992) Self-injurious behaviour: an overview of recent trends in epidemiological and behavioural research. *Mental Handicap Research*, **5**, 49–81.

Goode, D.A. (1988) *Principles and Recommendations from the Quality of Life Project*, Valhalla, New York.

Green, E., Hebron, S. and Woodward, D. (1990) *Women's Leisure: What Leisure?*, Macmillan, Basingstoke.

Guess, D., Roberts, S., Siegel-Causey, E. *et al.* (1991) *Investigations into the State Behaviors of Students with Severe and Profound Handicapping Conditions*, University of Kansas, Kansas.

Hogg, J. and Lambe, L. (1988) *Sons and Daughters with Profound Retardation and Multiple Handicaps Attending Schools and Social Education Centres: Final Report*, Mencap, London.

Lambe, L. (1986) MENCAP's PRMH project – hydrotherapy scheme helps handicapped children in major way. *Parents Voice*, Summer, 10–11.

Lambe, L. (1991) *A Leisure Resource Training Pack for Use with People with Profound Intellectual and Multiple Disabilities*, Mencap, London.

Latchford, G. (1989) *Towards an Understanding of Profound Mental Handicap*, Unpublished PhD thesis, University of Edinburgh.

Lees, A., Payne, A., Metcalf, C. and Hopkinson, P. (ND) *Leisure Link: A Scheme to Promote Integrative Leisure Activities in Stockport*, Leisure Link, Stockport.

Nash, J.B. (1953) *Philosophy of Recreation and Leisure*, CV Mosby, St. Louis.

Sanderson, H. (1990) *Leisure Link: A Scheme to Provide Integrative Leisure and Educational Activities in Manchester*, Leisure Link, Manchester.
Schaie, W. (1983) *Longitudinal Studies of Adult Psychological Development*, Guildford Press, London.

3

Leisure provision in Europe

Judith Cavet

INTRODUCTION

'They have to have leisure or they are not living.' This comment by a Belgian doctor about the needs of people who are profoundly and multiply disabled was made during the course of a European study carried out from 1988 until 1990. The aim of the study was to collect information about leisure activities available to people who are profoundly and multiply disabled. Detailed information about such leisure provision was collected from 28 services which were based in Belgium, France, Holland, Ireland, Germany and the United Kingdom.

The study sought to discover from as wide a variety of sources as possible how people with profound and multiple disabilities might enjoyably spend their free time. A broad view of what comprised leisure was adopted: the notion of free or non-obligated time was the key concept in deciding what might be considered a leisure activity, and activities labelled 'therapy' were included if they might have been regarded by a layperson as leisure. The aim of the project was to develop an extended view of the possible range of activities for people who are too often left unstimulated. In the words of one of the service providers interviewed, 'Boredom is the biggest handicap'.

The services from which detailed information was gathered were selected for the likely expertise of their staff in activity provision for people with profound and multiple disabilities. If services had innovative features, this was a particular bonus. The project collected information both from very small-scale services with a philosophy based on providing an ordinary lifestyle, and from much larger establishments which had particularly interesting features. Residential and day services were included, as were resource centres. Examples of resource centres were a centre which offered support in the use of microtechnology, an organization which worked to promote opportunities in sport and leisure for people with learning disability, a German family relief service and a centre which provided holidays and outdoor pursuits for people with disabilities. The smallest residential service offered a home to three people in a northern English city, while the largest, a Dutch institution, accommodated 670 residents. The smallest day service provided activities for five people and all these activities took place in the community, the service having no base at which users spent time. By contrast, the largest day service was a set of German workshops for 300 people with learning disability. Some services were highly specialized in the sense that all service users were profoundly and multiply disabled, whereas in some others people with profound and multiple disabilities were integrated into a group with fewer specialized needs. The project looked at services for both adults and children, but included a deliberate bias towards adult provision as it was felt that this was the area where deficits in service provision were greatest. Twenty-three of the services were run by non-profit making bodies and five were run by local authorities. All of these last five were UK-based. However, despite the voluntary nature of most of the bodies providing the services visited during this research, 23 of the 28 services received some public funding.

It would be impossible to make general comments about the pattern of service provision for people with profound and multiple disabilities in any European country from a study of this size. However, a few comparisons may be of interest to readers in the UK. The first point to note is that while all children of school age in the UK and in what was West Germany had a right to a school place at the time the study was carried out, this was not always the case in the other countries visited. In those countries children with profound and multiple disabilities might be excluded from school, although in this case day service provision in special centres was often available. It is also worth noting that investment was still taking place in some large-scale institutions in mainland Europe, and that in some countries children were still admitted to these institutions, although less frequently than formerly. Such institutions were not hospitals, but they were comparable in size to the smaller British hospitals for people with learning disability, although often the fabric of their buildings was more recent. This is not to suggest that community care policies did not exist in mainland Europe, but to point out that in some countries they had had a less marked effect on the pattern of service provision for people with profound and multiple disabilities than was the case in the UK.

ACTIVITIES

In the course of the study a frequent question from service providers was whether there was any activity for people with profound and multiple disabilities that they had overlooked. Table 3.1 is a list of activities arranged in ten main groups, with examples of the sorts of

Table 3.1 Types of activities

Number of services reporting activity	Category of activity	Examples of activities
18	Specially developed environments	Snoezelen rooms; snoezelen corners; vibrating floors, beds and chairs; sensory gardens; multisensory events; bubble machines; tactile cloths and boards; inflatables; waterbeds; 'feely boxes'; soft play equipment
27	Physical activities	Swimming and water-based activities; running and jogging; rebound therapy; wheelchair dancing; boating and canoeing; cycling; skating; parachute games; movement to music; yoga; ball games; use of gym equipment; 'rough and tumble' play; flying; horse-riding; horse-drawn carts
16	Task-orientated activities	Bathing and showering; hair drying; cooking; make-up and grooming; horticulture; handicrafts; domestic chores
23	Artistic activities	Music making; listening to music; painting; watching television; films and video tapes; dancing; photograph albums and scrapbooks; drama and dramatized story-telling; puppetry
14	Play and games	Toys; games; books; sand; specialized playgrounds; pethna machines
10	Microtechnology	Computers; toys operated by switches; cassette players operated by switches
4	Spiritual activities	Church attendance
24	Outings and holidays	
9	Nature-related activities	Ponding; country walks; becoming familiar with domestic animals and plants
9	Massage	Reflexology; aromatherapy combined with massage

activities included in each group. It should be made clear that, while people with profound and multiple disabilities participated in all of the activities outlined, their participation was often partial in the sense that it required a good deal of support from staff. Ways of providing the activities are described subsequently in this volume by authors with specialized experience of the particular fields in question. Here I have identified some of the common themes which emerged during the observation of the range of activities noted.

SENSORY STIMULATION

An emphasis upon sensory stimulation was a common motif throughout the study. The place of sensory stimulation in the education of children and young people has been well documented in the UK by Longhorn (1988) and others. Much of the activity provision observed rested on a similar approach, in that staff were seeking to develop sensory experiences for service users. However, the approach differed in that it was less structured and because the emphasis was upon pleasure rather than learning.

Some leisure activities observed took place in small-scale or large-scale environments designed especially to provide sensory stimulation for people with severe or profound disability (i.e. they fell into the first category in Table 3.1). One example of such specialized provision is the development of multisensory environments, as described in Chapter 4. A second approach to sensory stimulation which was discernible, which will be developed briefly here, was the enhancement of the stimulation to be gained from non-specialized leisure experiences. In this case everyday leisure activities were chosen for their sensory impact and carried out in a way that enhanced the sensory stimulation involved. For example, instead of using a saddle for horse-riding one Dutch institution sometimes sat service users on a sheepskin placed directly on the horse's back, with the aim of allowing the rider to feel in closer contact with the horse. In addition, the stimulation to be gained from horse-riding was said to include becoming familiar with the smell of a horse, the texture of its coat and the change of view given by riding on horseback.

Activities which are basic care tasks were also carried out with the emphasis on pleasure, enjoyment and sensory stimulation. As regards activities such as bathing, shaving and hairwashing, it was suggested that, particularly for people who are extremely disabled, basic care tasks are a major part of their experience and should be carried out slowly and in a way which introduces pleasure to the process. I was told in Belgium and Holland of such tasks: 'It makes no sense to rush', and: 'Washing and eating can also be snoezelen'. The philosophy behind such remarks was that it makes no sense to rush very disabled service users through basic care tasks in an apparently business-like way, if in the process opportunities for stimulation and pleasure are being overlooked. One example of a result of this approach was that the potential for sensory stimulation at mealtimes was emphasized to care staff by managers. Similarly, staff attention was also drawn to the potential of bathtimes for stimulation and enjoyment.

Another manifestation of this type of approach was the use of a variety of types of massage. Reflexology was a reported activity which is less familiar than the now popular aromatherapy. Reflexology operates from the principle that there are reflexes or responsive zones in the feet and hands corresponding to each part and organ of the body. Applying pressure to these zones is believed to be therapeutic and relaxing. The experience from the recipient's point of view is akin to that of having their hands and feet massaged. In Ireland, where I heard most about reflexology, the practice was to concentrate upon the feet. It was suggested that it was an unusual experience for staff to kneel at the feet of clients. The change in relative positions and the nature of the task performed were seen as positive for staff–client relationships.

A similar approach, i.e. with an emphasis upon sensory stimulation, was sometimes taken to the provision of water-based activity. The use of jets of water for stimulation was a common way of providing skin sensation. This might be provided in special swimming pools in Belgium and Holland, or perhaps in a jacuzzi elsewhere. On occasions a 'snoezelen' type approach was combined with water-based activities. For example, at a Belgian institution there were times when water in the swimming pool was heated to a higher temperature than normal and subdued lighting and soothing music were added. At one Dutch institution inflatable dinghies might be used at such special times to take service users out on the swimming pool. The bottoms of the dinghies were not fully inflated so that those in them were better able to feel the water underneath.

SOCIAL INTEGRATION

Participation in leisure activities offers opportunities for relationship making and a context in which relationships between service users and staff or volunteers might be fostered. Where volunteers were involved in activity provision a degree of social integration between service users and their local community developed. For example, in one French service volunteers took service users to the local church on a regular basis.

In addition, participation in leisure activities also offered other avenues for involvement in the wider community. One obvious example occurred when outings and holidays were arranged, although the degree of integration depended on how far such excursions were group or individual ventures. Staff showed imagination in the sort of outings planned. They kept in mind not only participation within the local community, but the pleasure that service users might derive from the specific experiences on offer. A trip to a French industrial museum with much press-button gadgetry enabled service users with profound and multiple disabilities to experience the notion of cause and effect and a sense of having control over their environment by pressing a button, while simultaneously participating in activities enjoyed by the rest of the community. A similar consequence resulted from the overnight stay of an English service user in a modern hotel with button-operated services.

Two Welsh services placed particular emphasis on activity provision organized on an individual basis within the community. In Wales I observed one service user, accompanied by a member of staff, take part in a movement to music session which was held in a local leisure centre and was open to the general public. In the same area two people with profound and multiple disabilities, again each with their own member of staff, attended a yoga class which was run for physically disabled people in a local leisure centre. Another service user with profound and multiple disabilities, a young woman, had joined a private health club where she used the jacuzzi. This was an activity she preferred to swimming because of the higher water temperature involved.

Anecdotal evidence suggests that public attitudes to people with multiple disabilities were not usually an obstacle to social integration, although a few disturbing incidents were reported. Some of the few difficulties which had arisen could perhaps have been avoided by better preparation of the members of the public involved. Practical problems also sometimes arose, a common comment being that water temperatures in public swimming pools were too low for the comfort of some people with profound and multiple disabilities. In this case, if the water temperature were raised on a regular basis to overcome this problem, then segregated sessions resulted and social integration was much less. Another potential danger of which some Welsh service providers were aware was the possibility of 'swamping' community leisure centres with people with learning disabilities, so that the composition of leisure sessions for the public became unbalanced, in the sense that they contained several people with learning disabilities, rather than one or two. Service providers were becoming aware of the need to communicate with each other and coordinate attendance so that sessions did not lose their integrated nature.

The majority of activities described in this study are familiar to the layperson and can be carried out in non-segregated settings. The performance of activities in community-based settings is likely to increase the familiarity of the public with people who are profoundly and multiply disabled, and encourages contact between people with disabilities and the general public. The comments of some Welsh respondents and my own observation of community-based activities in Wales reinforce this view. Staff there and elsewhere were engaged in the process of building up the confidence and familiarity of service users in an activity, while at the same time fostering the same attitudes in the public in its dealings with people who are profoundly and multiply disabled.

One beneficial effect identified by respondents regarding leisure provision in the community was that it gave people with profound and multiple disabilities the opportunity to develop socially valued roles. The organizer of a teenagers' summer activities scheme which utilized community facilities and included some service users with profound and multiple disabilities noted that the community at large had the opportunity to see such people 'doing things'. A staff member at a Welsh community-based day service reported: 'The local community has changed too. They have enjoyed people being there. People have been welcoming and probably will be welcoming in the future.'

STAFFING AND THE USE OF VOLUNTEERS

The training of staff in the services visited was varied, predictably so in the light of the varied nature of the services involved. Care-giving staff were predominantly female and often untrained, partly perhaps for economic reasons, although some service managers saw flexibility about formal qualifications more positively than this. Some respondents indicated that in their view the personal qualities of staff were of paramount importance – empathy, adaptability and initiative were three of the qualities mentioned. As regards trained personnel, nurses, teachers, psychologists and social workers were among those who were responsible for the organization of services. In addition, a number of services employed staff who had expertise in the particular leisure activities which were offered rather than formal qualifications in the disability field. The outside professional who was most likely to have been consulted for advice regarding activity provision was a physiotherapist. Most services offered some sort of in-service training to at least part of their workforce, although its nature was often, in the respondents' own words, 'ad hoc' or 'limited'.

Activity provision for people with profound and multiple disabilities requires high staffing ratios. For the time that an activity such as horse-riding, swimming or massage is being carried out a minimum ratio of one to one is likely to be necessary. It is possible to supplement staffing levels by the use of volunteers, although this device needs careful thought if it is to be used to the best effect.

About three-quarters of the services in the study utilized volunteers, a quarter of them to a very marked extent. Volunteers tended to be young and available primarily in the summer months, hence their usefulness was greatest to services which could cope with their cyclical availability and to those whose youthful service users benefited most from the company of people of a similar age. Play schemes and holiday centres fell into this category. One manager of a holiday centre described volunteers as 'a central part of the centre's operation – without them, we couldn't do half the things we do. At the same time they are an invigorating presence ... continually changing'.

Volunteers were employed overwhelmingly in capacities which brought them into very close interaction with service users. Despite this, the amount of vetting they received varied considerably from service to service. Most induction processes consisted simply of informing volunteers about the nature of the service and then supervising their work. One respondent felt that useful means of retaining volunteers' help included clearly defining the tasks to be accomplished, and offering people a time-limited commitment as an available option.

A few services noted problems in attracting volunteers. One respondent said, 'The biggest problem they have is in knowing what to do'. Direct observation of services suggested that there was some truth in this statement. The needs of the service users with whom interaction was the least immediately rewarding could be overlooked by volunteers, even when some sort of key worker system was in operation. This highlights the need for proper preparation of volunteers and bore out the comment of the respondent who, while commending the benefits volunteers bring, went on to say that volunteers must add to 'the quality of the icing on the cake. They are not and must not be the cake itself'.

SERVICE ACCESSIBILITY AND AVAILABILITY

Two important aspects of service accessibility are attitudinal factors and physical barriers. Staff attitudes are paramount in making available opportunities for enjoyment to people with profound and multiple disabilities, and are dealt with in more depth later in this chapter. As regards the use of community facilities, public attitudes were not found to be a major obstacle. However, an important barrier was the already well-documented one of a physical environment unsuited to the needs of people with disabilities. Complaints regarding the design of public buildings came from staff in France, Ireland and the UK. An Irish respondent said, 'You can't even get into the Post Office. It's worse since they redid it – little doors and so on – and we had the year of the disabled a few years ago.' A London-based respondent reported that her organization aimed to use community facilities with total access, but that in practice 'access is often diabolical'. A respondent in Wales reported: 'Specially designed changing facilities can be a nightmare. Obviously they haven't asked a disabled person's advice.' The same respondent felt that unless people with profound and multiple disabilities were taken into the community, the need for better access would not be demonstrated and therefore the need for improvement would not be raised. Nevertheless, the use of community facilities posed far more difficulties than ought to have been the case, and the question was raised as to who should lobby for change in this respect.

Transport is another important consideration when service accessibility is being considered. Although 25 services did provide at least one means of transport, one respondent spoke for many when she described transport as 'always an issue'. This was the case even in large-scale institutions with specialized facilities, such as those in Holland and Flanders. Here the distance between different parts of the same establishment, dispersed over a large site, might offer a disincentive to busy staff when they were faced with the prospect of a long walk with service users in wheelchairs from living quarters to specialized leisure facilities. One Dutch institution had its own electric bus service within the site to help overcome this difficulty.

When respondents to the study were asked how far the service they offered was available elsewhere locally and nationally, the picture that emerged was frequently one of an uneven pattern of provision and of long waiting lists for those services that did exist. This picture of unmet need was especially acute in relation to day and residential services. In Paris, one children's unit had closed its waiting list as it was impossible to know when the centre would be able to take in more children, while in a Brussels day centre for children with profound and multiple disabilities I was told: 'the difficulty is in finding a place'.

One effect of this state of affairs was that few services regarded publicity as an area requiring great effort. While some services had produced printed material about the service or raised awareness of their role by press coverage, one respondent spoke for many when she said, 'We don't canvas for students. We have too many applicants as it is'. This fear of being swamped by demand resulted in another respondent reporting: 'We have no neon flashing light'. In these circumstances referral of users was likely to be from another service, and the next most likely source of publicity was said to be word of mouth.

Another aspect of leisure activity availability relates to whether, in a given service, activities are available to all users if they wish to pursue them, or whether some are not offered the whole range of activities. Respondents usually affirmed that activities were available to all service users. One respondent said, 'We would change the activities to make them suitable ... modifying the activity and making it suitable ... It's this business of looking at what they can do, as opposed to what they can't do.' Other respondents pointed to the individual nature of the activities provided, and maintained that it was a question of each service user doing what suited them, rather than any question of exclusion of service users from particular activities.

There were, however, a few instances where people with profound and multiple disabilities had been excluded from some services as a whole, rather than purely from a particular activity. One user was seen as having excluded himself from a day service because his high level of anxiety led to seriously damaging self-injurious behaviour. Other grounds for exclusion cited by a small number of services included the need for tube feeding, the displaying of seriously aggressive behaviour or being a carrier of the hepatitis B virus.

MEDICAL AND LEGAL ISSUES

Medical and legal factors did not appear to pose major problems for most respondents, although a variety of issues were raised. Generally there was an acknowledgement of the importance of taking the medical aspects of activities into account. Respondents noted the need to have available adequate information from parents and care-givers regarding the nature of the disabilities of individual service users. Allied to this was the seeking of professional advice as necessary. Several respondents referred to the administration of medication, and reported that workers would give medication as necessary. Some respondents made reference to particular activities or conditions as being areas for special vigilance. These included swimming and rebound therapy.

In general, when discussing the medical aspects of activities, respondents noted the need for care but were positive about the provision of activities. One respondent noted: 'In 1974 it was never imagined that the children would go on outings, because of their fragility. Now all go out – although, of course, with precautions – e.g. on picnics which last a full day, epileptic medication is taken. For visits to the swimming pool, the water must be warm enough and one needs to consider the children's ears. But, despite the need for precautions, all go. Advice is sought from a physiotherapist concerning posture (e.g. of the hips) and from a doctor (e.g. regarding ears). Teamwork is seen as very important.'

With regard to the legal aspects of activity, concerns focused on two areas. Nine respondents raised the matter of insurance and reported that the service for which they worked carried some form of cover. The other matter concerned the seeking of parental consent for leisure activities. There was no unanimity upon this matter with regard to adults, as some of the minority of respondents who raised the matter felt permission should be sought, while others disagreed.

ENJOYMENT AND CHOICE

A very basic question arises when discussing the provision of leisure activities for people who are profoundly and multiply disabled: how can one be sure that, for the many service users whose communication skills are limited, the activities provided are associated with pleasure? Without enjoyment and choice, participation in the activities would merely be a pale imitation of leisure, a sort of 'going through the motions' in order to ape other members of society and perhaps satisfy pressures towards conformity.

The process involved in the provision of enjoyment and choice which emerged from service providers' responses had three aspects. First, it was suggested that it is important to provide diverse opportunities for activities. Secondly, respondents indicated that it is essential to observe minutely service users' responses to the activities. Thirdly, it was said to be necessary to persist in offering an activity until the service user has developed sufficient awareness of what is involved to be able to make an informed choice.

The provision of diverse opportunities demands that staff be as imaginative as possible about the range of opportunities they make available. Hence a wide variety of types of music, outings, food and video tapes was made available at the smallest service visited, the flat for three service users in an urban area of England. Four respondents, each a national of a different country, used the phrase 'trial and error' to emphasize that one must try different activities and then monitor users' reactions.

Observation of non-verbal communication and body language was seen as an important means of ensuring enjoyment. In Ireland I was told, 'We know E. likes us to work with his feet – by observation. His reactions tune me in. He's so clever. Unless you're a keen observer you'll miss these things. He listens to the cows chewing, and he likes the breeze on his face and likes to smell the lavender.' Similarly, in Germany I heard: 'Try something – see how they react. The most important thing is to watch them very closely. Be aware of their reactions. Maybe discuss them with others. You have to find the key to his personality. You have to understand the signals he gives and think very carefully about them.' Respondents noted the variety of individual responses that might indicate enjoyment or the reverse, ways of showing enjoyment being 'very specific to the person'. In the flat for three people mentioned above, I was told that one resident might be able to laugh and smile to show pleasure, whereas for another pleasure might be indicated by an absence of behaviours indicating distress, such as screaming or scratching.

The third part of this process of ensuring that enjoyment is the outcome of activity provision is the most contentious. Six respondents noted the need for persistence in the process of fostering choice and enjoyment. The point was made that if potential participants have no previous experience of an activity, they cannot make an informed choice about whether to pursue it. Hence at one of the holiday centres it was said of a novel activity: 'Lots of coaxing and persuasion goes on because the staff know the participants will enjoy it, if they (service users) can be persuaded to try.' In an Irish house for four residents it was said: 'If they really didn't want to do it, we'd stop. But we might try again – we wouldn't just give up.' Some respondents emphasized the need for repetition of activities so as to familiarize a person with a medium. Persistence was seen as necessary because a new experience may be frightening initially. The respondent for a small Welsh day service was clear about the need for persistence in opening up opportunities for community-based activities: 'It is .... necessary to set up an activity to happen a number of times – perhaps four – and then assess whether the individual likes the activity. Consumers need time to become accustomed to an activity and also time is needed for "fine tuning". The fine details of an activity may need adjustment. It is also necessary to give time for the community to welcome service users. This is a long process. Keep plugging away and keep fine tuning.' This approach, of course, gives rise to the question put by the same respondent: 'How far do you override the choice an individual is apparently making the first time you try an activity?'

For the three-part process described above to take place, some facilitating factors were said to be necessary. These included an individual knowledge of service users, positive attitudes among staff, adequate staffing ratios and a means of communication. Nevertheless, there are difficulties inherent in this process which were noted by some respondents. The subjectivity involved in the process was noted. In the words of a French respondent: 'There is no free choice – one must lead their choice.'

The respondent for a holiday centre pointed out that the alternative to taking out someone who is multiply disabled and apparently unresponsive might be inactivity. He felt that a walk by a river must be better than such inactivity, but recognized that this is difficult to evaluate. However, he felt that this is what he would want if he were in the position of a person with profound and multiple disability.

In Germany two respondents had the following dialogue regarding offering choice:

Respondent A: 'For me it can be difficult to be in such a powerful position. It is subjective on my part.'

Respondent B: 'It is the only way, for you to make some decisions about the choice to make available.'

UNDERLYING PHILOSOPHIES

Three different, though not necessarily mutually exclusive, philosophies were discernible as a background to service provision. These were:

- Emphasis on social role valorization, normalization, an ordinary lifestyle and social integration;
- Emphasis on education and the development potential of people with learning disability;
- Emphasis on leisure, relaxation and enjoyment as valid ends in their own right. A philosophical position which stresses acceptance of people with learning disability as they are is the background to this emphasis.

Those services which were inspired by the first philosophy, i.e. normalization, tended to mention concepts such as integration, participation, choice, individualization and independence. The need to give service users experiences appropriate to their chronological age was important to this type of philosophical position, which has been highly influential in the UK. A Belgian service provider also spoke in favour of people with profound and multiple disabilities adopting an ordinary lifestyle. He said, however, that in his opinion

'Normalization and integration are not an aim, but tools. It's dangerous when a tool becomes an aim. That's what's happened in Sweden – there normalization is the aim. Normalization – yes, if it's good for the disabled people – not because we find it important – it must be important for the person themself.'

A second philosophical position which has been highly influential in the UK is the idea that everyone has development potential, and that people with profound and multiple disabilities should be helped to acquire new skills. From this standpoint, leisure-time use offers people with profound and multiple disabilities educational and developmental opportunities. Respondents emphasized that service users might acquire new skills, and noted also that this could lead to gains in terms of confidence and self-esteem.

The third philosophical position emphasizes that leisure and relaxation should be regarded as legitimate ends in themselves, as is the case for the non-disabled population. A number of respondents noted the enjoyment, happiness, improved quality of life and physical wellbeing of people with profound and multiple disabilities as a result of leisure activity provision. The Dutch 'snoezelen' facilities described in Chapter 1 and 4 developed within this sort of framework, and although this type of equipment is now sometimes marketed as being 'therapeutic', the impetus for its formulation was concerned purely with the provision of pleasure.

There was a fair degree of unanimity from respondents regarding the types of activity which may be enjoyable to people with profound and multiple disabilities. Most of these are described in detail in this book. There was less agreement about the degree of specialization required in terms of equipment and the use of community resources. Some services saw it as a mark of quality that community-based non-specialized provision was being used for people with profound and multiple disabilities, while other service providers were proud of the high quality of their expensive specialized provision. These stances were consistent with their philosophical positions. Hence service providers who were most committed to a normalization philosophy were most enthusiastic about the use of community resources, while service providers who emphasized 'acceptance' as a philosophy were most likely to use specialized equipment.

STAFF MORALE: A KEY ISSUE

While carrying out this study I spent a good deal of time observing activity provision in a number of countries. This served to underline not only the variety of activities available but also the crucial importance of staff behaviour and morale. Observation of leisure activities highlighted how much of the time of people with profound and multiple disabilities is taken up by inactivity and by waiting for events to happen. Observation also underlined service users' dependency on staff in the making available of pleasurable experiences and in interpreting their responses. It was disappointing to observe staff, even in well resourced settings, talking to each other or watching television while service users engaged in self-stimulating behaviour. It was also disappointing how many times expensive equipment proved to be locked away, rather than available for use.

Difficulties regarding the maintenance of staff interest and morale were commonly reported by respondents, and this issue was raised in all countries visited. Maintenance of staff morale is a complex issue and one which has much wider implications and many more aspects than those raised by this study. However, the maintenance of the interest and motivation of staff working with people with profound and multiple disabilities emerged as a key issue and could legitimately be regarded as a priority area, both for future research and for service managers' attention. The observation undertaken during this European study underlines the experience in Ireland of Conneally and Boyle (1989) when they state that the quality of the relationship between staff and service users is 'crucial in the development of opportunities and a positive lifestyle'.

It may be that activity provision serves to raise staff morale. It is certainly the case that leisure activities provide the medium for the development of relationships between service users and other people, among whose number staff are very significant. The centrality of staff morale to the quality of life of service users cannot be overstated.

This study demonstrates that the provision of pleasurable activities is achievable for all, whatever their level of ability. Activity provision was not easy. In the words of the Belgian doctor, 'Progress is usually small, not sensational'. However, as a Welsh service provider pointed out, the debate is not about whether people with profound and multiple disabilities can benefit from the provision of activities, 'it is about support and money'.

Acknowledgements

This study was funded primarily by the Division for Action in Favour of Disabled People of the European Commission. Other financial support came from the Mencap City Foundation, the Mental Health Foundation and the International League of Societies for Persons with

Mental Handicap. I would like to acknowledge the contribution of these organizations and that of the directors of the study, Professor James Hogg, Professor Peter Mittler and Ms Judy Sebba.

REFERENCES

Conneally S. and Boyle G. (1989) *The INTOGAL Project. An Evaluation of a Model of Service for Adults With a Severe and Profound Mental Handicap*, Galway County Association for Mentally Handicapped Children, Galway.

Longhorn, F. (1988) *A Sensory Curriculum for Very Special People*, Souvenir Press, London.

Part Two

Environments and Activities

4

Multisensory environments

Judith Cavet and Helen Mount

INTRODUCTION

There is plenty of evidence to suggest that people with profound and multiple disabilities enjoy the same leisure activities as the rest of the population, and with the right sort of support and with attention paid to enhancing the sensory aspect of activities, such people can experience a wide variety of activities similar to those pursued by us all. Nevertheless, as more attention has begun to be paid to the quality of life of service users with profound and multiple disabilities there has also developed an interest in providing leisure environments which are designed with their particular needs in mind. Here we are concerned to explore the potential of the specialized environments which began in the Netherlands under the name of 'snoezelen'. This type of environment has become increasingly popular in the UK in recent years, and many examples are to be found in special schools, day services and long-stay institutions.

The inclusion of 'snoezelen' at the Hartenberg Institute in Holland has been documented by Hulsegge and Verheul (1987). The term has been used variously to indicate specialized environments and equipment as well as an overall approach to service users which emphasizes relaxation and pleasure. 'Snoezelen' is not a scientific word but a contraction of two Dutch words, the equivalents for 'sniffing' and 'dozing' in English. In the UK 'snoezelen' is the registered trade mark of Robinson and Sons Ltd., Chesterfield. Similar equipment is also made by other manufacturers under different trade names, and we have chosen to use the term 'multisensory environments' when describing this type of approach as it has developed in the UK.

It is our intention to examine the development of the original concept of snoezelen and consider its potential contribution to the leisure opportunities and quality of life of people with severe or profound learning and multiple disabilities. In order to assess the strengths and weaknesses of multisensory environments we have divided the chapter into three parts. The first of these examines the original development of snoezelen in The Netherlands. We also include a description of what we consider are the main components of a multisensory environment and offer some suggestions for developing such a resource on a limited budget. The final part of the chapter takes a critical look at some of the arguments surrounding the use of such environments and draws conclusions from the available evidence.

EXAMPLES OF MULTISENSORY ENVIRONMENTS

We all live in and experience a multisensory world. Therefore to use the term 'multisensory environment' in the present context requires some qualification. In order to clarify the type of environment under discussion we will first describe the original suite of snoezelen rooms which was developed at the Hartenberg Institute in The Netherlands by Hulsegge and Verheul. The Hartenberg is an establishment which houses several hundred residents, for whom it provides a number of potential activities. The snoezelen facilities were developed in order to extend the range of leisure opportunities open to the residents who, as a group, were becoming increasingly disabled. This change in the nature of the population at the Hartenberg was the result of community care policies which meant that less severely disabled people were often no longer living in such a large-scale setting. The Hartenberg was not the only Dutch institution to experiment with snoezelen facilities, but it was a pioneer in the field.

In 1989, the first author visited the Hartenberg Institute snoezelen facilities as part of the wider study described in Chapter 3 of this volume. The facility consisted of four rooms and a corridor, all of which contained specially developed devices that produced sensory effects. Throughout, lighting was dimmed and gentle music could be heard in the background. In general the overall effect was aesthetically pleasing. On the walls were collections of objects which might be interesting from a tactile point of view. For example, collections of sponges and elsewhere the heads of sweeping brushes were stuck together on wooden boards. In some places, soft materials of different compositions and colours hung from the ceiling so that they might be felt and handled. These objects and materials were placed at a height which was appropriate for a person using a wheelchair. Throughout the environment, careful attention had been paid to ensuring accessibility for wheelchair users.

Visitors to the snoezelen rooms removed their shoes. On the floor of the corridor was a checkerboard pattern of glass of different colours which was warm to the feet. Parts of the corridor floor, when trodden on, produced a ringing sound, while a light on the wall also flashed. In addition, there were tubes available which might be activitated by large switches to blow out various airborne smells.

The first room contained a ball pool, and the second room was called the 'white tower'. As its name suggests, it was round in shape with a high ceiling. The floor covering was soft enough to encourage one to sit or lie on it. A set of tall transparent tubes filled with liquid in which bubbles constantly rose was a feature of the white tower. While they had an immediate visual impact, their appeal for people with profound and multiple disabilities was said to lie for many in the fact that they vibrated slightly and were warm to touch. The white tower included special lighting effects, some of which were produced by the use of projectors plus a central revolving glass sphere. Other visual effects were produced by mirrors and lighting set within the walls. A hanging chair offered the option of rocking for those who enjoyed this experience.

A third room contained a water-bed and soft flooring covered by a very strong plasticized material. The windows had sliding shutters that opened to reveal coloured glass, which gave the outside environment a different appearance, in one case rose-tinted. The walls had a number of collages. These were soft to the touch and were made of materials such as satin or sheepskin. Also within the room was some soft play equipment, including a tent-like structure. The fourth room was known as the studio and had a raised floor which responded to noise by vibrating. Equipment for playing recorded music was available. On the walls patterns were produced which responded to different frequencies of sound, including those made by the human voice. The effects in this room were a little reminiscent of those to be found in discothèques. This was the level of development of the snoezelen rooms at the Hartenberg Institute in 1989. Some of the features described, perhaps most notably the white tower, the bubble tubes and the lighting effects, will be immediately recognizable to readers familiar with multisensory environments developed in the UK. The overall impression was one of a specialized environment where novel approaches had been developed in a well resourced institutional context which was visually attractive. Staff had collected together devices and equipment which offered sensory experiences thought to be enjoyable for people with profound and multiple disabilities. It is important to note that no attempt had been made to provide these sensory experiences in a context which would be regarded as consistent with the philosophy of normalization. This point will be discussed further later in the chapter.

In the UK one of the largest multisensory environments to have been set up is at Whittington Hall Hospital in Derbyshire. The Whittington facilities have many features in common with the Hartenberg's suite of rooms, although they include a jacuzzi pool as an additional feature (see Haggar and Hutchinson, 1991, for a full description). It is possible to visit and look at the environment and make bookings for use by groups or individuals not resident at the hospital. For further information, refer to the address given at the end of this chapter.

SETTING UP A MULTISENSORY ENVIRONMENT

Multisensory environments are big business. The equipment may cost anything from several hundreds of pounds for one item to hundreds of thousands of pounds for a complete system similar to the one at Whittington Hall Hospital. The sale of equipment and the commercial development of multisensory environments have been dominated by two major companies, but smaller companies also produce this type of equipment and several suppliers are listed at the end of this chapter. Some of the companies offer a wide range of services, including the design and installation of complete multisensory environments in either existing rooms or portable buildings. Other companies offer more specialist services as suppliers of certain types of equipment only.

Multisensory environments are in essence a collection of devices that offer sensory stimulation, some of which have been designed especially for people with severe or profound and multiple disabilities. Looked at from one point of view, they can be regarded as an extra leisure option for a group of people whose range of available activities has often been very limited. While snoezelen facilities were originally developed in large-scale settings, it is possible to install a less elaborate range of equipment for use in a smaller-scale service, or even in a domestic setting, and to incorporate some of Hulsegge and Verheul's ideas at a more modest cost. If the financial resources for expensive items of equipment are unavailable, the next section of this chapter offers some ideas for improvisation which may be no less effective.

There are several local 'play' resource centres in different parts of the country. These centres offer a recycling service by supplying materials surplus to production from various industries. They also sell new materials for mostly arts-based activities at competitive prices and provide an excellent selection of resources from which to develop multi-sensory environments. The scrap materials cost very little and it may be possible to purchase several yards of white netting or chiffon, plus 'curtains' of foil strips, mirror paper, tinsel, baubles, 'laser' paper printed with holograms and fabrics with different textures for less than £25. Among other useful items available are cellophane paper of different colours, sequin waste, textured papers, chunky pipe cleaners, empty plastic containers (for constructing sound-makers), fur fabric and glitter. There is a National Federation of Resource Centres, which will send you a list of those currently in business. Because these centres are dependent on grants and the support of local industry, some inevitably do go out of business. Please send a stamped, addressed envelope when you make your enquiries as this considerably helps their service.

Space is obviously one of the first considerations in setting up a multisensory environment, but if you are fortunate enough to have a separate room where equipment and materials may be left permanently, this is obviously the most desirable option. If a complete room is unavailable, a corner or other part of any room may be adapted on a smaller scale. This area could be partitioned by free-standing screens, but if this is not possible a parachute (preferably white) or mosquito net (available from IKEA) may be suspended from the ceiling using a few sturdy cup hooks and some clothes pegs where necessary. If a separate room is available, the walls will reflect any projected images more effectively if they are painted with a matt white emulsion paint. A curtain rail fixed to the walls and running round the perimeter of the room (close to the ceiling), will allow the use of curtains of different colours and textures which change the atmosphere in the room. One of the walls could be covered in large squares of fabric and other substances to provide a wide variety of textures, e.g. fur, fabric, silk, sandpaper, bubble wrap, rubber, foil, wood, plastic and coconut matting. If this is to be a permanent fixture, the different materials will need to be fixed to a board secured to the wall. An alternative would be to make a textured blanket or sheet which is easily folded away when it is not being used. A further adaptation would be to sew or stick musical instruments and/or other sound-makers to the blanket, e.g. tambourines, bells, maracas, cabassas, small drums and sticks, plastic containers filled with pulses, wooden spoons, pan lids and metal or plastic spoons. The magazine *Information Exchange* is full of imaginative suggestions for sensory exploration and the address is given at the end of the chapter. A third possibility for walls is to concentrate on visual stimuli such as tinsel wigs or 'skirts', baubles, mirrors, holograms, foil survival blankets and special reflective papers. Novelty torches, such as hand-held fibreoptic torches and torches which have lenses or glass of different colours, can also be purchased to provide a variety of light sources on limited funds. Tridias, Stocking Fillas and Webb Ivory are examples of mail order suppliers which supply some of these items.

If your budget is very restricted you may have to improvise your lighting by using coloured light bulbs, which will reflect on the white walls. The development of computerized Christmas tree lights is another source of illumination for the multisensory room. These are improving all the time, and can be obtained as lights that switch intermittently on and off or where individual bulbs are timed in such a way that the light appears to travel. It is worth exploring the possibilities of what is on offer at the local deparment store or larger garden centres, particularly before Christmas, and then to buy what you want in the sales when they are cheaper. Another way of introducing moving light if you cannot afford any of the commercially available equipment is to use a record player or turntable. There are different ways in which this can be used. Place a reflective object on the rotating turntable and direct the torch on to the object. The reflections will then be projected around the room. For example, it is possible to buy half a mirror ball (like the type used in discos and dance halls); if a torch is shone on to the mirror facets rotating light patterns will be produced on the walls and ceiling. An even cheaper option is to stick mirror tiles (available from most tile suppliers) on to the sides of a small cylinder (e.g. a piece of plastic drainpipe about 20 cm in diameter and 20 cm tall) and use this in a similar way. Alternatively, stick a piece of plastic mirror inside the lid of the record player, covering the whole surface. Any shiny object placed on the rotating turntable will also be reflected in the mirror and projected around the room if a torch or similar light source is used as before. If the multisensory environment is intended for children, a 'lullaby light' (made by Tomy) may be used. This is essentially a battery-operated nursery light which has coloured animal shapes printed on a translucent glass dome. The dome rotates when the mechanism is wound up and the lamp inside projects the animal images on to the wall. It should be noted that this light does play a nursery rhyme at the same time, so the age-appropriateness of this equipment has obviously to be considered if the environment is intended for the use of adults.

The piece of equipment we would recommend if you can only afford one expensive item is the Optikinetics Solar 250 projector. Originally developed for discos, the projector comes with a range of attachments as optional extras. Special-effect wheels are attached to the projector by a wheel rotator. These are essentially glass discs approximately 6'' in diameter, the surfaces of which are printed with various transparent images. When the projector is switched on, the effects wheel rotates and the images printed on the wheel are projected on to the desired surface. This may be a white wall, a curtain or even a piece of fine white netting held only a few feet away from a person.

The various images on the wheels include themes like clouds or under-water scenes in blues and white, which may provide a cool, calm, relaxing atmosphere. This may be enhanced by the addition of appropriate music and possibly aromatherapy and massage. For further information on aromatherapy and massage, please refer to Chapter 12.

Other effects wheels are printed with colours and images from the warmer end of the colour spectrum in yellows and reds, for example one called 'fire' and one called 'organic'. There is also available a liquid wheel, which is the type used at many discos. Different coloured bubbles of fluid flow into each other as they are heated by the projector lamp and when the wheel rotates. Whatever wheel is used, the overall effect is a series of large slow-moving images rotating around the ceiling and walls. By using a selection of these effects wheels in conjunction with coloured fabrics and background music it is possible to change completely the mood or atmosphere within the one space, or to incorporate a thematic approach which extends to other areas of leisure activity such as movement, dance or drama.

In addition to the effects wheels there are several effects cassettes available, and these are attached to the projector using a different rotator. These are smaller than the wheels (about 7.5 cm diameter) and most project images which result in a completely different atmosphere. The projected images are smaller, concentrated, pulsing vibrant patterns of light which are used extensively to stimulate vision in those people who have a visual disability. The images they create do not rotate in the slow, gentle manner of the effects wheels and they do not cover as large an area. A 'liquid' cassette, similar to the wheel, is also available. The effects wheels and cassettes should not be considered as an either/or option because each has a different function. A multisensory room employing both may therefore have more versatility than just one of the two options. It may also offer greater use of the room, which could have a dual function, as is the case in many special schools and adult training or social education centres. One function is to provide leisure activities and the other to carry out structured visual stimulation programmes with strictly educational or therapeutic objectives. The projector has other attachments as optional extras, which may be purchased as funds become available, but it is really worth buying a minimum to start with and learning from the full use of one piece of equipment.

A pin spotlight, focused on to a rotating mirror ball, can be installed at a reasonable cost and adds another relaxing dimension to the room. Coloured gels placed in front of the spotlight change the ambience of the room further. The pin spotlight is relatively easy to install, but it does have to be positioned where it can be easily focused on to the mirror ball. Mirror balls are most effective when they are connected to a motor and suspended from the ceiling. When switched on, the ball rotates slowly and any light source reflects and projects the hundreds of small facets around the room.

Two other items of equipment you may have the resources to purchase are a bubble tube and a fibreoptic light 'tail'. Bubble tubes are essentially clear plastic tubes about 6" in diameter which are held in a base containing lighting and an air source. The tubes are available in different lengths, usually 1 m, 1.5 m and 2 m. Once the equipment is assembled and ready for use the tube is filled with water. When switched on, the lighting, which changes from blue to green to red to yellow, illuminates hundreds of small bubbles as they float to the top of the water in the tube. Vibration may also be felt if the tube is touched or held in some way.

The fibreoptic light 'tail' is a small box containing a light source. Into this is plugged a 'tail' of long glass fibres (available in different lengths). When switched on, the light source illuminates the whole length of each fibre and the colour changes as a small plastic disc inside the metal box rotates. If the 2 m length 'tail' is chosen, this may be safely draped around individuals who enjoy the experience. Light 'tails' should not be confused with what are usually known as light ropes. The latter are long clear plastic tubes which look like a hosepipe, containing a series of tiny light bulbs. They are often used in shop window displays or at discos, and when switched on give the appearance that the light is travelling along the tube. Originally these all operated directly on 240 V main voltage, but it is essential to purchase low-voltage models where service users will come into close contact with the equipment.

An Optikinetics projector with several attachments, pin spot, mirror ball, bubble tube and fibreoptic light 'tail', offers a versatile multi-sensory environment, especially when music is added and aromatherapy and massage also take place in the same room. At the time of writing, such a set-up will cost £1500–£2000.

There is a wide variety of equipment available in addition to that described above, including, for example, devices which are activated by sound. The result of a service user making a noise may be anything from flashing lights to vibrating panels. Also available are bubble machines which, when filled with the appropriate liquid and turned on, blow hundreds of bubbles into the room. They are quite noisy and you can improvise by buying a small tube of bubble mixture, holding the loop in front of an ordinary electric fan and letting that do the work for you. There are also machines which blow out a variety of smells. It is best to consult the various manufacturers or marketing companies and get them to put on demonstrations to enable you to make your decision.

It is important to recognize that the environment described so far is essentially a passive one, where the person with profound and multiple disabilities has little control over what they experience. There is considerable scope for development of any basic system, and it is essential to consider the level of involvement of service users with profound and multiple disabilities. It is obvious that they may be able to respond to the environment and display their pleasure by smiling, vocalization or in another way. They may enjoy some of the experiences in a completely passive way by listening to the music and watching the light patterns presented to them. Fragrances may be added by the use of incense, joss sticks, perfumed oils and lotions, and these may produce similar responses, all of which is acceptable as one way of spending leisure time.

More active and challenging situations, however, may be presented by the introduction of switching devices used to control the equipment in the room (see Chapter 11 for a full description). There are numerous options available, of varying complexity and cost. However, one of the cheapest and simplest is a box which connects to the mains and has one piece of equipment plugged into it. A choice of switches may then be connected to the box and there are two ways in which the equipment may then be controlled. In one mode, if the person controlling the equipment, e.g. a bubble tube, uses the switch correctly, it will operate for a set period of time and then switch itself off. The length of time the piece of equipment stays on can be varied and the person operating it has to press the switch again to make it work. In the second mode, the switch is operated and the equipment stays on until the switch is pressed again, when it will be turned off. Using a multisensory environment in this way offers more scope for objective assessment and monitoring of the responses of service users. Moreover, the opportunity it offers for the development from passive recipient to active choice-making participant results in a more rewarding leisure pursuit for that person.

Whatever equipment you are purchasing, it is in your interest to shop around for a good deal. Biggest is not always best, and you could save enough money to buy an extra piece of equipment if you are prepared to invest some effort. Some of the smaller companies may have more specialist knowledge of the equipment, and the person who comes to demonstrate it may be the person who has designed and made it. It is also worth establishing what sort of maintenance will be provided by the company and what sort of guarantee comes with the equipment.

It is possible to view the special effects described in this chapter on video tape. Doubletrees School in Cornwall have available for purchase a video tape which displays much of the equipment described above. While the emphasis on this tape is on children and young people, and the context is educational, the possibilities for leisure applications are evident from the images it projects of service users relaxing and enjoying themselves. The focus in this video tape is upon demonstrating equipment and offering practical tips about its operation. Also available is a video tape from Rompa which shows snoezelen equipment being used by people with learning disabilities and by elderly people living in institutions. Both tapes are relatively inexpensive and give an impression of the effects to be gained in the operation of a multisensory environment. The Leisure Resource Training Pack for People with Profound and Multiple Disabilities (Lambe, 1991) also describes examples of the use of basic snoezelen equipment and ways of creating your own multisensory environment. Other videos about multisensory environments are availble from Toys for the Handicapped and information on all of these is given at the end of this chapter.

SAFETY AND MAINTENANCE

All electrical equipment should be installed, if possible, by a qualified electrician and most local authorities have strict checks on its purchase and use. For example, the rope lights (not the fibreoptic tails) that operate on 240 V mains voltage have been banned by one authority because they are thought to be a potential hazard. Manufacturers' instructions must be strictly followed and the installation of circuit-breaker sockets, although costly, provides an additional safety check.

Lighting and projectors should be kept well away from any fabrics as the heat generated can cause a fire. All materials should be non-toxic and care should be taken with fabrics, as the pile may come away easily or they may tear into small pieces on which someone could choke. These are obvious preventative measures, especially when there is a dimly lit environment where potentially dangerous behaviour may be difficult to observe.

Choice of seating or cushions for people to lie on usually makes the floor uneven and it is essential that all electrical equipment is secured on a stable surface where it cannot be knocked or pulled over. The covering of the cushions or seating should be made from a material which can be easily wiped down to ensure that the environment remains a hygienic, as well as a relaxing, place to be. This does not mean that it should continually smell of disinfectant: any fabric which cannot be wiped should be periodically washed or thrown away. The inflammability of any materials must also be considered, and when purchasing cushions it is essential to establish that they meet British Standard requirements with regard to toxicity and flame-retardant qualities.

Anyone using the fibreoptic 'tail' should never be allowed to put the ends of the strands into their mouth, as these are made from glass-fibre. These fibres are perfectly safe to handle in an ordinary way, and may even be draped around someone or bent quite sharply to change the pattern of light, but like any other electrical equipment they must be treated with respect.

Never put projectors, light 'tails' or other equipment which generates heat directly on to plastic-coated surfaces because the plastic will melt and may even catch fire. Projectors or any equipment containing lighting should never be moved while they are still hot, as this is likely to shorten the life of the bulb, especially if they are moved with the light still turned on. When changing the bulb in most types of equipment you will find that the new bulb is covered with a clear plastic sleeve. This should only be removed after the bulb is securely in place, as touching quartz–halogen bulbs with the fingers can damage them. It is also good organization if one or two named people take responsibility for the room, to ensure that it is maintained, especially as the facility can so easily be rendered inoperative because no-one knows how to change the projector bulb. Incidentally, a good question to ask the designers/suppliers of bubble tubes in particular is 'How easy is it to change the bulb and can you demonstrate?' (This can prove difficult, even when the bubble tube is not full of water.) Bubble tubes purchased from at least one manufacturer have to have all the water syphoned out and need to be virtually dismantled before the bulb can be changed. As a point of practicality rather than safety, it is sensible to keep a spare stock of bulbs for the various items of equipment.

MULTISENSORY ENVIRONMENTS AND THE AIMS OF SERVICE PROVISION

It is worth noting that it was in a large-scale institution that Hulsegge and Verheul set up their facilities which were intended to provide a relaxing ambience for people with severe and profound disabilities. The development of snoezelen needs to be understood in this light. The originators devised the rooms in an attempt to offer stimulation that was pleasurable and which offered choice to the institution's residents. Some of the types of stimulation they made available have been shown to have a particular appeal for people with profound disabilities. For example, vibration has been shown to be especially pleasurable (Ohwaki, Brahlek and Stayton, 1973; Byrne and Stevens, 1980; Prosser, 1988), as has the type of stimulation to be gained from a water-bed or a swinging chair (Sandler and McLain, 1987). Indeed, most people find a first visit to an environment such as that at the Hartenberg Institute a pleasant experience. In this sense the environment is a success. It is also a success in that the originators have provided a soothing contrast to the residents' living quarters. Moreover, it offers to some service users with profound and multiple disabilities choice of stimuli, the possibility of being able to activate devices, the exercise of a degree of control over their environment and the opportunity to understand cause and effect. For all these reasons Hulsegge and Verheul were successful in enhancing the institutional setting of the Hartenberg's residents.

Likewise, there can be little doubt that the facilities at Whittington Hall have widened the leisure options available to the hospital's residents. This was the view expressed by staff and reported by Hutchinson and Haggar (1991) in their evaluation of the snoezelen facilities. These authors further reported that one group of ward staff intended to set up a 'relaxation room' on their ward, as a result of their positive view of service users' responses to the hospital's snoezelen facilities. An allied phenomenon to be observed in a number of Dutch-speaking institutions in Europe is 'snoezelen corners' (Cavet, 1990). These are small areas in the residents' communal living quarters where staff have placed sources of sensory stimulation (soft hangings, reflective surfaces, special lighting, mobiles, etc.) in a designated place to provide a particularly pleasant environment for residents. They represent an attempt by staff in Dutch and Belgian institutions to reproduce in residents' living quarters the positive effects they associate with 'snoezelen rooms'. Thus there is some evidence that staff in large-scale institutions in the UK and mainland Europe consider multisensory environments to be beneficial to service users.

However, although multisensory environments may have had positive effects in large-scale settings there are differing views about how far they are a useful feature in community-based services. Some schools for children with severe learning disability have developed multisensory environments with great enthusiasm (as the video tape from Doubletrees School demonstrates), although their emphasis is necessarily upon education rather than leisure. In addition, we have suggested ways of adapting multisensory environments to small-scale or even domestic settings. Nevertheless, service providers who are adherents of the philosophies of normalization (Wolfensberger, 1972) and social role valorization (Wolfensberger, 1983) need to consider how far their service's aims are compatible with the introduction of environments designed especially for people with severe or profound learning disabilities. A sophisticated critique of normalization has now developed. It is indeed possible to hold the view that people with profound and multiple disabilities have a right to an environment which meets their particular needs, regardless of its compatibility with an 'ordinary' lifestyle. Nevertheless, it is important to consider arguments against the use of specialized environments and certainly against too exclusive a dependence on their use as a means of leisure activity provision.

One aspect of this debate relates to the potential of leisure activities for the promotion of the social integration of people with learning disability within their local community. If this is an important consideration for you, you may prefer to offer your service users only activities which can be carried out by and with the rest of the population. Alternatively, if you feel this course restricts the choice available to service users in an unacceptable way, you may wish to consider whether it is possible to set up a multisensory environment in a location which is accessible to and used by the general public.

Another argument which has been put forward in opposition to the development of multisensory environments relates to the fact that they do not prepare people for an ordinary lifestyle. When Whittaker (1992) asks 'Can anyone help me to understand the logic of snoezelen?' (p. 15), this is the phenomenon he is pinpointing. You may feel that service users with profound and multiple disabilities have a great deal of free time, and that therefore they have time available both for the leisure experiences open to the rest of the population and for leisure experiences designed especially for them. Nevertheless, there may be a danger in providing an environment which is intended only for people from devalued groups, that other forms of leisure activity which permit more interaction with the rest of society and more variety of environment for service users will not be actively pursued.

Whittaker refers to a snoezelen room as 'a bizarre and absurdly isolated place' (p. 15), and considers any assessment carried out there as of dubious validity. In fairness to Hulsegge and Verheul, it should be pointed out that they do not advocate that multisensory environments like theirs should be used for assessment purposes, although workers elsewhere have felt that documenting service users' reactions to the different stimuli has a clear utility. The rationale for this may be as simple as keeping a note of which experiences appeared pleasurable to different service users in order to facilitate communication of information between staff.

If we are to provide multisensory experiences in more integrated settings, it is worth addressing the question as to how this is to be achieved. There are numerous opportunities for making available activities enjoyed by the general public to people with profound and multiple disabilities and for enhancing and emphasizing the sensory aspects of those activities with the needs and abilities of service users in mind. For example, the sensory gardens and aromatherapy with massage, described respectively in Chapters 7 and 12 of this book, can provide environments which are designed to offer sensory stimulation to people with profound and multiple disabilities. Likewise, activities which are physical in nature can be devised with the production of a sensory environment in mind. For example, at a leisure centre the use of a trampoline, combined with a parachute and perhaps an item of large play equipment, could fall into this category. Similarly, engaging in a cookery session or a drama session can be to experience a multisensory environment, taking a less rigid definition of the term. Clearly, these latter ways of engaging in multisensory experiences have the advantage of being connected with an ordinary lifestyle, and therefore being more acceptable to many service providers. Moore (1991) adopts this view when she asks, with reference to snoezelen facilities, 'Whose needs is this type of facility actually serving?' (p. 126). She considers that instead of making available safe, secure, special environments, service providers should be working to develop high-quality leisure facilities which are accessible to everyone within their local community.

Multisensory environments are expensive to provide unless less sophisticated approaches similar to those described in this chapter, or in Hulsegge and Verheul's Chapter 7 about 'do-it-yourself "snoezelen" equipment' are adopted. However, it is often not as difficult to obtain money for the purchase of such equipment, which is both tangible and novel, as it is to gain funds for maintenance and for staffing ratios which enable service users to gain the most from the environment. Of fundamental importance is the need to recognize that the quality of staff input in such an environment is paramount. Although the emphasis is upon service user choice, the most disabled users will be dependent on sensitive staff to make available a wide variety of experiences. They will also be dependent on staff to ensure that they are not left exposed to stimuli which may become unpleasant to them over a period of time, or which may simply become unstimulating. Kewin (1991) writes that it is essential for the carer to be responsive to the communications of participants within the snoezelen environment. If you are in favour of the development of a multisensory environment as a way of expanding the leisure opportunities for service users, it is crucial to consider how staff can provide the greatest choice and pleasure for them.

Claims have been made about the therapeutic nature of multisensory environments. For example, Williams (1991) writes of a snoezelen room: 'It is an active treatment setting and as such can have profound effects on the individuals using it' (p. 129). Such claims should be treated with caution, as there is little evidence to support such a thesis. Hulsegge and Verheul did not research the effects of their environment in any systematic way, and what research there has been (Hutchinson and Haggar, 1991) does not claim this type of 'profound effect'. Verheul (Cavet, 1990) reported that some service users with aggressive behaviour did appear calmer in the Hartenberg's snoezelen rooms than they did in their living quarters in the institution, but he felt this may have been due simply to the fact that the snoezelen rooms were quieter and therefore had a soothing effect. The evaluation carried out by Hutchinson and Haggar (1991) has evidence of a similarly soothing effect on people with difficult behaviour. However, it is not apparent whether the calming effects were the result of a visit to the snoezelen rooms, or whether other sorts of activities which were undertaken away from the ward would have had a similar effect. In other words, there is no evidence as to whether the snoezelen rooms were important in inducing the reported drop in difficult behaviour, or whether any pleasant activity undertaken in a novel setting would have had a similar outcome. However, the debate about whether multisensory environments are a form of active therapy, rather than merely 'therapeutic' in the sense of being relaxing, should not be a major issue when considering their leisure applications. This is the point which Hutchinson and Haggar (1991) make when they ask whether we justify our own leisure pursuits in terms of their therapeutic value.

CONCLUSION

The aim of this chapter has been to describe multisensory environments and to indicate how some low-cost environments can be established by service providers. Despite some reservations that have been expressed, multisensory environments have become very popular in recent years. What can be learnt from the popularity of such environments?

First, the most highly developed multisensory environments, and especially that developed at the Hartenberg, are aesthetically pleasing and well resourced. This is in marked contrast to the relative impoverishment which affects many environments available to people with profound and multiple disabilities. Well resourced, expensive and technically sophisticated environments are highly valued and considered attractive in our society. This accounts, in part, for the appeal of the environments under discussion. In so far as any service users associated with such an environment may be revalued in the light of this general appeal, such environments might be said to have something positive to offer. Fundamentally, however, arguments of this type do not specifically favour multisensory environments, but support the notion that other more impoverished environments for people with profound and multiple disabilities should be upgraded and better-funded.

Secondly, the popularity of multisensory environments highlights the need for deliberate and careful attention to be paid to the need of people with profound and multiple disabilities for sensory stimulation. This need is well recognized in the UK, although service provision does not necessarily reflect this.

Thirdly, multisensory environments were originally developed within a philosophical framework which emphasized that it was acceptable to develop an environment which promoted service users' pleasure for its own sake. Hence the popularity of multisensory environments has highlighted the need for leisure provision for people with profound and multiple disabilities that incorporates well resourced environments, sensory stimuli and a recognition of the value of pleasure for its own sake.

Multisensory environments can be described as leisure facilities which are 'specialized' in function, or may be regarded more negatively as being 'segregationist'. They can be seen as an extra leisure alternative for service users whose options are often limited, or as being in opposition to patterns of provision which emphasize an ordinary lifestyle. Perhaps one of the most salutary comments Hutchinson and Haggar (1991) make is that residents at Whittington Hall spent, on average, no more than 1 extra hour per week away from their ward as a result of the development of the hospital's multisensory environment. Prior to the development of the snoezelen rooms, the most disabled residents spent on average only 2 hours per week away from their ward, in sensory, play or recreational activities. These facts provide a sufficient rationale for the development of the facility, while also drawing attention to the more major need for alternative community-based facilities for the hospital's residents. The future of the essentially specialized multisensory environments discussed in this chapter will be affected by the extent to which people with profound and multiple disabilities are integrated into the community and included in activities taking place there. The present need is for further research into the effectiveness and utility of this type of multisensory environment.

REFERENCES

Byrne, D.J. and Stevens, C.P. (1980) Mentally handicapped children's responses to vibrotactile and other stimuli as evidence for the existence of a sensory hierarchy. *Apex*, **8**, 96–8.

Cavet, J. (1990) *Leisure Opportunities for People who are Profoundly and Multiply Handicapped*, MPhil Thesis, University of Manchester.

Haggar, L.E. and Hutchinson, R.B. (1991) Snoezelen: the approach to the provision of leisure resource for people with profound and multiple handicaps. *Mental Handicap*, **19**, 51–5.

Hulsegge, J. and Verheul, A. (1987) *Snoezelen: Another World*, Rompa, Chesterfield.

Hutchinson, R.B. and Haggar, L.E. (1991) *The development and evaluation of a snoezelen leisure resource for people with profound and multiple handicaps* in *The Whittington Hall Snoezelen Project*, (ed. R. Hutchinson), North Derbyshire Health Authority, Chesterfield.

Jenkins, J. and Kewin, J. *Snoezelen, The Way Forward into the 1990s. User's Guide*, Rompa, Chesterfield.

Kewin, J. (1991) *Snoezelen user guide*, in *The Whittington Hall Hospital Snoezelen Project*, (ed. R. Hutchinson), North Derbyshire Health Authority, Chesterfield.

Lambe, L. (ed) (1991) *Leisure for People with Profound and Multiple Disabilities – A Resource Training Pack*, Mencap, London.

Moore, W. (1991) Snoezelen. *Mental Handicap*, **19**, 126.

Ohwaki, S., Brahlek, J. and Stayton, S.E. (1973). Preference for vibratory and visual stimulation in mentally retarded children. *American Journal of Mental Deficiency*, **77**, 733–6.

Prosser, G. (1988) Vibratory reinforcement in the field of mental handicap: a review. *Mental Handicap Research*, **1**, 152–66.

Sandler, A.G. and McLain, S.C. (1987). Sensory reinforcement: effects of response-contingent vestibular stimulation on multiply handicapped children. *American Journal of Mental Deficiency*, **91**, 373–8.

Whittaker, J. (1992) Can anyone help me to understand the logic of snoezelen? *Community Living*, October, 15.

Williams, C. (1991) Book review of 'Snoezelen – Another World'. *Mental Handicap*, **19**, 129.

Wolfensberger, W. (1972) *The Principle of Normalisation in Human Services*, National Institute on Mental Retardation, Toronto.

Wolfensberger, W. (1983) Social role valorization: a proposed new term for the principle of normalization. *Mental Retardation*, **21**, 23–9.

ADDRESSES

Whittington Hall Hospital, Old Whittington, Chesterfield, Derbyshire S41 9LJ. Tel: (0246) 277271.

Suppliers

Mike Ayres and Company, Unit 14, Vanguard Trading Estate, Britannia Road, Chesterfield, Derbyshire S40 2TZ.
 Tel: 0246 551546.
Toys for the Handicapped, 76 Barracks Road, Sandy Lane Industrial Estate, Stourport-on-Severn, Worcs DY13 9QB.
 Tel: 0299 827820.
Kirton Litework, Unit 2, Woodgate Park, White Lund Industrial Estate, Morecambe, Lancashire LA3 3PS.
 Tel: 0524 844808.
Sense-Ability, Unit 1, Woodgate Park, White Lund Industrial Estate, Morecambe, Lancashire LA3 3PS.
Ayn Thurston (Chair), Federation of Resource Centres, 25 Bullivant Street, St Anns, Nottingham NG3 4AT.
 Tel: 0242 221700. (Please remember to enclose an s.a.e. with your enquiry)
Rompa, Goyt Side Road, Chesterfield, Derbyshire S40 2PH.
 Tel: 0246 211777.
Information Exchange, c/o Wendy McCracken, Oakes Green, Royal Schools for the Deaf, Stanley Road, Cheadle Hulme, Cheadle, Cheshire SK8 6RF.
 Tel: 061 437 5951.
Tridias (Mail Order), 124 Walcot Street, Bath, Avon BA1 5BG.
 Tel: 0225 469455.
Stocking Fillas (Mail Order), Tennant House, London Road, Macclesfield, Cheshire SK11 0LW.
 Tel: 0625 511511.
Edu-Play Toys, 10 Vestry Street, Leicester LE1 1WQ.
 Tel. 0533 625827.
Environmental Electrical Services, Manywells House, Manywells Industrial Estate, Cullingworth, Bradford, West Yorkshire BD13 5DX.
 Tel: 0525 274068.
Webb Ivory (Mail Order), Primrose Hill, Preston, Lancashire PR1 4EL.
 Tel: 0772 200700.
Selections Catalogue, Innovations Mail Order, The Response Centre, Euroway Business Park, Swindon, Wiltshire SN5 8SN.
 Tel: 0973 514666.
IKEA (Croydon), Valley Park, Off Purley Way, Croydon CR0 4UZ.
 Tel: 081 781 9003.
IKEA (Gateshead), Metro Park, West Gateshead, Tyne & Wear NE11 9XS.
 Tel: 091 461 0202.
IKEA (Warrington), 910 Europa Boulevard, Warrington, Cheshire WA5 5TY.
 Tel: 0925 55889.
IKEA (Birmingham), Park Lane, Wednesbury, West Midlands WS10 9FS.
 Tel: 021 526 5232.

Video tapes

Rompa, Goyt Side Road, Chesterfield, Derbyshire S40 2PH.
 Tel: 0246 211777.

Doubletrees School, St Blazey, Par, Cornwall PL24 2DS.
  Tel: 0726 812757.
Toys for the Handicapped, 76 Barracks Road, Sandy Lane Industrial Estate,
  Stourport-on-Severn, Worcs DY13 9QB.

5

Physical activities

Mark Leach and Howard Bailey

INTRODUCTION

There is a very real sense in which all leisure activities entail physical activity, whether this is minimal, as in moving our eyes to scan a picture or orienting our ears to sound, fine motor, as in painting, or gross motor as in horse-riding. Yet physical movement, whatever level we are viewing it at, cannot be abstracted from a wider psychological and social context. In order to place physical activities in this context, we must consider the role that communication plays in encouraging movement skills, how complex sports and games available to us all can be adapted to the competencies and needs of people with profound disabilities and how motivation can be maintained.

The present chapter deals in turn with each of these issues before considering, first, specific activities within the setting of a person's school, day service or leisure club or centre or, space permitting, home. We then illustrate the availability of physical activities in a wider context, noting, for example, the potential of horse-riding and carting and water sports, among others. Here access may be to situations specially tailored for individuals with disabilities, or to mainstream community provision in leisure centres or sports clubs. In these last instances the challenge confronts not only those providing direct services for people with profound disabilities, but also those running community provision, often with an explicit commitment to equal opportunities.

COMMUNICATION AND PHYSICAL ACTIVITY

At the heart of our position is the view that all activity entails communication in as much as it tells us something about the person. Communication is central among the many issues associated with the inclusion in physical activities of people who have multiple disabilities.

For many such people communication is at the preverbal stage. Nevertheless, the expression of feelings and needs through gesture and emotion is common to us all, providing the key to understanding the responses of people with profound and multiple disabilities, idiosyncratic though such expression may be. It is our consistent response to such communication that underlies the development of relationships and precludes the person withdrawing from active interaction. When communication occurs between two people, a two-way process of interpreting signals begins. Each action must be thought of as communication. Actions only become intentional communication when a consistent regular response is generated.

Within some mainstream sports, however, the surroundings and players' position in those surroundings is constantly changing, and it is this inconsistency that may create confusion for the person who has not yet developed the appropriate communication skills. Any opportunity for self-development is highly dependent on receiving a consistent response to existing activities from which a suitable system of communication can be devised, with sufficient time to respond ensured.

Important as the assessment of the person's individual needs is, an understanding of his or her response to the surroundings is also crucial. This is particularly important for people who have difficulty conceptualizing a particular activity, however much it may be enjoyed. If the surroundings offer familiar activities which can be understood and enjoyed, the promotion of choice and communication is possible and the conditions for development are greatly improved.

ADAPTING PHYSICAL ACTIVITIES

Many of the games and sports played in mainstream society are of quite a high conceptual order, and will therefore present special challenges to the person with profound and multiple disabilities. Short-mat bowls, for example, is a game which local authority recreation departments often promote among people with disabilities. To fully appreciate the game each player must understand the following:

- The biasing principles of the weighted bowl;
- The principles of competition;
- How to distinguish colours;
- The variable three-dimensional target in space;
- Numeracy skills;
- Have hand–eye coordination;
- Have developed fine-tuned perceptual skills.

Overall, the majority of people who have multiple disabilities have not yet acquired all or, in some instances, any of the skills listed above. Carpet bowls, therefore, would not appear initially to be an appropriate activity for them. However, if the skills needed to participate in an activity are examined and married to the skills that a player has acquired, the chances of success are greatly improved. This situation is well illustrated in the development of the Meldreth Games. In Meldreth Roboule (Reed, 1991), for example, the bowls are unbiased so that they will travel in a straight line and be seen to do so. The target, i.e. a three-dimensional bridge with three archways, is stable and also offers visual and auditory signals of success when the delivered ball disappears out of sight. The issue of numeracy is addressed in Roboule using coloured blocks, which are given as rewards when the bowl disappears under a colour-designated arch. The rule system of this game has been developed to encourage achievement by offering recognizable success signals. Although for some this game is set at too high a skill level, it highlights how a physical activity can be adapted to take account of a person's ability to understand principles and concepts.

Offering informed choice is very important if people are to take the initiative and communicate their own preferences about physical activity. In some educational establishments, objects of reference, which are associated with an activity, are given to the person before starting an activity (Park, n.d.) so that they can choose whether they wish to engage in the activity or not. For example, Sarah usually goes for a swim on Tuesday morning each week. Her key worker gives her a towel and swimming costume before setting off. She usually accepts them and enjoys the swim, although on occasions she will reject involvement by rejecting the object of reference. She has been given the choice to communicate her wishes through the objects.

ENCOURAGING SUCCESS

Opportunities for physical activity for people with profound and multiple disabilities should be carefully planned and prepared, aiming both to challenge and to provide the experience of success. The starting point upon which everything else is built is the assessment of individual needs and abilities, and planning should reflect the outcome of this assessment. Different needs, interests and abilities should be reflected in differing activities.

An activity must encourage success and provide everyone involved with the experience of achievement. Though this may appear small or insignificant, success provides motivation, improving confidence in movement and developing motor skills that lead to controlled and purposeful actions. Pointer (1992) notes that, in creating a movement opportunity, it is worthwhile looking beyond the activity itself towards carefully structured learning, which enriches the individual and promotes a degree of independence. By learning progressive physical activities, people can discover the ability both to complete successfully and to initiate positive movement patterns.

PHYSICAL ACTIVITIES THAT ENCOURAGE SKILL ACQUISITION

Although successful performance of an activity is important, developing new skills that can be reinforced and built upon is also a key element. The range of movement abilities of people with profound and multiple disabilities is extensive, from full physical development through to near-total absence of voluntary movements. An individual's ability and motor characteristics will influence the types of activities and experiences offered. Pointer (1992) suggests that, ideally, activities should encourage active directed movements which are self-initiated, whereas passive directed movement will be necessary for people who have limited voluntary control and a restricted range of movements.

Some people experience difficulty in initiating effective movement and may need help from an enabler when participating in physical activity. In other instances, movement development has been affected because some motor skills have not been learnt. This produces an apparent lack of coordination in movement, although the flexibility of movement is perceived to be impaired. Physical activities need to provide and stimulate the motor skills of the individual in a functional way. The breakdown of skills to identify and act upon an area of need may be required.

FACTORS TO CONSIDER

Pointer (1992) has listed several important factors that need to be considered before deciding upon activities which provide fun experiences and encourage success. These are:

- The duration of an activity, i.e. how much time a person needs to complete a task, and the time needed to provide a quality experience. If the experiences are to be consistent then continuity and progression must be offered within the activity. The rate at which progression is developed is important. If the progression is too quick or the person has to think of too many new ideas, confusion will result and a sense of failure rather than success will be encouraged.

- The number of participants involved in any activity is important, as is the number of enablers available to provide support. All participants should be given the oportunity to be included in the activity so that they are offered the experiences that the activity provides. The numbers affect the type of activity offered, e.g. parachute games (see Lambe, Mount and Jackson, 1991). If there are two participants and only one enabler the type of parachute activity offered would be passive, such as relaxation, whereas with six participants and six enablers the range of games would be wider.
- Resources: using adapted, or adapting, equipment is often helpful in either stimulating or initiating or motivating movement. Balloons, bean bags, blankets, parachutes and bubbles are examples of movement-stimulating equipment. Helpers can also be used as physical resources to provide movement experiences. An open-minded awareness of the possibilities and potential in both adapting equipment and the use made of other people is often invaluable.
- The environment must be suitable to the physical activities being planned. For example, for a relaxation session a noisy, large, cold room will not be appropriate and an alternative must be found.

CLASSIFICATION OF MOVEMENT TASKS

Brown (1987) has commented that physical activity tasks vary from simple to highly complex, and that we must analyse the component factors that affect the degree of task difficulty. He noted that the demands placed upon the individual when performing difficult types of movement tasks may result in different performance in the spatial and perceptual elements of the task, or in integrating both aspects. All movement tasks, he suggests, contain elements that we describe as cognitive and perceptuomotor, and that the degree of difficulty facing any person will vary according to the individual factors encountered with each element.

A model for classification of movement tasks was proposed by Sugden (1984). This model is simple to use and useful when arranging problems into a progressive order. The degree of task difficulty is obvious, although this classification system was not originally intended to be applied to the levels of profound disability with which we are concerned here. Nevertheless, a programme of activities based on progression of skill, and its achievement within each of the identified categories, may be used when planning physical activity opportunities so that the person taking part participates at the appropriate level. Sugden examines the demands placed on the individual when performing different types of movement under each of the following conditions: when the body is stable; when the body is moving and in tasks requiring limb manipulation; where the environment is constant; and where the environment is changing (Table 5.1).

Table 5.1 Brown's (1987) classification of body stability-movement and environment constant-changing in physical task performance

	Body stable	*Body moving*
Environment constant	Relaxing Sitting Aiming activities Boccia Bowls Massage	Crawling, wheeling Swimming Gymnastics Distance beanbag
	1	2
Environment changing	Parachute games Sherbourne movement Catching a balloon Striking a balloon Computer game	Wheeling, crawling Meldreth cricket Volleyball Trampoline Polybat
	3	4

Table 5.2 Progression of physical activity (Brown, 1987)

		Social interaction
Level 4		*Complex motor action* Gross body movement/ variable environment Team cooperation Fast decisions Direct opponents
Level 3		*Simple motor actions* Limited movement/ variable environment Decision-making opponents, no direct contact
Level 2	*Simple motor actions* Body moving/environment constant Limited range of movement, fitness factor Limited decisions	
Level 1	*Simple motor actions* Body stable/environment constant; Limited decisions, repetitive actions No interference, e.g. beanbag games, Meldreth Roboule	**Individual**

Totally predictable tasks such as aiming a beanbag at a target or a ball at a skittle occur when the body and the environment are both stable. When two people pass a balloon to one another they are stable but the environment is changing. This task demonstrates an increasing difficulty dependent on the type of balloon used, the distance between the players and the flight of balloon related to the way it is passed, for example high and slow or fast and low. In team games both the body and the environment demands become unpredictable and therefore the task is more difficult.

Table 5.2 shows the progression of activities based on the skills needed to participate in an activity.

EXAMPLES OF PRACTICE

The following activities are taken from Pointer's (1992) examples of various movement experiences which may be used with people who have profound and multiple disabilities. They will need to be modified according to individual need, but the essence of encouraging movement motivation and the pleasure of sensory or tactile movement experiences is embedded within each example. The contribution of either the teacher or the leader–enabler in shaping each session, not only in catering for the wide variety of extreme needs but also in creating a happy and fulfilling experience for all concerned, cannot be overemphasized.

Tunnel slide

Each person is placed on a blanket which is dragged by helpers through a series of tables, arranged in a circular fashion. Underneath each table are stuck a variety of different hanging objects, such as balloons, quoits, string and airflow balls. From the blanket, the individual can look up at the various swinging objects and may attempt to grasp or feel them as they travel from one 'table tunnel' to the next. A different set of objects should be hung from each table.

Crash-mat roll

Three soft cylindrical rollers are spaced evenly across a crash mat. Another crash mat is put on top of this, creating a rocking and swaying structure. All those involved surround the crash mats and an individual is placed on top. By holding on to the sides of the top crash mat, the helpers gently push it from side to side, creating a gentle, rhythmical rocking and swaying experience, which is also very soothing and relaxing.

Washing line

String or rope is attached between two stands with some balloons pegged on to the string. The individual is placed in front of, or underneath, the line, and supported or cradled by a helper from behind. With support, the individual may tap the balloons with hands and then feet. The balloons can be unpegged and a game started between individuals and their supporters.

A variation is to have another line of objects that the individual can explore or investigate at close range, with support. This may be a line of quoits, some brightly coloured beanbags or some air or sponge balls that are easy to grasp and manipulate. The practice may be varied to suit the individual's need.

Chalk shapes

Working with a partner, an individual has a star shape drawn on his or her back. The partner slowly draws with a piece of chalk around the body so that the person with profound and multiple disability can both feel the shape being drawn and afterwards be lifted or moved into a position to see the outline.

Elastic shapes

Strips of elastic are sewn or tied together for use by a pair of individuals, both of whom explore its stretching properties by wrapping it around different body parts and at different levels (e.g. kneeling, lying on the side, etc.). Using a larger elastic strip, everyone can be joined or linked by a body part to the elastic. Also the partner can 'twang' the elastic, creating vibrations on different parts of the body.

Parachute games

Mushrooms: Everyone sits around the parachute and holds the edge. The parachute is pulled taut in order to get the creases out and to give people time to become aware of the new experience. The leader asks the group to raise their arms and take one step forward, which allows the parachute to form a giant mushroom. Once the parachute has mushroomed the players can then lower their arms.

Whirlpool: Ask for a willing volunteer to experience this activity. The volunteer with an enabler sits in the middle of the parachute with his or her knees close in to the chest. A floor mat placed underneath the parachute will ensure safety. The enabler acts as a support behind the volunteer. The arms of the two people in the middle are then raised above their heads. The other participants move in a circular clockwise direction around the couple, wrapping the parachute around them and ensuring that the material goes under their shoulders and not around their necks. When the couple are wrapped up in the parachute everybody will be asked to move back a metre and pull; the parachute will unravel, making the couple spin round.

Breeze: Everyone sits around the parachute. Two or three people lie underneath the parachute on floor mats, while the people around the edge mushroom the parachute. Air rushes in and out and cools the people underneath. The parachute can be moved from side to side, tickling the people underneath. This needs to be done in a sensitive way as it can frighten some people.

The activities described above illustrate the potential of physical activities for people with profound disabilities. For a fuller account of such pursuits, the equipment required and safety factors, see Lambe, Mount and Jackson (1991). In addition, the Pro-motion Project, in conjunction with the United Kingdom Sports Association for People with a Mental Handicap, aims to increase access to opportunities in physical activities for people who have multiple disabilities.

THE WIDER CONTEXT

The preceding sections focused on the processes involved in physical activities for people with profound disabilities. Such principles clearly underlie a wide range of activities, the breadth of which is clearly indicated in Cavet's (1989) European study of leisure in general, and the physical activities potentially available to people with profound and multiple disabilities specifically. Cavet demonstrates that, in the 28 services surveyed, water-based activities were the most popular type of physical activity undertaken, followed by horse-riding and going for walks. Also reported as potential activities were running and jogging, trampolining, use of waterborne craft, ice and roller skating, parachute games, music and movement, yoga, ball games and the use of gymnastic equipment. Thus it has been demonstrated that a wide variety of physical activities can be made available to people with profound and multiple disabilities.

Some of the activities outlined above were undertaken on a group basis; others were carried out by an individual service user in a community setting in the company of members of the general public, accompanied by a staff member from a support service. One example of a participant in this type of approach was a young man described as 'very frail' who went for a flying lesson. Another instance occurred when a young woman with profound and multiple disabilities joined a private leisure club and regularly used their jacuzzi. A third example was a service user who, with her support worker, attended a weekly music and movement session at her local leisure centre.

The individual needs and preferences of service users should dictate what activities are undertaken and the ways in which they are put into operation. For water-based activities, the optimum water temperature will vary from person to person. For service users who are susceptible to the cold, raising the water temperature of pools or utilizing other environments, for example hydrotherapy pools or jacuzzis, will need to be explored.

Physical adaptations to sports equipment and environments may be necessary to maximize participation and enjoyment. Mounting a horse may be made easier by the use of a specially built ramp which raises the level of the rider. Alternatively, a channel may be cut in the ground which lowers the height of the horse relative to the position of the rider. Horse-drawn carts and wagons are another way of promoting contact with horses and providing a variety of new experiences for people with profound and multiple disabilities. Some horse-drawn carts are available which allow wheelchair users to gain easy access by a rear door.

Water-borne craft provide a further example of a leisure activity where physical adaptations may improve access for people with profound and multiple disabilities. Specially designed boats which allow for ready access for wheelchairs are one possible type of craft, as are adapted barges. For relatively adventurous service users who would like to canoe but require more stability than a canoe can usually offer, it is possible to lash two canoes together. Staff and service users can then enjoy the experience of canoeing, with a much reduced possibility of capsizing. This type of major adaptation is perhaps most easily made available to service users by spending time at specialized holiday or field centres. An example of these are The Calvert Trust Adventure Centre for disabled people, which is in the Lake District, and Churchtown Farm in Cornwall (see end of the chapter for addresses). Both of these centres have adapted facilities which encourage the active participation in outdoor leisure pursuits of people with profound and multiple disabilities. Attendance at such centres can widen the horizons of such people, and in some cases will provide a transition to engagement in community-based provision for physical activities available to the wider population.

REFERENCES AND FURTHER READING

BAALPE (1989) *Physical Education for Children with Special Education Needs in Mainstream Education*, BAALPE, Leeds.

Barlin, A. and Kalev, N. (1989) *Hello Toes! Movement Games for Children*, Princeton Book Company, Princeton.

Booth, D.(1968) *Games for Everyone*, Pembroke Publishers, Ontario.

Brown, A. (1987) *Active Games for Children with Movement Problems*, Harper and Row, London.

Cavet, J. (1989) *Occupational and Leisure Activities for People with Profound Retardation and Multiple Impairments*, Report to European Commission, Hester Adrian Research Centre, Manchester.

Heseltine, P. (1987) *Games for All Children*, Basil Blackwell, Oxford.

Lambe, L., Mount, H. and Jackson, R. (1991) Module B Book 3: Sports, games and their adaptation, in *Leisure for People with Profound and Multiple Disabilities*, (ed. L. Lambe), Mencap, London.

Leach, M. (1993) *Pro-motion Resource Guide – Activities for People with Multiple Disability*, The Spastics Society, London.

Loscher, A. (1990) *Everybody Play*, Sports Book Publishers, Toronto.

Masheder, M. (1989) *Let's Play Together*, Green Print, London.

Orlick, T. (1978) *Co-operative Sports and Games Book*, Pantheon Books, New York.

Ouvrey, C. (1987) *Educating Children with Profound Handicaps*, BIMH Publications, Kidderminster.

Park, K. (n.d.) Using objects of reference. *European Journal of Special Needs Education* (in press)

Pointer, B. (1992) *Movement Activities for Children with Movement Difficulties*, Jessica Kingsley, London.

Price, R. (1980) *Physical Education and the Physically Handicapped Child*, A.C. Black Ltd, London.

Reed, L. (1991) *Games with a New Look for all Ability Levels*, Spastics Society, Meldreth, Herts.

Sugden, D. (1984) Issues in teaching children with movement problems. *British Journal of Physical Education*, **15** (3), 68–70.

ADDRESSES

Calvert Trust Adventure Centre for Disabled People, Little Crosthwaite, Underskiddaw, Keswick, Cumbria CA12 43QD.
Tel: 07687 72254.

Churchtown Farm Field Studies Centre, Lanlivery, Bodmin, Cornwall PL30 5BT.
Tel: 0208 872148.

Lifequest. The Spastics Society Recreation Services, 11 Churchill Park, Colwick, Nottingham NG4 2HF.

6

Task-orientated enjoyment

Freda Abbro

For parents and carers of people with profound and multiple disabilities the everyday tasks of washing, changing, feeding and dressing their charges take up so many hours of the day that to suggest adding a further and separate chore – that of providing entertaining leisure occupations – seems almost gratuitous. Yet both parents and professional carers admit that the hours spent between carrying out the tasks of meeting basic bodily needs can be both unrewarding and unproductive for both parties. As parents we take pride in the performance of these routine tasks for a new baby – bathing, feeding, dressing and changing can be occasions of fun, and are recognized as opportunities for early learning. The baby's first responses of sound and recognition are celebrated as important milestones in their development, and shared with all who care to listen. Contrast this with the situation of those caring for people whose response repertoire is very limited and all too familiar.

Over the years carers become expert in the performance of those routine care tasks required to maintain health, so that they are carried out as speedily and efficiently as possible. Professionals from medicine and education advise all concerned that the person being cared for is so severely handicapped that their basic needs demand 'special care'. This usually becomes a recipe for total physical care, with a 'no-risks' policy being actively encouraged, and the rule of self-fulfilling prophecy comes into force. Rarely is reference made to those other needs, which all people have in common, and which can facilitate development towards adult status, however disabled the person may be. These latter needs encompass the encouragement of choice, in all its aspects, engagement in activities which are rewarding in themselves, and social interaction linked to the constructive use of leisure. This chapter outlines the work of a Further Education Centre which aimed to meet some of these needs, in normal domestic environments, using everyday and routine tasks, to promote enjoyment in carrying out the tasks and to facilitate the development of adult status.

The Orchard Hill Further Education Centre was set up in 1983 to provide some form of further education service to the 200 young adults who live on Orchard Hill. This was, and remains, a long-stay residential District Health Authority facility for people with profound and multiple disabilities, and is situated in the grounds of a children's hospital. What helped to make the Orchard Hill resident population unique was the severity of their disabilities and their narrow age range, since 85% were aged between 20 and 30 years. In contrast to the population of most other mental handicap hospitals, where only 15% could be classified as 'least able' by the National Development Team criteria, 85% of the Orchard Hill residents come into this category. This resulted in severe challenges to both care and teaching staff. The statistics were daunting:

- 170 of the residents were wheelchair or spinal carriage-bound;
- Only 10 residents had any spoken language;
- No resident used more than three communication signs;
- More than half the residents had significant sight and/or hearing loss.

Most of the residents lived in 'bungalows' with up to 15 other 'patients', and frequent changes of care staff meant that a maximum of two on a shift was the norm. The majority of the residents had been in institutional care since early childhood, and since only 10% were visited with any regularity, their contact with the wider community had been strictly limited.

When setting up the Centre it appeared essential to put into practice those philosophies which lie at the heart of all education, and which distinguish it from a whole range of other activities. These philosophies dictated that the progression of these students towards adulthood should be facilitated, with emphasis being placed on autonomy and independence, the opportunity to engage in rewarding activities, and social interaction linked to leisure skills.

The purpose of each experience presented was to ensure that, first and foremost, it was enjoyable in itself; secondly, that it supported the pursuance of the Centre's philosophies; and thirdly, that it provided a learning opportunity for the individual, regardless of handicapping condition. To achieve this it was essential to travel from what the student already knew, at whatever level, towards the unknown but essential next step along the way. Thus the range of activities designed for teaching sessions formed part of a learning continuum for the students. These were broadly divided into five main areas:

- Communication (language and/or signing)
- Mobility (gross motor skills)
- Knowing and understanding (cognition and perception)
- Manipulation of objects (fine motor skills)
- Stimulation of vision and hearing (visual and auditory discrimination).

Each of these areas was staffed by a team of three 'teachers', few of whom had any previous experience of teaching or caring for profoundly and multiply handicapped people. Conversely, this in itself brought enormous benefits to the student group, and to the work carried out in the Centre, since these staff approached the work with an open mind and few preconceived notions. Staff were largely recruited by standard newspaper advertisements, but before any formal interview they were placed in a teaching team for two differing sessions. The attitude of the students and staff towards the prospective applicant was a critical factor in the selection process, and the applicant had an opportunity to assess their own suitability for this type of work. Everybody using or visiting the Centre was addressed by their forename, there was no 'staff room', no door was locked and all equipment was used in common.

The tasks and activities selected by the teaching team in each of the areas outlined often overlapped, and since each team was given timetabled access to every facility and resource within the Centre, the opportunity to build on and generalize the skills learned was facilitated. Essential to the teaching task was the emphasis placed on individual teaching, with staff working with an individual student for much of any session.

Parents, direct care staff, or any other person with knowledge of the individual could refer a student to the Centre, although in practice it was usually a member of the care staff who actually completed the referral form. The student was then offered a 6-week 'taster' course, of 2 hours each week, containing some elements of the intensive course selected, to determine whether they actually liked the sorts of activities involved, (for example, if a person is afraid of water, the water games component of the Mobility Course would be unsuitable), or whether they had already mastered the basic skill but had been prevented from practising it. This often happened with wheelchair 'driving' lessons, when students were taught to propel their own wheelchair or to use an electric one, but were prevented by institutional constraints from practising the skill in their own ward/home. Once accepted on an intensive course, each student had an individual teaching programme drawn up which contained at least one specific objective to be met within a fixed 9-week timescale. This was regarded as a 'contract' between the student and the teaching staff, and ensured that the student actually benefited from attendance at the Centre. Each staff team designed their particular course skills continuum to enable any student to progress from their base level, which would have been assessed throughout the 'taster' course, to mastery of the skill or terminal behaviour. To demonstrate achievement of the specific objective set criteria were used: for example, performance of the skill or terminal behaviour on four out of five consecutive attempts. This broad background sets the scene for the Centre's activities.

The Centre was designed to facilitate activities taking place in normal and appropriate domestic environments, therefore, of the two kitchens, one was designed on the 'Phlexi-plan' system for people with physical handicaps. It contained a sink which could be raised or lowered by a simple hydraulic lever action, pull-out work surfaces, one of which had a circle cut out in the centre to allow a mixing bowl to be fitted in, cupboards fitted with 'carousels' or pull-out deep trays for easy access, and a small glass-fronted oven fitted on a shelf at table-top height, so that students could actually see food cooking, an automatic front-loading washing machine and tumble drier, and a halogen hob. The other kitchen was designed to meet the needs of people with visual impairments: textures were used as 'markers', items of equipment were obtained in one colour – we discovered that dark brown was easily obtainable and made a sharp contrast to the pale-coloured walls, table and work surfaces – and all equipment was arranged in set places, which were labelled to ensure that new staff knew where each item belonged. At the end of each session every item used was returned to its correct place, since this helped visually handicapped students to gain confidence when using the kitchen. Both kitchens were of normal domestic size and contained many standard electrical items of normal kitchen equipment, including hand-held mixers, food processors and electric can openers.

The value of using a microwave cooker in helping people with profound and multiple disabilities cannot be stressed too highly: microwave ovens were used in both kitchens, placed at table-top height, and students were encouraged to sit and watch the changes that occurred during the cooking process. The experience of actually watching the cake rise, or the egg scramble, reinforced the connection between the uncooked food they had prepared and the final cooked product. The speed of the microwave also helped students with a limited attention span, because they could quickly see the changes brought about during the cooking process. Yet another advantage is that the plastic cooking vessels used in microwave cooking are light and flexible, thus helping people with physical disabilities or clumsy movements to participate fully in the cookery class.

The emphasis throughout the Centre was on the process and not the product, so all students were expected to use the appropriate piece of equipment, even if modifications were sometimes needed to allow physically disabled students to take an active part in the process involved. This also meant that for some students, especially at the start of a course, considerable physical assistance and prompts were required to help them complete a task. Over time, and by using specific and constant language sequences, students learned to carry out quite complicated tasks with minimal assistance.

It is salutory to reflect that most babies and young children spend many hours in the kitchen 'helping' their mother, and we cannot overestimate the learning that takes place in what is normally a warm, familiar and friendly environment. Often children are given the bowl and spoon, which have been used to stir the cake, to scrape and lick, thus learning to manipulate objects, before helping with the washing up, which provides an opportunity to learn some properties of the weight and volume of water. The smell of the cakes cooking, the anticipation experienced while waiting for food to come out of the oven, learning by experience what 'hot' means, and the satisfaction of eating the food that the child has helped to make, provide invaluable opportunities for growth and understanding. These early learning opportunities had been denied to the Centre's student group (and to many others with profound disabilities), since they were normally denied access to a kitchen.

A cookery session always started with washing hands and putting on aprons, because this created a sense of anticipation and identity of the activity. The students needed to feel secure and comfortable in what was initially an unknown environment, so sitting round a table was found to be preferable to standing, especially for those whose gait was unsteady. In this way social interaction was fostered, since students faced each other with the teacher acting as facilitator. The desired end-product was visually portrayed and verbally described, and for students with a visual handicap the 'Blue Peter' method was used (producing an identical item made previously). Every ingredient and item of equipment used was either tasted or touched – often both – by each student. Students were invited to participate in the actual processes involved, with no pressure put upon those who initially showed reluctance. As the activity progressed, constant verbal prompts were given to remind students of the aim of the session, and to encourage their awareness of the processes involved. When the food or drink was ready, and each person had helped with the clearing and washing up, the students were encouraged to sample the final product. This also progressed to the stage where students took some of their produce 'home', or shared it with a friend of their own choosing. We all made – and learned – from our culinary disasters: cakes that wouldn't rise, jellies that didn't set, etc., but these were often the cause of more fun than our successes!

Simple recipes which required little or no cooking, such as milk shakes or Instant Whips, were used in the earliest sessions of the course, but over time students gradually progressed to more complicated food preparation and cooking skills. Wherever possible packet mixes were used, since students could choose and buy these on their weekly outing to the shops. A set of coloured photographs, identical but in large and small sizes, were invaluable in carrying out these shopping excursions. Having decided what items were to be purchased, each student was given the small photograph of the one specific item they were to buy. This meant that they had to identify the item in the large supermarket that we used and as familiarity of the layout grew, many students learned just where to look for 'their' item. At the end of this course complete meals were chosen, cooked and eaten by the students involved. In addition, to mark the different festivals of the year, more complex foods were made, such as hot cross buns or individual Christmas puddings (when everybody present in the Centre was called in to 'have a stir' for luck!). We also took advantage of the 'pick your own' fruit and vegetables service available at local smallholdings, since this helped to give our students an awareness of how some food was grown, as well as providing an enjoyable outing.

Each student had a 'Communication Book', in the form of a diary, which staff collected when they went to escort the student to the Centre. In this, a pictorial illustration was used to describe the task undertaken by the student in a particular session. Fixing in the picture from a packet mix, or a simple line sketch of the finished product, was usually sufficient, although for students with visual impairments differing textures and scents were added. Photographs and video films were also taken of sessions, so that students had a visual reminder of an activity, and a useful aid in encouraging their communication skills. The use of these simple means of recording added to the pleasure gained in any activity, and provided the student with a personal record of their achievements. Naturally, these much-used 'Communication Books' became rather dog-eared over time, so at the end of an intensive course they were re-covered and bound. Care staff reported that students appeared to enjoy looking or 'feeling' through their old Communication Books as a leisure activity, and the tasks and experiences portrayed gave visitors and volunteers a starting point for initiating communication with people whose speech was limited or non-existent.

Our awareness of our body, and knowing how we are seen by others, is an important step towards adulthood. The use of personal care skills in an unhurried and relaxed environment can facilitate this knowledge, as well as providing a wide range of pleasurable experiences. To enable students to develop this body image each Centre team used the bathroom, hairdressing salon and toilets as teaching areas. Inevitably, most of the activities were carried out on an individual basis, with the emphasis always placed on respect for the dignity of each student. There were two toilet areas, one shower room and one bathroom in the Centre, each containing standard items of sanitary ware, but with some special additions. For many of the Centre's students, used to the communal facilities that were the norm in their wards, the introduction to these areas of personal care as places of relaxation and enjoyment came as a pleasant surprise.

It had been salutory to observe the awareness of our incontinent students to the negative facial expressions and body language of staff when a change of soiled clothing was necessary. In an effort to change this we discovered the use of the Clos-o-mat Toilet (the self-washing and drying model). This removed much of the indignity usually attendant upon this essential function, and in our experience actually promoted continence. We found it advisable for the teacher to demonstrate the actions of this toilet in front of the student before their initial use of it, for the surprise of a warm water spray and the subsequent jet of warm air could be frightening if the student was not aware of what would happen. The benefits, especially to women students with physical disabilities, were obvious, for many of them had achieved continence only to be placed back in 'nappies' at the onset of menstruation. Normal women can change 'stick-on' pads and wash or shower frequently when menstruating, yet care timetables dictated that only three changes of the 'nappy' in 24 hours were the norm for our young women with multiple disabilities.

One toilet contained a urinal, because observation of our young men had demonstrated that they invariably sat down to use the toilet, whereas the majority of public toilets for men contained urinals. The safety and hygienic aspects of this piece of equipment should not be overlooked. Naturally, very few homes possess a urinal, yet to teach a young man to urinate standing up can be invaluable if they are to use public facilities. Hand-washing following use of a toilet was insisted upon, even for those who were confined to spinal carriages, offering many the first chance they had had of carrying out this task.

The strict language sequence to be used by all staff, as well as a pictorial illustration of hand washing, was placed prominently above each handbasin, to encourage each student to develop this independent skill. The availability of 'sensing' equipment, which dispenses water or soap or warm air automatically when hands are placed underneath, has proved to be invaluable for people with severe disabilities, especially if their movements are lacking coordination. It is sad that equipment of this type is not more widely available since it is invaluable in giving a sense of positive achievement to people with severe disabilities, by promoting the skill of independent hand-washing. Similarly, the use of a wall-mounted hair drier, as used in most large hotels, facilitates drying the body independently.

The Centre possessed a domestic model of the Parker bath, with a thermostatically controlled central tap, whirlpool spa and shower attachments. For an individual whose regular daily routine is to be bathed 'by numbers', as still happens in some old-style hospitals and hostels catering for people with profound and multiple disabilities, or for the person whose parent/carer had come to regard the daily hygiene and changing routine as a necessary set of chores, the luxury of a complete 'body care' package provided an enjoyable experience, if the reaction of our students was any guide. The aim was to allow the individual to experience a bath, with time and comfort to actually enjoy it, with a staff member of their choice (facilitated by photographs of the staff available), choice of bath foam, choice of still water or whirlpool spa, a hair wash with their choice of shampoo and conditioner, the choice of towel colour and their choice of clothes to wear afterwards.

This element of choice was vital if we were to encourage autonomy, as was promoted in every area of the Centre's work. Choice in routine tasks is often refused to people with profound and multiple disabilities, especially if they have additional sensory handicaps, thus denying them the chance to develop autonomy. Staff members soon learned, by acute observation, how each individual student expressed choice. True, it initially took much longer to accomplish a task, and often what might be considered unwise choices were made, especially as regards clothes, yet this in itself was seen as a positive stage in developing adulthood. Everyone has made the wrong choice of clothes at some time in their life – wearing formal dress to an informal gathering or vice versa – yet by always choosing the clothing we consider appropriate for a person with disabilities we deny them this learning experience.

Next to the main bathroom was a hairdressing salon, with a hairdresser in attendance for some sessions. Here, as part of the total grooming package, students could have their hair trimmed or cut, set or permed, again with the emphasis on choice, with a manicure and pedicure as optional extras. For women students, a facial massage or face-pack was available, and they were helped to apply make-up, taking an active part in the application and choice of colours. For men the use of electric razors was encouraged with their choice of aftershave lotion. The use of good-quality non-allergenic toiletries was regarded as essential, and care staff were always consulted in advance, so that any individual skin or hair problems were allowed for. At the end of the session 'before' and 'after' photographs were taken and fixed in the Communication Book.

The total body care package took some 2 hours, and although most students demonstrated their enjoyment of the activities by smiling, laughing and vocalizing, it was notable that those students who were seen by care staff to present the most 'challenging' behaviours seemed to gain most enjoyment from the activities involved in these sessions. Whether this was due to the concentrated one-to-one situation, or because their bodily comfort had previously been a low priority for care staff, was not clear, but with rare exceptions this was the activity most opted for when offered as one of three choices. The use of large mirrors around the Centre, at varying heights, was invaluable in promoting body awareness, and emphasized the change in appearance of the student after the body care package. The use of the instant photographs also served to highlight the difference in appearance, and these raised awareness of care staff regarding the importance of good grooming.

We developed an Intensive Communication Course, which consisted of daily 2-hour sessions on a one-to-one basis for a period of 6 weeks. The aim of the course was to develop some form of communication system, using language, sounds, signs, eye-pointing, etc., or mechanical aids, such as a Touchtec computer screen, so that the individual student could exercise choice in their lives. One of the tasks of this course was carried out in a small room in the Centre called the 'sounds room'. The activities carried out here could equally be carried out in a person's home, and could be used to provide a worthwhile leisure occupation, since they do not require specialist training or equipment. A student in the early stages of the Intensive Communication Course would be escorted to this room and invited to sit at a table with a mentor. Once comfortable and settled, they would be fitted with earphones attached to a cassette recorder. We had several different pairs of earphones to choose from, since some students objected to certain kinds, especially the heavy padded type, and for students in spinal carriages we used 'sound pillows'. The aim of the initial sessions was to build up a pattern of sounds to which the student reacted positively, and to this end we had acquired a wide range of music and sounds on tape. These were played in random order (for example 1 minute of piano music, 10 seconds of laughing, 30 seconds of fast drumming, 1 minute of the latest pop sounds, etc.), and the student's reactions noted. After some 15 minutes the student went off to the next activity, and those sounds which had evoked a positive response were taped together. Subsequent visits to the sound room built up the pattern of sounds, with frequent checks to ascertain whether the positive response to particular sounds remained.

If a response to one particular sound or song was very marked we made further inquiries of the care staff as to its known relevance in the life of the student. Often these inquiries produced remarkable results, which proved rewarding to both the student and staff. For example, one student did not react positively to any sounds presented on his first two visits. On the third visit the teacher tried, among other sounds, a 1-minute excerpt from the popular Beatles song 'Yellow Submarine'. The young man looked up, smiled and moved his head in time to the music. So marked was this response that the teacher persisted in her inquiries, and eventually wrote to the young man's mother requesting her views on why this piece of music should evoke such a response. The mother came to see the teacher and explained that, prior to the road traffic accident at the age of 4 which had caused the young man's severe brain damage, his father used to play this particular record to his son before putting him to bed. A visit from his father, for the first time in many years, followed this exchange of information, and within weeks the young man was spending alternate Sundays with his family.

The next stage of this course was gradually to extend the listening time to the length of a standard 45-minute cassette. The known sounds were interspersed with the student's name, and gradually other words and music were introduced. Over time a repertoire of different tapes was produced, each tailored to the individual. The next step was to teach the use of an autoreverse cassette recorder, using simple on/off switches. The majority of students eventually mastered this skill, although many had individually tailored switches made or adapted for their personal use. At the completion of this aspect of the communication course, the student was provided with their own cassette recorder, earphones and switch and, with minimal assistance from care staff, they were enabled to listen to rewarding sounds and music in their ward/home for up to 90 minutes.

The positive aspect of leisure made a welcome change from the ever-present television and/or radio for some students, and care staff became very enthusiastic about this aspect of the activity. This course component proved of greatest value to students who suffered additional visual impairments, but its success for all students taking part made it one of the most popular. The element of built-in success appeared to be vital if the student was to gain maximum enjoyment from these aspects of the courses which required some effective concentration. A 'no-fail' situation guaranteed that students were rewarded, often for the first time in their lives, by a guaranteed end-product.

One large room was devoted to those tasks which involved making a mess, and possibly getting dirty, as an integral part of the activity. The room, which we likened to a utility room, contained an ordinary kitchen sink with draining boards, two domestic-sized tables and several sturdy chairs with wooden arms. These chairs were used throughout the Centre, for students lacking mobility were usually taken out of their wheelchairs and given the opportunity of sitting at the same level and at the same work place as everybody else, and needed the security of chairs with arms. Students with disabilities which resulted in a clumsy gait, those recovering from a recent seizure or others taking heavy doses of certain medication all demonstrated security when seated in these chairs. For students who could not be moved out of their wheelchairs or spinal carriages, tilting work surfaces on variable-height stands were made, to allow them to take an active part in the selected task. The activities undertaken in this room ranged from washing flower pots, filling them with compost, inserting cuttings, planting bulbs, stripping lavender, pressing plants and leaves, making plant pictures, keeping plants watered, etc. Compost was placed either in old plastic washing-up bowls or in wooden boxes with two sides cut away, and a wide range of variously sized spoons and trowels were tried until a suitable one was found for each individual student. Similarly, watering plants was carried out using any piece of normal domestic equipment that enabled the student to carry out the task with minimal assistance.

Everybody taking part in these sessions was involved in washing the tables, cleaning the sink and sweeping the floor at the end of the chosen activity. We considered that helping to clear up and put things away was an important and integral part of any activity, and even the student with the most profound disabilities was expected, and helped, to take part. It became important to warn care staff that a student was likely to get dirty in these sessions, because for some reason the appearance of a person with profound disabilities covered in compost, soil, mud or other messy substances was regarded as totally unacceptable! The logic behind this attitude escaped us, for the obvious enjoyment of the students taking part in these activities and then taking their produce 'back home' was obvious to all.

When the Centre first opened it had been presented with sand and water-play equipment for the utilities room, because it was felt that these items were appropriate for the 'developmental age' of the student group. The Centre's policy of only engaging in age-appropriate activities meant that the first task undertaken with this equipment was to make planters of them, to demonstrate that compost and sand were interchangeable, and that cuttings regularly watered could provide plants to enhance the environment, regardless of who grew them. Bulbs dropped on to plates of shingle flowered and smelled sweetly, and helped to develop an awareness of growth, regardless of the 'developmental age' of the person dropping the bulb. From the earliest months plants and bulbs grown in these sessions were used to brighten up the Centre, and many students demonstrated an awareness that they remembered the plants or bulbs that they had grown, especially as they were involved in the weekly watering sessions. Within 2 years of opening, the students were taking houseplants and other produce 'home' and to the offices of the hospital managers and the local education department, accompanied by a small notice stating that these were the produce of the Centre!

Another small room was developed into a woodworking unit, using a standard workbench and a Workmate (made by Black and Decker). This piece of carpentry equipment was necessary because its height could be varied to accommodate the individual needs of a student, and its central clamping mechanism assisted those students with severe physical disabilities to use the tools available in comfort and safety. In woodwork sessions students used tools found in most homes, e.g. saws, hammers, nails, screwdrivers and others, including an electric drill. The majority of the tools were mounted securely on the walls, and were outlined in red to ensure that they were put back in the same place. As always, the emphasis was on the process and not the product. A brief description of some of the tasks involved in the making of simple hanging baskets will therefore suffice to demonstrate the sorts of activities carried out in this area.

Because the Centre was situated in large grounds containing many old trees, students would go on expeditions to pick up fallen sticks. In the woodwork room the sticks would be sorted by size and thickness and, using a simple jig, sawn into equal lengths. It was not lost on us that the actions required to use a saw were identical to the use of a knife to cut up some kinds of food, for example roast potatoes, meat, bread, etc. – another example of the opportunity to generalize skills. By fixing the electric drill in a sliding clamp, students drilled holes at both ends of the sticks, using a simple up-and-down movement of the drill's lever attachment. The sticks were then placed, one at a time, on to a square base board and attached to it by threading through both with strong cord. After five layers of sticks had been fixed alternately into a square, sufficient cord was left to allow for a reasonable amount of plant height and growth before the ends were secured to a brass curtain ring, thus creating a simple rustic hanging basket. Square plastic ice-cream containers, filled with either compost and plants or 'oasis' and dried flowers, were fitted into the baskets, producing an end-product that was both aesthetically pleasing and useful for brightening up the environment.

Some professionals visiting the Centre, or seeing videos of the work carried out in the woodwork room, expressed considerable surprise at seeing people with such profound disabilities actually using tools which were potentially dangerous. Allied to this, the concern expressed by many care staff over the taking of risks was an issue which was never satisfactorily resolved. We believed that any risks taken were justified, provided that every possible precaution was taken to secure the safety of the individual. Since all students had equal access to the woodwork room we ensured that protective clothing, goggles and, essentially, the one-to-one ratio of teacher to student, was maintained. Students with epilepsy were encouraged to wear a protective helmet, and for all students tasks were carried out in a seated position wherever this was practically possible.

Another regular weekly activity for students on intensive courses was a weekly outing, the risk factors involved in these being carefully examined by all Centre staff. The staff team members of the Mobility Skills Course usually selected a ramble or walk in some nearby woods, and inevitably students fell over, scraping hands and knees. The staff team members of the Manipulation of Objects Skills Course (designed to help students develop the use of their hands) normally went shopping – and yes, they did on occasions knock over piles of stacked groceries, select the wrong item from the shelves or refuse to pay at the checkout. The Communication Course team invariably selected a cafe or snack bar for their outing, and of course sometimes the tea or coffee was too hot, or a cake would spurt cream over other people. The teams teaching students with visual impairments and the Knowing and Understanding Skills Course were far more adventurous, since they actually presented students with challenges. Since all our outings were planned well in advance, and were always on a one-to-one basis, we believed that any risks taken were justified.

Elementary safety measures, which should be present in every home, are neither expensive nor complicated. Crucially important is the floor covering, which should ideally be of non-slip linoleum, with quarry-tiled surfaces in bathrooms and showers. The growth in use of rugs, dhurries, ceramic tiles and the like, especially in areas where liquid is liable to be spilt, can result in falls, because it is difficult to maintain one's balance, and propelling a wheelchair can become hazardous. Carrying out tasks from a sitting position aids stability, and the use of a small trolley to transfer articles from one place to another, especially when they are hot, adds another element of safety.

Electric plugs should always be switched off when not in use, and some of the worst hazards – leaving the live lead of an electric kettle loose on a work surface, or leaving hot pans with handles within reach – are obviously dangerous. Guards which can be easily fitted around the tops of stoves are available, and the use of electricity rather than gas for cooking should be seriously considered. Old-style gas cookers require two operations – the turning on of the tap and at the same time pressing the lighter or striking a match; electricity, on the other hand, only requires the use of a switch. Halogen hobs, with their instant change of colour and surge of heat, are safe to use, and the new conduction hobs promise to be safer still, since they only become hot when in contact with metal containers. Cupboards which are too high, too deep or inaccessible are danger spots, and should be reserved for rarely used goods. Everyday items of kitchen and bathroom materials, such as bleach and toilet or oven cleaners, can be obtained with safety-top containers, and the contents of pressurized spray containers can now be obtained in screw-top or flip-top plastic jars. Drawers should be fitted with stops to prevent them coming out when pulled with a jerk, and should be easy to close. Other hazards which cause concern are kitchen/bathroom equipment with sharp edges, such as knives, scissors and razors. These should be safely stored away. (Experience of hospital casualty departments indicates that pencils, pens, forks, etc. are equally hazardous.) Accidents can and do happen in every household, but by applying common sense and using our imagination, we can ensure that any person, however severe their disability, can enjoy and participate in all normal domestic activities: it only requires time, a positive attitude and a sense of humour. The result, at the lowest level, is a marked reduction in boredom and all its attendant problems.

Many of the activities described above require a one-to-one ratio of teacher to student, and this would appear to rule them out as viable pursuits in situations where more than one person with profound and multiple disabilities lives, or in a busy household. Our student population was unique relative to that of other day care centres, since every student had profound and multiple disabilities, but the activities described could all be carried out by one teacher with a group of four or five, providing that each person was actively engaged at some stage of the activity. As already stated, few of the Centre staff team had undergone any training, and the use of the word teacher was interchangeable with assistant, facilitator, mentor, companion or friend. To increase the number of students to whom we could offer a service, we actively recruited volunteers from churches, golf clubs, the fifth form of local schools, the local branch of the Council for Voluntary Services and by word of mouth. Each volunteer was paired with a named student for a particular session, and this promoted friendships, some of which persisted over years. This constructive use of volunteers effectively allowed the Centre to double its student intake, and demonstrated that respect for the individual and a friendly welcoming attitude were more essential attributes than training in specialized skills. Effective management of the Centre, and weekly in-service training, helped to develop the teaching skills of the Centre staff, and many went on to obtain qualified teacher status or degrees in allied subjects.

I hope that some of the tasks and activities outlined in this chapter will encourage both parents and carers to look again at everyday routine tasks and, by using their imagination, determine to include the person with disabilities in carrying them out. If enjoyment and choice are included as elements of the tasks, the results in terms of personal satisfaction for both the person with profound and multiple disabilities and his or her carer are inestimable.

APPENDIX

Copies of the Orchard Hill Further Education Centre's Prospectus and a professionally made video film of some of the Centre's activities are available from the Centre. Please write to:

The Head of Centre, Orchard Hill F.E. Centre, Queen Mary's Hospital, Carshalton, Surrey SM5 4NR.
    Tel: 081 770 8319.
Details of specialized equipment can be obtained from:
Disabled Living Foundation, 380–384 Harrow Road, London W9 2HU.
    Tel: 071 289 6111
or from:
RADAR, 25 Mortimer Street, London W1N 8AB.
    Tel: 071 637 5400.

Advice on horticultural activities can be obtained from:
Horticultural Therapy, Goulds Ground, Vallis Way, Frome, Somerset BA11
  3DW.
  Tel: 0373 464782.
For more specific information concerning the activities described, simple
adaptations to standard equipment, or design details of individually made
items, please contact the author at:
6 South Drive, Banstead, Surrey SM7 3BH.
  Tel: 081 643 3393.

7

Gardening:
a multisensory experience

Loretto Lambe

INTRODUCTION

Gardening is one of the most popular pastimes in Britain, second only to fishing, and its popularity is on the increase. The panel of 'Gardeners' Question Time', one of the longest-running programmes on BBC Radio, recently dealt with the query: 'What section of the population is not interested in gardening, and does not garden?'. The answer was, not surprisingly, 'teenagers'. However, even for teenagers, this lack of interest in gardening was confined to their adolescence. By definition, then, all other sectors of the public either garden or gain pleasure from gardens. People with disabilities form a part of this great gardening community. People with profound and multiple disabilities may be limited in how they can actively garden, but they do derive a considerable amount of enjoyment from gardens.

Gardens provide us with a host of natural, multisensory experiences. Quite often, garden planners do not consider this when designing a garden, but sensory gardens are now increasingly being created. Usually they are attached to a school, an adult day service facility or a residential unit for people with disabilities. The Chelsea Flower Show, the gardening event of the year, has for a number of years featured gardens that are designed with the needs of elderly persons or people with disabilities in mind. There is no reason why your own back garden cannot be turned into just such a sensory garden. So, what is a sensory garden? Basically, it is just like any other garden, with the same features and elements. Gardens have an overall design that includes **hard landscaping**: walls and/or fencing, formal paths, a pond or water feature, raised beds, terrace or patio, etc; **soft landscaping**: planting, e.g. shrubs, flowers, trees, lawns, hedges; **colours and textures**: e.g. flowers, foliage; and **wildlife**: birds, insects, fish, etc. The only difference in a sensory garden is that all these components must be carefully chosen and designed to appeal to the senses in such a way that they provide maximum sensory stimulation. A sensory garden could also be described as offering the range and diversity of sensory stimulation to people with profound and multiple disabilities that are to be found in multisensory or 'snoezelen' rooms. The difference is that in a sensory garden the stimuli are natural and cost considerably less.

DESIGN AND PLANNING

Sensory gardens are not just for people with disabilities: everyone will enjoy and derive pleasure from such a garden. However, to ensure that a person with profound and multiple disabilities will gain the maximum pleasure from a garden, care and attention must be given to each element in its design. With careful thought and planning a garden can offer stimulation to all the senses: sight, sound, touch, taste and smell, all vitally important when planning any leisure activity that may involve people with profound and multiple disabilities. Many books on gardening suggest that gardens should be designed as a series of 'rooms', with each room focusing on a particular theme, with colour, style or type of plant contrasted. This idea of different rooms could be adapted when creating a sensory garden, with the theme for each room or area being an emphasis on a different sense. This is not to say that each element of the garden should be devoted to appealing to just one of the senses, but it would be a help in the initial planning stages to concentrate on each sense separately. I will now expand on this theme and deal with how you can begin to think about employing plants, shrubs, shape, form, texture, etc. for each sense in turn.

It is not the intention in this short chapter to give detailed information on the specific plants or features that could be incorporated in the garden, but reference to such detail will be given. However, the general principles underlying the design of a sensory garden will be described and some practical suggestions presented. With regard to the names of plants suggested, do not be put off if Latin names are not familiar: for our purposes the common name will usually serve when dealing with a nursery or garden centre.

Sight

The overall design and appearance of a garden is vitally important. Visual interest is provided in a number of ways. First, the shape and form of trees, plants, shrubs and flowers should be used to create pictures. Every plant has a natural form and silhouette and the variety from which to choose is vast. The shapes of trees and shrubs include spreading, pyramidal, conical, weeping, round-headed, arching, columnar and so on. In one species, conifers, we find all these shapes and forms. Conifers also have the added advantage of coming in a range of sizes, from miniature to full-sized trees. They are also evergreen, which means you have colour all year round. I am not suggesting that you only consider conifers: too many would give a boring and artificial look, but in moderation careful selection will add shape, form and year-round colour. There are numerous other tree species from which to choose. For example, **Japanese maples** (acers) have beautiful shapes and forms and come in a variety of colours. Many can be grown in tubs or containers, which means that they can be within visual range of a person with limited vision or movement. One good example is *Acer palmatum 'Dissectum Atropurpureum'*. This has light feathery leaves and a lovely shape and colour, and in autumn turns a wonderful vibrant coppery red. Many herbs and bulbous plants have striking foliage and flower spikes. **Hostas** are plants that are grown primarily for the shape of their foliage. There is such a variety of plants to choose from that there should be no difficulty in using shape and form in the 'visual' pictures you create.

Secondly, the movement and rhythms of the garden provide a different form of visual interest. In addition to being pleasing to look at, plants and trees also create moving pictures or shadows. Interesting patterns are created by the sun shining through leaves and branches. Movement is also provided by the wind, soft breezes and rain. A whole series of still-life and moving pictures can be presented to a person with profound disabilities, who need do no more to enjoy them than view them from their wheelchair, seated on the lawn or garden bench. Being in a garden in this way offers visual stimulation and at the same time is also pleasurable and peaceful.

Thirdly, using colour to its optimum is another very good way to bring visual stimulation into the garden. Flowers are the obvious choice, but do not forget that foliage can also be very colourful. When choosing plants for a sensory garden, bear in mind that many people with disabilities will have visual impairments. In addition, the side-effects of a number of medications cause blurred vision. Therefore, be careful not to provide a confusion of colour by planting drifts of multicoloured annuals that mix the whole colour spectrum. Instead, plant flowers and shrubs in bands of single colours, but break up the bands with foliage plants, hedging or paths. Plant all whites, all blues, yellows, reds and so on in this way. Think of the impact that beds of single-colour annuals in our public parks and gardens make. Endeavour to choose bold, vibrant colours and also soft but strong calming tones. One of the most successful well known gardens in the country is the 'white garden' created by Vita Sackville-West at Sissinghurst. If you get the opportunity, do visit this garden to see just how effective one-colour planting can be. Do remember that it is not just flower blooms that come in strong different colours: the foliage of many shrubs and trees is not green but yellow, red, silvery white and so on. Grasses and sedges come in a wide range of colours, from a bright yellow-gold to almost black. Many gardening reference books list the different flowers and shrubs by colour, so you should have no difficulty in choosing a variety from each colour range to suit the specific conditions in your own garden. An excellent book as a comprehensive reference is The Royal Horticultural Society's *Gardeners' Encyclopedia of Plants and Flowers* (Brickell, 1989). This may appear an expensive outlay (it is approximately £29) but it is the major reference source of information on over 8000 plants. If you have only one gardening reference book, it should be this one, which, together with its companion *The RHS Encyclopedia of Gardening* (Brickell, 1992), would provide a comprehensive source of gardening information. It may be possible to borrow both these books from your local library or to consult them in the reference section. Another very useful plant identification book is *The Plant Finder*, published by the Hardy Plant Society (1994) and updated annually.

Smell

A vital element of any garden is fragrance or scent. The inclusion of plants and flowers that provide scent should be to the forefront of our thinking when planning a garden that will be used by people with disabilities. Van Toller (1988) makes many references to the sense of smell as a powerful evoker of old memories, and also how olfactory preferences colour our judgement. As with colour, care must be taken not to bombard the senses by providing an assortment of strong-smelling flowers. Plants, shrubs and flowers have two distinct but very different types of scent. One is 'floating' scents. These are released by warmth or a breeze, and they float or drift in the air. You will find that many plants with a summer flowering time will have floating scent. Some examples are old roses, honeysuckles and lilies. The **honeysuckle** *Lonicera americana* has clusters of strong fragrant yellow flowers. From the **jasmine** family, *Jasminum polyanthum* and *Jasminum officinale* both have lovely fragrance. Many other climbers and creepers have lovely scent and they are excellent examples of floating-scent plants. Grow them against a trellis, up a wall, near a seating area or close to a window, to gain maximum benefit. There are numerous lilies with good floating scent, and the very popular *Lilium regale*, which has a strong sweet scent, can be grown in pots and moved after the flowers have died down. Roses have long been regarded as the queen of plants, for the beauty of their blooms and their wonderful scent:

> Roses have long been prized for their scent; most old garden species and some modern roses possess enchanting and diverse perfumes with hints of clove, musk, honey, lemon, spice and even tea, as well as the 'true rose' fragrance.
>
> *Encyclopedia of Gardening* (1992 p. 116)

If this does not convince you that roses are a 'must' in a sensory garden, then visit a rose garden and convince yourself. It is worth noting that the types of perfumes listed above could equally be describing aromatherapy essential oils, covered in Chapter 12. The number of varieties of roses available can be bewildering, but remember that they fall into the broad categories of shrub, bush, climbing, rambler and miniature. You can also now get thornless varieties.

There are numerous books on roses. One good inexpensive reference source is *The Rose Expert* (Hessayon, 1992). There is a series of 'Expert' gardening books by Hessayon, all of which are good basic reference books. *Roses* (Beale, 1992) provides another comprehensive reference source.

The second type of scent is 'held' scent. As opposed to plants with floating scents you must get close to plants with 'held' scent to smell them, or touch or rub the leaves or foliage to release their perfume. For this reason, plants with held scent should be planted close to the edge of the border or raised bed to ensure that a wheelchair user, or a person with mobility difficulties, can enjoy their perfume. Herbs are excellent examples of plants with this type of scent. They also serve many purposes in the garden. They are pretty and decorative, have varied and interesting fragrances, are edible and can be enjoyed by the whole family in cooking. Additionally, they can be grown in a number of situations, directly in the soil in the garden, in pots on the patio, in hanging baskets or on a windowsill. The variety to choose from is enormous. For example, there is mint – many different kinds – parsley, sage, thyme, rosemary, fennel, chives, basil, chamomile, lavender, geraniums and so on. Thyme (*Thymus vulgaris*) and chamomile (*Chamaemelum nobile*) were often used by the Victorians as lawns. However, unlike grass these will not take heavy or continual wear. You could try this type of lawn if you have limited space or to give added interest to an area of the garden. The non-flowering chamomile '*Treneague*' is fairly robust, and therefore more suitable for lawns. A wheelchair pushed gently over this 'lawn' will release an abundance of its sweet apple-like fragrance. The leaves of many other herbs, such as the 'curry plant' *Helichrysum angustifolium*, have wonderful pungent fragrance. Many geraniums, or rather **pelargoniums**, which the experts now tell us is their correct name, have highly scented leaves. Although they are almost all tender, that is, they will rarely survive a hard winter or a severe frost, they are worth growing for their scent in containers in the garden and over-wintered in the greenhouse. **Eucalyptus**, which can be grown as a shrub or a tree, has a most interesting aromatic fragrance. Its leaves also make wonderful sounds when blown in the wind (see the section on 'sound' for more on this and other plants that produce sound). Eucalyptus is also very useful for flower arranging. You will need to crush or press the leaves of plants in the held scent category between the fingers to release their scents. This will not harm or damage the plants and a person with profound and multiple disabilities may be encouraged to do this to enjoy fully their perfumes.

There are a great number of plants with held scents that do not require handling to release their fragrance. However, in order to enjoy their full fragrance you must get close to them. **Dianthus**, or pinks and carnations, all have this type of held scent. The old-fashioned pinks have masses of fragrant flowers, and *Dianthus 'Mrs Sinkins'* is just one example from this group. Remember, too, that fruit and vegetables also have wonderful fragrances and they can be included in any garden, but particularly in a sensory garden. These will be dealt with under the heading 'taste'.

Touch

Many plants, shrubs and trees are very interesting to touch. With some it is their shape and form, with others their texture. Always give some thought to their tactile element when choosing plants. The foliage or leaves of many plants are tactile. Foliage and plant textures can be velvety, lacy, feathery, shiny, sharp, rough, smooth and ridged. Christopher Lloyd, an eminent horticulturalist, has this to say about leaves and foliage:

> Leaves are two-faced because of the different finish on the upper and lower surfaces, which brings us to the sensuous subject of leaf texture. Sensuous because so many leaves seem to be inviting us to touch them: to feel their attractions through our finger tips. They may be waxy, woolly, silky, clammy or crinkly; these are all

conditions requiring tactile recognition. And while some leaves, like a fully expanded banana frond as yet untorn by wind, may charm us by their fragility, others are no less fascinating for being thick and solid; my pet *Senecio reinoldii (S. rotundifolius)* comes to mind.

(Lloyd, 1987, p. 11)

The appearance of many plants invites touch. Some people will remember 'lambs' ear' (*Stachys lanata*) from their childhood. This and others in the species have very soft leaves that are woolly or velvety to the touch. The lacy fronds of a number of ferns are very attractive as well as being interesting to touch. Another plant with a 'lacy' feel is *Alchemilla mollis*. This is a good plant for colour and interest. It also self-seeds, which means you will have plants to swap with friends and can also increase your stock at no cost.

Plants that have a 'feathery' texture include **asparagus fern**, which smells of aniseed, and **fennel**, which also smells of aniseed and comes in two colours, bronze and green. **Astilbes** also have a feathery feel and come in a variety of colours. The shape of the blooms of a number of flowers are interesting to touch. Mop-head hydrangeas (*Hydrangea macrophylla*) and many chrysanthemums and dahlias, particularly the 'pom-pom' varieties, have large round blooms that are lovely to touch. The seedheads of some flowers and shrubs are also interesting to touch and feel: **sedum** and **euphorbia** are just two that fall into this category. *Sedum spectabile*, with its rich brown seedheads, is a good example. As well as being tactile the seedheads will provide colour in the garden in autumn and winter if left uncut. In addition, its leaves have a matt, waxy feel, i.e. it is a plant with a number of sensory elements. Many plants commonly found in the rock or alpine garden have most fascinating shapes and textures to explore. Cacti and other succulents have intriguing shapes and forms. However, as most will have sharp spikes or spines, great care should obviously be exercised when exploring this type of plant tactilely. The rosettes of **sempervivums** or **saxifrages** are good examples of 'touch' plants. Trees and large shrubs that have coloured, ornamental or textured bark should always be considered when planning the 'touch' areas of the garden. Some examples are silver birch (*Betula utilis* var. *jacquemontii*), which is silvery white; cherry (*Prunus serrula*), with its silky sheen and bright burnt-orange colour; as well as acer (*Acer capillipes*), which has an interesting rough-textured bark.

These are just suggestions and are provided here, together with the many other examples of plants, flowers and shrubs, to give you a guide as to what to look for. The final choice will of course be governed by the specific type of soil in your own garden and the climate in your area of the country and, just as importantly, the needs of those who will enjoy your efforts.

Another good way to include 'touch' in the garden is through the use of garden ornaments and statuary. There are many types and styles from which to choose, some inexpensive, others relatively costly. You can get garden ornaments, statues and pots in a variety of media and textures – plastic, stone, terracotta, lead, bronze and wood. All shapes and sizes are available, from very formal classical Greek urns and statues to the much-maligned but well loved garden gnome! A recent introduction to sensory gardens is specially designed free-standing garden 'mobiles'. These can be commissioned as one-offs from an artist, as they are not yet commercially available, or you could try to make one yourself. They can be any shape or size, but the most attractive ones I have seen have been shaped like a weeping tree, or a maypole. You can hang a variety of interesting objects from the 'branches', for example, mirrors of different shapes, or birds, butterflies and flowers made from stained glass or rigid coloured plastic.

Taste

The sense of taste can be stimulated in numerous ways in the garden. The most obvious choice is herbs, already discussed in the section on 'smell'. The range of herbs available is vast and they can be grown in a variety of ways: in a formal herb garden, in the herbaceous border, in pots and hanging baskets or on a windowsill. Try some of the new interesting herbs that are becoming available in garden centres such as **coriander** (*Coriandrum sativum*) and **cumin** (*Cuminum cymium*), with their lovely oriental smell, both of which can be used in Indian and eastern cooking. Vegetables and fruits will add interest to the garden, provide many learning experiences and are also a good food source.

It is not possible to list the many varieties of fruits and vegetables that can be grown, but whatever size the garden some fruit trees should be included. Fruit trees in the garden can be highly ornamental. They have many seasonal interests, with their blossom in spring and summer and their edible and often highly perfumed and decorative fruit in late summer and autumn. In most areas of the country a range of fruits may be grown. Even where space is limited some fruit trees can be grown, either in pots or in the herbaceous border. There are many new varieties now available as bushes or the tall slim 'ballerina' type fruit trees that are becoming increasingly popular for small town gardens or for patios. Soft fruits, for example strawberries, raspberries, loganberries, black and red currants, are just a few of the many types of fruit that are available in tree, bush or shrub form. Bear in mind that, as male and female flowers are often borne on separate plants, you will have to grow both to ensure successful fruiting. Tomatoes, with the many varieties now on the market, are fairly easy to grow in the greenhouse, the garden, in containers or in 'growbags'. Vegetables for all seasons are readily available and most can easily be grown from seed. Growing fruits and vegetables from seed, planting out and finally eating the produce, is both an exciting and a very pleasurable activity. Although herbs, fruits and vegetables are included here in the 'taste' section, they can equally be incorporated in the other sense sections, as they are often very colourful, perfumed, attractive to look at and to touch. Additionally, they will encourage wildlife to come into the garden.

Sound

There are a variety of ways of introducing sound into the garden. First, many trees, shrubs and plants provide engaging and varied sounds through the movement of leaves and branches. The leaves of **eucalyptus**, already mentioned under 'smell', make a wonderful 'quivering' sound in the slightest breeze. The wind and rain create rustling sounds in **bamboos** and **grasses** (of which there is a great variety), as well as in the leaves and branches of trees. Secondly, very different sounds and tones can be introduced by using windchimes and other sound-producing wind instruments. Hang windchimes from the branches of trees: they are particularly effective if positioned near a seating area. There are numerous shapes and styles to choose from; charity and craft shops, and Indian, Chinese or Japanese stores are all good places to search for windchimes. Aeolian Chimes is just one company that supplies hand-made windchimes. They will also create one to your own specification (address at the end of the chapter). Some of the specialist suppliers of equipment, such as Rompa, Toys for the Handicapped and Mike Ayres and Co, sell free-standing musical instruments that can be used out of doors and are very suitable for a sensory garden if you have the space. The catalogues of these and other similar companies are a very useful source for further ideas. The garden mobile mentioned above could equally be listed here in the 'sound' section.

The inclusion of a pond or water garden will provide auditory and visual stimulation through a constantly changing pattern of sound, movement and reflections. These will attract many forms of wildlife, such as birds, frogs, dragonflies and other insects. Still or lightly running water is inherently tranquil and gives great pleasure. The sun shining on water creates patterns. Trees, shrubs and the sun will reflect in the water, creating ever-changing pictures. If possible, aim to include moving or running water. A fountain or stepped waterfall will add sound and movement interest. A 'bubble fountain' will create a very effective jet of water and, if used in conjunction with stones or large pebbles, the sound of the water trickling over them will give added interest. The sound of running or moving water will also help orientation and will act as a marker to let people with visual impairments know where they are in the garden. Fish, frogs and newts should all be included, and the users of the garden should be encouraged to feed the wildlife and care for the plants. The water feature should, ideally, be raised and made accessible by surrounding it by a flat, even path or surface. Most garden centres will have a section devoted to water gardens, and their staff should be knowledgeable about all aspects of this type of gardening. Stapeley Water Gardens in Cheshire is the largest company devoted to water gardens and equipment. Coach trips to Stapeley and Bridgemere Garden World, its near neighbour, are arranged from many major cities. They are both worth a visit to obtain ideas, having an enormous range of plants and equipment and also demonstration model gardens.

One of the most pleasurable sounds in any garden is birdsong. There is a vast range of plants and shrubs that attract birds. Plants with berries, such as **pyracantha**, with its bright red, orange or yellow berries, are essential. They are also evergreen and have flowers in spring or summer. These and other fruit-bearing plants should be included as a priority. Care should be taken to ensure that there is food for birds all year round, so aim to include plants that fruit at different times. A bird-table and nest boxes should also be considered. Putting food out in winter will attract a variety of wildlife, and if you are lucky you may even entice hedgehogs into the garden. These are most useful animals, as their favourite diet is slugs. Butterflies and other wildlife should be encouraged in the garden through the planting of flowers and shrubs that attract them. **Buddleia**, the 'butterfly bush', as its common name suggests, is very attractive to butterflies. The bright red flowers of **salvias** not only provide a blaze of colour but also lure butterflies into the garden. **Lavender** (*Lavandula angustifolia*), planted as a hedge, edging a border or path, or in pots on the patio, will not only ensure that bees are visitors to the garden but will also provide an abundance of perfume. If space allows, why not develop an area of the garden as a wildflower or meadow garden? Seeds for wild flowers are now available from specialist nurseries and many garden centres. Please do remember that it is illegal to dig up flowers, plants and bulbs from the wild, and do check that bulbs offered for sale are cultivated and not from the wild.

Overall design

Most gardens have an overall design plan. The design will be governed by the size of the garden, its location, e.g. south- or north-facing, type of soil, i.e. acid, alkaline, neutral, clay, chalky, heavy, etc. and, most importantly, the needs of its users. The same is true of a sensory garden. There are a number of factors you must take account of when initially laying out the garden. As the majority of people with profound and multiple disabilities will be wheelchair users, the garden will have to be accessible. Paths are a very important component of garden design. They link the different parts of the garden and often lead to a specific feature, such as a water garden, a piece of sculpture or a seating area. Paths in a garden that will be used by people with disabilities should be wide enough to take a wheelchair as well as being smooth, flat and even. This does not mean that they have to be boring slabs of concrete. The choice of paving materials is very varied. You can use old stone, such as York stone, bricks, cobbles, concrete paving stone, 'stepping stones', logs, etc., or any combination of these. For people with visual impairments, paving can effectively be used as markers. For example, always use one type of paving material to indicate seating areas, another to indicate flower beds and so on. It is often suggested that paving in a garden that may be used by people with disabilities should be of a variety of textures to give different sensations. Although this is recommended to offer variation and also to assist orientation, do bear in mind that being wheeled over rough or bumpy terrain may not always be a pleasant experience, particularly for someone with limited movement.

Avoid using steps. If the garden has different levels, use a gentle slope as access. It is important that the garden users can get close to the plants, shrubs and garden features. Therefore, try to include a number of raised flower beds. For wheelchair users to be able to reach and touch plants, beds should be just below average waist height, and not more than 2'6" in width. You can, of course, plant large shrubs and trees beyond this point as a backdrop, against which to grow the plants and frame the pictures you create.

GARDENING INDOORS OR IN CONFINED SPACES

It must be said here that not everyone will be lucky enough to have a garden. This does not mean, however, that you cannot enjoy aspects of gardening: some wonderful gardens have been created on the balconies of high-rise flats. Roof gardens are also a feature of many city flats and tiny back yards have been turned into an abundance of colour and fragrance. Amazing effects can be created using a variety of containers and pots. You can achieve height by building up tiers using planks or bricks and, as mentioned before, many species of trees and shrubs can be grown in tubs. If space is confined – say you only have small back yard – you could consider a vertical garden. Containers can be fixed to a wall or fence at different levels. Choose some plants that trail, such as ivy *Hedera (Araliaceae)* or trailing pelargoniums. Plants that climb and those with interesting foliage and flowers should also be included. Any type of container can be used, from specially designed commercially available containers for this type of garden, to wire and plastic baskets. Do ensure that the garden commences at wheelchair level, to enable a person with profound and multiple disabilities to be able to work with the plants and soil.

The residence or service facility may, however, be in an inner-city area with no outside space. You will still be able to create a sensory garden indoors. Different types of plants will have to be used and this will depend on the conditions in the room or area where they are to be situated. Seek advice from your local garden centre or nursery on what is suitable. Herbs and tomato plants can be grown very successfully on a windowsill, and there is a wide variety of indoor plants and flowering shrubs available specifically for indoors. To ensure that the garden offers maximum sensory stimulation, follow the same principles as for outdoors. Incorporate plants with good strong single colours, those that are interesting to touch, some with rich fragrance, and do not forget taste through herbs and fruits. Most gardening books will have a section on indoor gardening, and there are also many volumes available devoted to this type of gardening.

Conservatory gardening is a very different and exciting way to garden. Again, there are many reference books available to help you plan and gain the most from a conservatory.

EQUIPMENT AND TOOLS

A certain number of basic gardening tools will be required, for example a spade, fork, rake, hoe, trowel, hand fork, weeding tools, lawnmower, wheelbarrow, etc. Information on tools specifically designed or adapted for use by people with disabilities is available from The Royal National Institute for the Blind (RNIB) and Horticultural Therapy (addresses at the end of this chapter). Both these organizations also give advice and information on gardening for people with disabilities. The RNIB have published a very useful booklet *Gardening without Sight* (Flint, 1989). Horticultural Therapy produce a quarterly journal, *Growth Point*, available by subscription.

SAFETY

A great number of accidents happen in the garden, many of which are easily avoided by following a few basic ground-rules. For example, plant stakes, the cause of many eye injuries, should not be left unmarked or uncovered. It is much safer and also more efficient to support plants with special circular plant supports, known as 'grow-throughs', available from most garden centres. Alternatively, blunt the ends of the stake and cover with special rubber caps (available from garden centres), or even yogurt cartons. All electrical equipment should be fitted with a circuit-breaker and always switched off and stored after use. Many plants are toxic, poisonous and/or irritant, and the Consumers' Association is campaigning to have them labelled as such at the point of sale. Although there is as yet no legislation to enforce this, many garden centres are taking responsibility to label harmful plants. *Gardening Which?* has produced a factsheet listing known harmful plants (Consumers' Association, 1991). This is available free of charge from *Gardening Which?* (see address at end of chapter). Weedkillers, fertilizers, etc. should be stored out of reach and clearly marked. All paths should be kept clean of algae and slime, as these make surfaces slippery and unsafe. Never leave a person with profound and multiple disabilities or someone in a wheelchair close to a water feature unaided. There will always be some accidents in the garden, but many can be avoided by taking a little time to tidy up after working, having the correct tools for the job, reading carefully the instructions on all garden products, including plants, and using your basic common sense.

SOURCES OF HELP AND ADVICE

Although sensory gardening as a concept is relatively new, there are a number of organizations to which you can turn for help, advice or inspiration. Some of these have already been mentioned but will be listed here again, along with others that spring to mind. The charity Horticultural Therapy (HT) produces a range of information leaflets on such topics as tools, raised beds and design principles, as well as a number of books on the topic. HT also runs demonstration gardens, and details of these are available from their head office. The Royal Horticultural Society (RHS) have recently redesigned their model garden for the disabled – though, regrettably, they have not changed its name – at Wisley. This was reopened in June 1993. The Royal National Institute for the Blind (RNIB) provide information on gardening for people without sight or with visual impairments. They also publish booklets and information pamphlets on the subject. Action for Blind People, a London-based voluntary organization, have had a garden designed for people with visual impairments at the annual Chelsea Flower Show for a number of years. They provide information on gardening and visual impairments and also have details of people with visual impairments who provide quality goods and services, many of which are related to gardening.

National disability voluntary agencies such as Mencap, Help the Aged, Spastics Society, etc. will be able to provide information on the needs of people with disabilities. Very good free information sources on gardening in general are the many programmes on gardening on TV and radio. Most towns and cities will have organizations associated with gardening, whose members would, I am sure, be happy to advise on plants, etc. suitable for your area. You should be able to find their addresses in the telephone directory. Garden centre and nursery staff should also be knowledgeable about gardening in general and local conditions in particular.

GARDENING AS A TEACHING, LEARNING, MULTISENSORY EXPERIENCE

The above is just a brief introduction to creating a sensory garden. There is still very little written on the subject of gardening as a leisure activity for people with disabilities. Some suggestions for further reading are given in the reference section. However, the best way to proceed is to think about every aspect of the garden and to consider how this can be adapted or modified to enhance the experiences offered. As mentioned before, the plants suggested here are to give you some ideas and to get you started. The layout and design will depend on the size and location of the garden and most importantly, the needs of its users. What has not been covered in any detail is how to involve a person with profound and multiple disabilities in gardening. This we will cover briefly.

You will have your own ideas and methods; it may be that the person for whom you are organizing leisure activities already participates in horticultural therapy in their school or day service. Involvement in a sensory garden would be an obvious way to extend those experiences. A number of schools and adult day service facilities include horticulture in the curriculum. Byers (1990) has shown how the garden could become the organizing topic for an integrated scheme within a whole school. He suggests that, first, the staff meet to conduct a brainstorming session to come up with a general idea for a topic web of activities for pupils of all ages and abilities, including those with profound and multiple disabilities, around the theme of the garden. Secondly, these topics are related to the National Curriculum, e.g. making a map of the garden ties in with map-making in geography, keeping a diary of gardening activities involves the use of English, and so on. Horticulture also plays an important part in the curriculum of the Orchard Hill Further Education Centre in Carshalton. Abbro (1989) suggests that the most valuable lesson gardening teaches is the natural order of living things, the natural cycles of birth, growth, death and decay. She also gives many examples of how gardening tasks are related to developing self-help skills. Here are just a few of her examples:

Task	Teaching objective
Planting bulbs and seeds	Illustrating cause and effect
Filling pots with compost	Use of spoon (self-feeding)
Watering plants	Pouring skills
Arranging plants/flowers	Visual discrimination

Although these are primarily teaching and learning experiences, and the focus of this book is leisure, they are the tasks that are involved in gardening. As discussed in the foreword to this book, leisure, education and therapy cannot be clearly separated if we are to adopt a holistic view of the person with profound disabilities.

The comparison of a sensory garden with a 'snoezelen' or multi-sensory environment has been made here, and we will now expand this theme a little. A garden, particularly a sensory garden, is a truly natural multisensory environment. In a 'snoezelen' room or area we strive to ensure that the user has control over the environment in whatever way possible. This is done by their activating the controlling devices to change the visual stimuli, choosing the music, the aroma-therapy essential oils and where to be positioned in the area. This level of involvement should be attainable in a sensory garden – in fact it should be much easier to achieve. In a sensory garden, to receive visual, auditory, tactile and olfactory stimulation – all elements of a multisensory environment – and additionally to involve taste, a person with profound and multiple disabilities does not have to become involved with high-tech electrical equipment: all that is required is that the elements suggested above to provide these are incorporated in the design of the garden and that it is fully accessible. This means not just including accessible paths, which are of course essential, but ensuring that planting and features are within reach and vision.

Finally, something should be said about the interactive aspect of gardening. Gardening can be enjoyed alone, on a one-to-one basis, and as a small- or large-group activity. There is, first, involvement with the soil and plants; secondly, the interaction with others developing the garden; and thirdly, meeting people involved in gardening in the wider community. For people with profound disabilities it is also an activity that is age-appropriate. The creation of a sensory garden can be undertaken by a family, as an assignment for a class or group within an adult day service, or as a whole school or centre project. It will encourage integration, enhance the environment and the local community and, as will all leisure pursuits, enrich the experiences and improve the skills of all participants.

REFERENCES AND FURTHER READING

Abbro, F. (1989) Why horticulture? Gardening as an activity for profoundly or multiply handicapped people, *Growth Point*, Autumn, 8–10.
Beale, P. (1992) *Roses: An Illustrated Encyclopedia*, Harvill, London.
Brickell, C. (ed) (1989) *The Royal Horticultural Society: Gardeners' Encyclopedia of Plants and Flowers*, Dorling Kindersley, London.
Brickell, C. (ed) (1992) *The Royal Horticultural Society: Encyclopedia of Gardening*, Dorling Kindersley, London.
Byers, R. (1990) Topics: from myths to objectives. *British Journal of Special Education*, **17**.
Consumers' Association (1991) *Factsheet: Poisonous and Irritant Plants*, Consumers' Association, Hertford.
Flint, K. (1989) *Gardening Without Sight*, Royal National Institute for the Blind, London.
Hardy Plant Society (1994), *The Plant Finder*, (eds C. Philip and T. Lord), Moorland Publishing, Ashbourne.
Hessayon, D.G. (1992) *The Rose Expert*, PBI Publications, Waltham Cross.
Lambe, L. (1991) Creating a sensory garden, in *Leisure Resource Training Pack*, (ed. L. Lambe), Mencap, London.
Lloyd, C. (1987) *Foliage Plants*, Penguin, Harmondsworth.
Nuffield Orthopaedic Centre (1991) *Gardening: Equipment for the Disabled*, NOC, Oxford.
Please, P. (ed.) (1990) *Able to Garden*, Batsford, London.
Squire, D. (1986) *The Scented Garden*, Hodder & Stoughton, London.
Taylor, J. (1987) *Fragrant Gardens*, Ward Lock, London.
Van Toller, S. (1988) Odours, emotion and psychophysiology. *International Journal of Cosmetic Science*, **10**, 171–97.

USEFUL ADDRESSES

Action for Blind People, 14–16 Verney Road, London SE16 3DZ.
  Advice and information on gardening and visual impairments. Details of services provided by people with visual impairments.
Aeolian Chimes, Higher Knowle, Aveton Gifford, Kingsbridge, Devon TQ7 4NJ.
  Suppliers of hand- and custom-made musical chimes.

Bridgemere Garden World, Bridgemere Nurseries, Bridgemere, Nr Nantwich, Cheshire CW5 7BQ.
Very large garden centre, model gardens, vast range of plants and equipment.
Gardening for the Disabled Trust, Old House Farm, Peasmarsh, Rye, East Sussex TN31 6YD.
Information on gardening and disability, award small grants towards adapting gardens, special tools, etc.
Gardening Which?, Castlemead, Gascoyne Way, Hertford X, SG14 1LH.
Monthly journal, available on subscription. Send an A4 stamped addressed envelope marked 'Factsheet' for a free copy of their factsheet on poisonous and irritant plants.
The Hardy Plant Society, Bark Cottage, Great Comberton, Worcester WR10 3DP.
Publish a plant-finding directory, The Plant Finder, *which is updated annually. Information on hardy plants.*
Help the Aged, St James's Walk, London EC1R 0BE.
Information on garden design suitable for elderly persons and those with mobility difficulties.
Horticultural Therapy, Goulds Ground, Vallis Way, Frome, Somerset BA11 3DW.
Advice and information on horticulture and people with disabilities. Quarterly journal Growth Point *available on subscription. Details of demonstration sensory gardens.*
Mencap, 123 Golden Lane, London EC1Y 0RT.
Information on learning disabilities.
Orchard Hill Further Education Centre, 6 Elm Avenue, Queen Mary's Hospital, Carshalton, Surrey SM5 4NR.
Videotape and booklet on the curriculum (including horticultural therapy) available from the Further Education Centre at Orchard Hill.
Royal Horticultural Society (RHS), 80 Vincent Square, London EC15 0BE.
Information and advice on all matters pertaining to gardening. The RHS publish many books on gardening. Monthly journal by subscription. Organizers of the Chelsea Flower Show. Model garden for the disabled at their Wisley garden (see below).
Royal National Institute for the Blind (RNIB), 224 Great Portland Street, London W1N 6AN.
Advice on gardening for people with visual impairments. Suppliers of adapted gardening tools.
Sissinghurst Gardens, Sissinghurst, Nr Cranbrook, Kent TN17 2AB.
Famous garden created by Vita Sackville-West. House also open to the public. Now owned by the National Trust. Limited access to house for people with disabilities.
Wisley Garden, The RHS Garden, Wisley, Woking, Surrey GU23 6BQ.
The garden of the RHS. Shop, information and plant centre. Access for people with disabilities. Model garden for the disabled.

The following companies supply large free-standing musical instruments, suitable for out of doors. They also supply equipment for multisensory environments.

Mike Ayres & Co, Unit 14, Vanguard Trading Estate, Britannia Road, Chesterfield, Derbyshire S40 2TZ.

Rompa, Goyt Side Road, Chesterfield, Derbyshire S40 2PH.
Toys for the Handicapped, 76 Barracks Road, Sandy Lane Industrial Estate,
    Stourport-on-Severn, Worcester DY13 9QB.

8

Art, drama and music

Helen Mount

INTRODUCTION

The importance of participation in the arts for people with disabilities is now well documented, including the benefits derived from such participation (Attenborough, 1985). Through participation in the arts in the broadest sense, whether this is music, dance, drama, arts or crafts and related therapies, people with disabilities can interact more fully with their environment.

A variety of activities can be enjoyed, some of which will need little if any adaptation, whereas others may need a little more thought. Opportunities to participate may help to develop fine and gross motor coordination and may also enable individuals with the most profound disabilities to express themselves, communicate through different media and enjoy the activity for its own sake. Here, these activities are described under two different headings, **Arts and crafts** and **Music and drama**. The first of these will encompass examples of painting and printing techniques, also outlining some craft activities. The second will incorporate movement and dance, drama and music activities. At the end of the chapter there is a list of useful addresses for contacts and suppliers, as well as some of the recipes described.

ARTS AND CRAFTS

Although access to the high-tech facilities described in Chapter 4 offers a highly desirable leisure activity, the capital outlay is beyond the reach of many organizations, let alone individual families. Enjoyment of the arts, however, may be achieved at a relatively low cost, and the two types of activity should not be considered as mutually exclusive, with one competing against the other. Multisensory environments should be viewed as complementary to other activities, including arts and crafts. They are all different elements of a programme which should offer as wide a range of leisure choices as resources permit. If a little creativity is used, an apparently limited range of arts and crafts materials can be applied to a wide variety of associated activities, and for very little outlay. It will also be shown that it is what can be done with the materials that is important. For example, finger painting and sponge printing are often only considered as activities for nursery children, and are therefore seen as inappropriate for older individuals, yet they are a few among a vast range of techniques used by practising and successful artists, both past and present. The American artist Jackson Pollack applied paint to his canvases by dripping, pouring and throwing. Some of his influence came from Max Ernst, who tied a piece of string to a can of paint, pierced a hole in the base of the can, then swung the can across the canvas. L.S. Lowry and Helen Bradbury produced some paintings which may be considered at best as naive and immature, and at worst as childish, by certain critics, but this merely emphasizes that the techniques used and the end results are a combination of the creativity of the artist and the taste of the observer.

One of the key issues in providing choice is being able to offer access to a range of opportunities. Activities may then be undertaken by anyone, not just people with profound and multiple disabilities. Many people have difficulty holding implements such as artists' brushes, but it is possible to overcome this in several ways. Home decorating paintbrushes have thicker handles, which are easier to grip than artists' brushes if fine motor control is difficult. They also have thicker bristles, which make bold lines and cover a surface less laboriously than finer brushes.

Painting

There are commercially produced aids which can provide access to painting implements. Selectagrip, Multistrap, Ultralite and hand straps (available from Nottingham Rehab, see address section) were developed primarily to help the handling/gripping of feeding utensils. They can, however, provide a means of access to creative activities if they are placed around the shafts of paintbrushes, crayons, felt-tipped pens, pencils, etc. Dycem non-stick mats, available from the same source, can also be used to stabilize paint pots and dishes.

Fluorescent paints offer a more visually interesting and brighter alternative to ordinary poster paints. There are also paints containing glitter to add further interest. (A list of suppliers is provided at the end of the chapter.) Paint can be applied to surfaces by using rhythmic strokes, dabbing, splashing, flicking and even blowing through large straws. It can be applied to a variety of different surfaces, not only plain paper and card but also textured papers, wallpaper, plastic, glass, cellophane and fabric, among others. If paint is to be applied to shiny surfaces such as plastic, glass or cellophane, a few drops of washing-up liquid added to the paint will make it stick to the surface, otherwise it just forms small blobs and peels off when dry.

If it is not possible for the person with profound disabilities to hold a brush, even with some assistance, there are alternatives. Marbles in boxes are one way of applying paint to paper or card and it is a particularly effective method to use when people have limited hand and finger movement. The basic method is to cut a piece of paper or card to fit the bottom of a shoe box. The next stage is to have two or three shallow dishes containing about a tablespoon of fluorescent paint. A large marble is then dropped into each dish. The marbles are pushed around in the paint until they are coated, then the first one is dropped on the paper at the bottom of the shoe box. The box can then be positioned between the hands/arms or on the lap of the person with profound disabilities. Next, encourage or prompt the person to tip the box in a rocking motion so that the marble rolls around and deposits its paint on the paper. Any slight movement will create a pattern, and once the first marble has deposited all its paint the process is repeated with marbles covered in different-coloured paints until a 'picture' is produced.

Results can be varied by changing the shape and size of the box, or by using balls instead of marbles. If a round or square biscuit tin is used this will have an added advantage of providing sound and vibration for people with limited vision. It is also interesting to vary the consistency of the paint, or to use one colour (instead of three) on contrasting paper, e.g. white paint on black paper.

Deodorant bottles provide another alternative for people with restricted movement but, as with other suggestions in this chapter, can be used by anyone. For this activity the 'roller ball' is carefully removed from an empty plastic deodorant bottle with a fine screw-driver or knife. The bottle can then be washed out and is ready for refilling with a solution of water, a few drops of food colouring and a very small drop of washing-up liquid. The roller is then replaced and is ready for use on paper or card. This method provides a spiral or circular motion, different from more traditional brushing. As the solution is thin the quality of the surface to which it is applied needs to be quite close-textured, otherwise it will soak in and smudge. The result is similar to drawing inks, but without the expense, as food colourings are cheap and readily available at most supermarkets. If a wide variety of colour is required, food colourings can be obtained from specialist cake-decorating suppliers, whose addresses will be found in Yellow Pages. The solution may be left in the bottles for several months without deterioration.

Brusho is a very fine powder paint used primarily for tie-dyeing. It can also provide a very useful medium for generating interesting colours and patterns on paper. Like the deodorant bottles, it is advisable to use good-quality paper and card which is not too absorbent, otherwise the colours will not spread. Attractive pictures which are very popular can be produced in the following way. First, the surface of the paper is coated with water, using a paintbrush. The amount of water applied will alter the speed at which the Brusho spreads, and the depth of colour. One colour of the Brusho is then sprinkled on to the wet surface. The Brusho spreads quickly and should be sprinkled from discarded spice jars, or cruets with very fine holes. When not in use the holes can be sellotaped over to keep the powder dry. Different colours may be added until the required design is achieved, and then the finished article may be left to dry.

It is important not to put too much water on the surface of the paper/card, otherwise there is no control over the blending of the colours. Brusho is obtainable from the supplier listed at the end of the chapter. If it is not available, however, it is possible to use powder paint as an acceptable, if less dramatic, alternative.

Printing

The scope of printing activities is virtually unlimited, as it is possible to print with a vast range of objects and materials. Commercially produced printing blocks and rollers are available, but they are expensive and often geared to younger age-groups, which limits their use. Alternatively, it is possible to make your own printing material, which could be built up into quite a large resource offering plenty of choice. Printing presents an opportunity not only to make repeating patterns to produce a picture, but also to decorate presentation boxes or make wrapping paper and cards at Christmas time.

Sponges cut to an irregular or particular shape make interestingly textured prints. It is possible to purchase shaped sponges, usually of animals, but these are not always age-appropriate and it is often more fun to make your own. Sponge packaging material is an excellent 'recyclable' resource and sometimes comes with finger-sized holes in it to make gripping easier.

Paper can be used as a simple and quick way to print by merely crumpling it into the hand of the person doing the printing and leaving enough surplus to print with. Tissue paper is excellent, but like other papers (kitchen roll, cellophane, foil) it cannot be reused and should be discarded when finished with. As with other painting techniques, different colours can be built up and overprinted to produce a variety of results.

Blocks can be made from thick card, but wood and polystyrene will last longer. A simple printing block can be made by wrapping string around a block of wood approximately 10 x 5 x 2 cm thick. The paint will stick to the string but not the gap in between, and produce a print of stripes. If a handle is required to facilitate participation by a person with profound and multiple disabilities, then a block of wood approximately 3" square and 1" thick can be given a handle by screwing an empty cotton reel to it. The pattern on the base of the blocks can be varied by sticking different thicknesses of string to the base in random, geometric or symbolic shapes (see Figure 8.1). Grooves or holes can be cut into the base of the blocks to give different patterns.

Balloon printing is a good method to use, particularly with people who have limited use of their fingers and hands, but who have some movement of their arms. Partially deflated balloons can produce effective prints with interesting patterns, especially if they have been left inflated for a few weeks and have partially deflated of their own accord. At this stage they are softer, wrinkly, very flexible and therefore easier to grip than newly inflated balloons. They can be dipped in paint and applied to an appropriate surface.

Finger printing/painting can be used both as a creative activity and one which will offer additional sensory experience to people of all ages and abilities. The paint consistency needs to be fairly thick and not too wet, otherwise a poor-quality print will result. Prints can be achieved simply by moving the hands/fingers around in paint which has been placed on to a wipeable table top or wheelchair tray. For example, open both hands, place them into the paint and, using

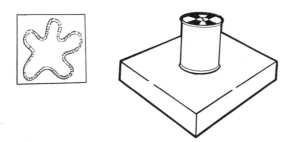

Figure 8.1 Printing block with string on base.

circular movements, create a pattern. Different colours and textures can be added, as for other activities, and if oil or lotion is mixed with the paint it does not dry out on the skin so quickly (a sensation which some people may find unpleasant). The resulting patterns may then be printed if a piece of paper is pressed on to the 'painted' surface and then peeled off. Alternatively fingers, thumbs and different parts of the hands may be placed directly into paint and printed on to paper. Fingertips will produce small dots, which can be positioned to look like flower petals, and the side of the hand to represent leaves and stems. Finger prints can have further 'features' added to them once they are dry, using paint, ink or felt-tip pens. Some recipes for finger painting are given at the end of this chapter, but it is quite acceptable to use ordinary poster paints. Some manufacturers make paint especially for finger painting/printing.

Crafts

There are many craft activities which may be adapted for the enjoyment of people both with and without profound and multiple disabilities, and which they can enjoy together.

Collage can provide an interesting textured piece of work. Sewing, glueing and stapling or pasting may all be used to stick fabrics, pasta, wood shavings, feathers, nuts, etc. on to a variety of surfaces. The tactile nature of this activity makes it of particular interest to this group of people as, with a little imagination, the collage may be felt, seen, heard or smelled. Ideas for the collage may be taken from different seasons and the material may be collected by the person with profound multiple disabilities, e.g. a collage could be made from a collection of feathers, shells, sand and driftwood collected during a day at the seaside.

Puppetry is an ancient art form which deserves greater consideration as a leisure activity. China and Japan in particular have an ancient tradition of using various types of puppetry, which should not be considered and dismissed simply as an activity for children. Combined with drama, puppets can be used to enhance communication and produce theatrical events for different audiences. Simple puppets may be made by painting facial features directly on to the fingers, or by using socks with features stuck or sewn on to them. Alternatively, fluorescent towelling socks are a particularly versatile and cheap resource for making into a variety of character puppets. They stretch to fit most hands and gently but firmly grip the arms, so that they are comfortable but difficult to shake off (Figure 8.2). These socks offer visual stimulation with their bright colours, and if bits of ribbon and bells are sewn on securely, they will also make sounds.

Figure 8.2 Sock puppets.

Besides glove puppets, shadow puppets, finger puppets, rod puppets and string marionettes can be made and used (see Hawkesworth (1984) for further details about making puppets and putting on shows).

Papier mâché is made up of strips of thin paper (newspaper works very well) soaked in wallpaper paste, and layers are built up into a given shape that eventually hardens and sets. This is quite a slow process, as a 'creation' approximately 0.3 cm thick can take several days to dry out at room temperature. Newspaper can be pasted around an inflated ballon and the balloon popped when the papier mâché has hardened. The resulting sculptures can be painted and varnished and/or have collage material stuck to the surface. They may also be sawn in half vertically and made into face masks with holes cut for eyes, nose and mouth, or made into hats. Papier-mâché sculpture may be made around wire frameworks to give a basic shape or around small card boxes of different shapes. These may then be painted, varnished and used as gifts.

Colouring fabrics can be achieved with ordinary paint, but this will obviously become lighter and eventually disappear in the wash. Special fabric dyes give a more permanent alternative, and these are produced as crayons, pens or liquids. Some fabric dyes require a special fixative but the colours of fabric crayons and pens can usually be fixed using a hot iron. In every case it is important to follow the manufacturer's instructions. It is possible for several people to contribute to one large-scale piece of art work, or alternatively decoration can be made more personal by adding it to a garment such as a T-shirt.

Some special fabric paints such as Slick-Writers leave a raised pattern on the material to which they are applied, offering additional tactile qualities. This solution comes in a squeezy bottle and is applied directly to the surface. It takes several hours to dry and this needs to be borne in mind, especially as smudges cannot be removed. For this reason it is also advisable to practise on a piece of scrap material or paper. Slick-Writers can be applied to canvas, leather, plastic and ceramic as well as fabric, so the choice and content of the activity is quite wide. The range of colour is also comprehensive and includes fluorescents and pearlescents, as well as gold and silver.

To tie-dye, bunch a piece of fabric (usually cotton) in one hand and twist a rubber band tightly around it or tie it tightly with string. Repeat the process all over the garment or fabric. Submerge the fabric in water so that it is completely wet. Then, following the directions on the dye packet, make up the dye in an old pan. Submerge the fabric in it, then put the pan on a cooker for the required time, adding salt as specified. Remove the fabric when ready and rinse until the water is clear. Take off the rubber bands or string and the process is complete. Every tie-dye pattern is different and can brighten up T-shirts, pillow cases, hankies, tea towels, tablecloths or serviettes. Large pieces of fabric may be made into wall-hangings or cushion covers. It is recommended that participants wear rubber gloves for this process as the dye stains very easily. Alternatively, Tulip Productions make 'Easy Tie Dye' markers which are applied to cotton fabric in a small squeezy bottle. The surface of the fabric is then sprayed with water and the dye spreads, giving the effect of tie-dyeing less laboriously.

Dough of various textures and smells is good for modelling or squeezing, especially when warm. A number of recipes for making dough are given at the end of the chapter. Try using warm dough either by handling it when it has just been made, or by putting a piece of leisure dough in a tightly sealed plastic bag and placing it in a container of boiled water for about 10 minutes. For more permanent results, some dough recipes can be cooked in the oven or left to dry at room temperature after they have been modelled into desired shapes. It is possible to produce jewellery, badges or small dishes, which can be painted and then varnished.

Organization

It is important to emphasize the versatility of the small selection of activities described above, which can be engaged in and enjoyed as leisure pursuits just for fun, as creative occupations, or as a means of producing an end-product. They are suitable and adaptable for people of all ages. The making of papier-mâché objects and jewellery or dyeing clothing have distinct outcomes that may enhance self-esteem through the person's involvement in their production. They may wish to keep the finished article or offer it as a gift to someone else.

They may also wish to use paintings and prints in a similar manner, therefore the importance of presentation cannot be overemphasized. A completed painting, print or collage will have more impact if it is mounted on a coordinating piece of stiff paper or card. One parent who attended an arts and crafts workshop was enthusiastic about the marbles in boxes, and could envisage that her son would, for the first time, be able to make something himself, i.e. Christmas cards, which he could send to friends and relations.

If you are organizing any of the activities described and working with people with profound and multiple disabilities, they may need considerable physical assistance to take part. However, this does not mean that you should do the activity for them, reducing their involvement to a token. If being helpful means taking over completely, then it is the 'instructor' and not the person with profound and multiple disabilities who has produced the work of art. Allow them the dignity and respect for their own efforts which they deserve and to which they are entitled. Some people will need a lot of help, but you should always be ready to reduce your physical control of their limbs and give them the opportunity to take over.

All the activities described can be undertaken by one person, with help as necessary, or by a group of people. They can therefore be carried out in the person's home, school, college, Adult Education Centre/Social Education Centre or leisure club, such as that offered by the Gateway Federation. All that is required is a room with tables/work surfaces, chairs and the necessary equipment outlined in each activity. Do remember that wheelchair trays can double-up as a work surface. These trays are often more effective than tables, which may be at incorrect heights for wheelchair users.

The person organizing the activities will need to assemble the required materials, often from non-commercial sources, and teach her/himself how to carry out the activity. Forward planning is the key to success, and many materials can be accumulated as a resource without too much effort and at little cost. In most large towns and cities there are 'Play Unit Resource centres' which are an invaluable source of inexpensive equipment and materials for art and craft activities. They sell paints, T-shirts, paper and other new materials at competitive prices, but are also an additional source of waste fabrics, plastics and papers from local manufacturing industries, which they sell at very modest prices. Details of such centres in your area can usually be obtained from the Town Hall Information Department, and it is recommended that you subscribe to or join your local Centre.

Group participation in art and craft activities can extend beyond the school, club, ATC or college if wider use of community facilities is encouraged and organized. For example, Arts Ability Projects, such as those run by the SHAPE organization, may be available in your area. SHAPE may be willing to become involved in creative arts activities, ranging from setting up an art class to providing live music concerts.

Art galleries and museums are also developing more considered access for people with disabilities, and most local authorities have a person with responsibility for providing information on the arts. Several museums, including the British Museum, have undertaken initiatives such as 'touch' exhibitions, the provision of information in Braille and audio commentaries. There is still, however, a long way to go and it is important to exert pressure to improve the facilities offered. Ask for details regarding access and special facilities for people with disabilities. If there are none, keep writing about the existence of your group and their special needs. Access to community arts facilities is the right of all people, including those with disabilities, and visiting an exhibition can enhance or extend an activity started at a club or centre. It also provides greater choice in participation of the arts as exhibitions change and widen individual experience.

Safety

The cardinal rule in all activities is to make sure that you know the person or group you are working with. Some participants may have a propensity to eat non-food items. It is therefore recommended, when painting using the 'marbles and box' method described above, that you use large marbles, as the smaller type could be more easily thrown or swallowed. Alternatively, large rubber balls could be used. Collage materials and beads may also be easily swallowed, and polystyrene has been known to have fatal consequences. Never leave the person with profound disabilities unaided when using this or other equipment and materials that could potentially cause injury or danger.

Some participants may tend to throw objects, so if using the deodorant container method, always use plastic containers not glass. The latter could break if dropped, could cause serious injury if thrown and are also heavier to hold and use.

All materials used should obviously be non-toxic. This inevitably limits the range of activities offered, but if the participants are closely supervised and all manufacturers' instructions carefully followed, activities such as tie-dyeing and using varnish are feasible.

Some activities require the use of very hot water, so clearly common sense dictates that extreme care needs to be exercised to ensure that containers are out of reach and cannot be knocked over.

When engaging in sticky or messy art and craft activities, it is a matter of consideration rather than safety to make sure that the participant's clothes are well protected. A collection of unwanted large shirts provides adequate cover over the top of clothes and prevents parents having to cope with additional washing and ironing.

Anyone can have an allergy, and it is important to be vigilant if participants show signs of developing a rash when in contact with certain substances. This is particularly relevant when using adhesive and wallpaper paste, as the latter may contain fungicide. It is therefore advisable to purchase one without fungicide or buy from an educational supplier.

MUSIC AND DRAMA

Music plays an important role in all societies and we are directly exposed to it from a very early age through television, radio, stereo music systems or live concerts. 'Background' music is played in stores, supermarkets, cinemas, theatres and other public places. We listen to music and may choose a particular kind, depending on our mood. We can relax to music or be invigorated by it. It is therefore difficult to imagine life without it.

If we offer people with profound and multiple disabilities the musical choices available to the rest of us, we are presenting them with opportunities to develop aesthetic awareness and develop their self-confidence and assurance in responding to the medium of sound (Addison, 1989). People with severe hearing impairment can feel the vibrations of guitar strings or a percussion instrument, or the body rhythm of a partner with whom they are in contact. Music can also provide a means of communication to people with profound and multiple disabilities for whom words can have little meaning. Above all, music gives pleasure.

Including people with profound disabilities in such activities does not need to be the realm of the specialist music teacher. If the person offering the activity is sufficiently interested to do some background reading, a comprehensive music programme can successfully be built up. It is best to start with something enjoyable with which you feel confident. For example, a music session may be planned to consist of an opening theme or song, a variety of activities as the central core and a final 'goodbye' song, as outlined below.

Start of session

It is important to tell the participants with profound disabilities what you are doing. If you begin and end the music session with consistent music/song cues, these will eventually become familiar to the participants and will give them an indication of what to expect. Sessions can and should be developed over several weeks. This will involve gradually changing one or two elements while retaining some familiar cues. If this type of format is followed, greater experiences for expression and participation can be offered. Continuity, however, is achieved over a period of several weeks, without the inevitable boredom resulting from constant repetition.

Core

The core part of the session could include the use of instruments, with or without accompanying music, activities to develop listening skills and/or rhythms, songs to encourage communication/speech or guessing games to identify different sounds. For example:

Introduction (to tune of 'Frere Jacques')
Whole group sings:
Hello Carol, Hello Carol
How are you, how are you?

Carol is encouraged to reply, or one person replies on her behalf:
Very well thank you,
Very well thank you.

Shake hands on last line:
How do you do, how do you do?

or (to tune of 'Michael Row the Boat Ashore'):
Hello Michael how are you?
Hello Michael,
We are pleased to see you here,
Hello Michael.

Body percussion can be a particularly enjoyable activity. Those who are able can use their own body parts; others may need a partner to help them join in. For example, without music, clap a simple rhythm of about four beats and get everyone else to copy the pattern. Use slapping thighs, patting stomachs, stamping feet, etc. as alternatives. Put a few different rhythms together, set it to music and use pauses, e.g. 'The Skater's Waltz', with musicians only playing at the end of each bar. Use percussion instruments in a similar way, asking participants to copy the pattern. Use individual names to clap or beat out the rhythm, e.g. De-borah; Da-vid; Con-nie. Use a variety of percussion instruments to accompany music from all over the world. Encourage the development of understanding of loud/soft, fast/slow, high/low.

Use BBC sound effects recordings as a guessing game. It may be necessary to accompany these with visual stimuli in order to provide clues. Alternatively, use objects/articles behind a screen, e.g. grating carrots, stirring coffee, rustling paper or leaves. Participants have to try to guess the sound either without seeing the object(s), making the sound or choosing from a selection of 'duplicated' objects laid out on a table, which may also give clues.

End of session

Use a piece of music which relates to part of the session or a sequence of notes/beats played on instruments which you want participants to recognize as the finale. Alternatively you could devise a 'goodbye' song modified from a simple tune. For example, you could consider using the Peter Cooke and Dudley Moore song, 'Goodbye, goodbye, we're leaving you ... etc.' or part of the Beatles' 'She's Leaving Home'.

These suggestions provide a basic framework for numerous activities, i.e. exploration of sounds/music as a leisure activity which goes beyond the opportunity to participate simply at a seasonal show or performance. It is, however, recognized that the last are also valid musical/dramatic experiences which can form part of wider creative arts activities. Details of the BBC sound effects and other musical sources referred to in this section are given at the end of the chapter.

Music/sounds can be an independent activity, but may also be incorporated into movement and drama activities, as outlined in the next section. It is useful to build up resource banks which are well labelled and can be adapted for use during different activities. Musical instruments can be very expensive to purchase from specialist suppliers, so they need to be chosen with care to make sure that they are durable and offer some versatility.

Making your own instruments

Shakers are easy to make and decorate and some ideas of how to make them and other simple instruments are outlined below.

Empty plastic spice jars or shampoo bottles filled with dried pulses, rice, buttons or beads, then sealed with strong glue, will produce an interesting selection of sounds. If you are fortunate enough to live near a Play Unit Resource Centre which sells industrial waste and craft produce cheaply, you may be able to obtain plastic bottles without printing or labels on them. This makes decorating them a simpler task and they look more authentic.

Elasticated wrist bands, socks or short pieces of dowel (0.5 × 0.75 cm diameter) will provide different sounds if bells and ribbons are attached to them (Figure 8.3).

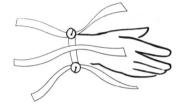

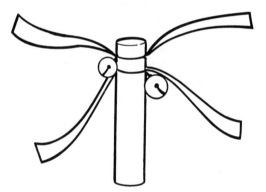

Figure 8.3 Elasticated wrist band and dowel shakers with bells and ribbon.

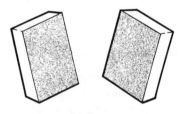

Figure 8.4 Sandpaper scraping blocks.

Old tyre inner-tubes cut and stretched over tins or large cardboard cartons or cylinders provide a selection of percussion 'drum' instruments. Beaters can be made from 1 cm dowel as a variation from using your hands.

Two blocks of wood approximately 10 cm long × 5 cm wide and 10 cm deep, with sandpaper stuck to one large face of each block, produce scrapers (Figure 8.4).

An alternative scraper can be made by cutting grooves at approximately 1 cm intervals on one face of a 15 cm-long piece of 1.5 cm deep dowel, then scraping the cut surface with another piece of dowel to produce sounds (Figure 8.5).

Figure 8.5 Large dowel scraper.

Sound resource

Building up and adding to a sound resource need not be expensive. Party blowers, squeakers and balloons are readily available and easy to replace. There are numerous alternative 'sound-makers' to choose from, and the main point to bear in mind is the appropriateness of the objects for the age of the groups or individuals with whom you are working. It is also important to consider offering a good selection of instruments which can be blown, hit, shaken or plucked, e.g.

Blow: Range of squeakers
           Range of party blowers
           'Whoopee' cushion
           Balloons

Recorder or similar instrument
Bubble pipe (or tube to blow in water)
Whistle
Bird warblers
Kazoo
Paper and comb

Hit: Drum
Tambour
Cymbal
Wood block
Chime bars
Tambourine
Xylophone
Glockenspiel
Home-made instruments

Shake: Maracas
Cabasa
Rattles
Bells
Castanets
Shakers
Tambourine

Pluck: Guitar
Violin
Home-made instruments

A good sound resource should also contain a wide variety of prerecorded music, e.g. folk, pop, classical, jazz, rock, brass band, Japanese, African, etc. Sound-effects records produced by the BBC offer a range of sounds, from a fairground to a rocket taking off, and can be reproduced on tape without violating copyright restrictions. It is also useful to develop your own library of everyday sounds, such as household noises, animal sounds, transport sounds, street sounds, etc.

It is well worth investing in a good stereo cassette tape recorder with tape-to-tape copying facilities and a built-in microphone which offers quality sound reproduction at both low and high volumes. Sound and music activities lose much of their effectiveness and interest value if the quality of sound is poor or if the sounds cannot be heard. Just because the person operating the tape recorder can hear it does not mean that everyone else can. Test the quality of sound in different places in the room you are using.

Organization

Music can be appreciated at an individual level by a person choosing to listen to specific songs, operas, symphonies or musicals on their own. The home is probably the most natural environment for this type of activity. The advent of personal stereos has facilitated an individual's participation in music which may not be to the taste of others in the immediate vicinity. This therefore offers the potential for exposure to a greater choice of musical experience, which should not depend on the preferences of the person putting the tape into the player.

Individuals or groups can also attend a variety of live music concerts, operas and musicals at the theatre or cinema. Activities with another person or a larger group can also take place in the home, at local clubs or adult training centres, etc., and the scope for participation in a wide variety of experiences can be increased with a little imagination.

There are many performing artistes who will put on a concert at a club or centre, ranging from steel bands to jazz musicians. Artistes may also be interested in providing 'workshops' for participants in which they become actively involved. This may involve a fee, and SHAPE may be able to help towards the cost of funding, so it is worth contacting them and/or your regional arts centre.

Safety

When engaging in musical activities, be aware that some people may have sensitive hearing or that a seizure may be brought on by loud noises. So check if you are unsure before blasting them with a cymbal two inches from their ear! In no way does an unstructured and unplanned series of events bear any resemblance to a music session; have fun by all means, but do not expose people with profound disabilities to confusion and possible distress in this way.

Some instruments have sharp edges which could cause cuts or scratches. Take extra care when using these. Ensure that drumsticks or 'scrapers' do not have sharp pointed ends which could cause injury if inadvertently poked in an eye, and do not use very small hand-held instruments, e.g. bells or whistles, which could be swallowed.

Move heavy instruments out of the way of people sitting or lying on the floor, and always use non-slip mats to stabilize equipment and instruments used. If using electrical equipment use circuit-breaker plugs and always unplug all equipment after each session.

MUSIC AND MOVEMENT

Movement to music has been used in educational contexts for many years as a means to establish contact and interaction with people with profound disabilities. Movement has also been used to develop and enhance sensory perception of fine and gross motor skills. The ideas and structures governing music and movement programmes can easily transfer to a leisure setting. Through music and movement with the appropriate help and assistance, people with profound and multiple disabilities can experience spatial and body awareness. As well as being a learning experience, movement to music can also be fun. The choice of music to accompany the movement is most important. It should be instrumental music not song, and have a clear rhythmical beat. If the person has a favourite piece or type of music you could use that. You should also try out different styles of music and observe the person's responses, ensuring that you allow sufficient time for her/him to react before changing the music, and then use the piece that elicited the most favourable response.

Music and movement follows a clearly defined pattern or set of moves which are timed to the beat of music. For example, the person's left arm is moved/guided and so forth. This could be followed by rocking, bending, rolling, stretching, etc. Always explain what you are going to do using plain simple language. If the session is a group activity, it is a good idea for one person to act as leader and call out the changes of movement, e.g. 'right arm, stretch', repeated say five times, according to the beat of the music, change to 'left arm, stretch', etc. If the degree of physical disability prevents the person's limbs/body being moved or stretched fully, then move the hands or fingers, etc. to the same rhythms. If even such movement is not possible, then tap or touch the limb or part of body in time to the beat of the music.

Organization

Music and movement sessions can take place in the home, a school, ATC/SEC, college, a leisure setting such as a Gateway Club, or a residential unit. All you require is a quiet room or space and the necessary equipment.

To organize a music and movement session you will need floor mats (physiotherapy mats are ideal; if you do not have access to these a carpeted floor will do: make it more comfortable by using either a sleeping-bag or floor cushions to sit on); a cassette tape recorder; a selection of music tapes covering a wide range of music styles; and helpers to act as facilitators on a one-to-one basis or as required,

Figure 8.6 Position for supporting someone in movement activities.

according to the degree of disability of the people participating in the session.

It is important that the person with disabilities is comfortable and, if possible, is in a sitting or upright position. To do this you will have to provide some physical support. For example, the helper/ facilitator should sit on a floor mat with legs apart. The person with disabilities may then sit between the helper's legs, facing in the same direction. The body is then secured and supported by the facilitator (Figure 8.6).

A mirror may be placed in front so that she/he can see the movements and you can observe reactions. An alternative position would be to sit facing the person you are assisting and, by clasping her/his hands, guide them in the movements. If the person is unable to sit up, they could lie over a wedge or on the mat, using a cushion or beanbag to help prop them up and give additional support. The important point is to find the most comfortable position for each individual and create the actions according to their abilities.

There are commercially produced music and movement packages available. Two of the best known are 'Activity Programmes for Body Awareness' and 'Communication' produced by Learning Development Aids. This package contains four music tapes, with voice-over instructions, a teacher's handbook and recording sheets. Full details of this package are given at the end of the chapter. It is recommended that you use a structured programme such as this one to begin with. Once you are familiar with this programme, you could develop your own by using your own movements, music, etc., following the format of the package. In addition, the activity could be developed or incorporated into a drama or mime session. Music and movement activities can be undertaken by people with or without disabilities and are a good example of how integration can be introduced.

Safety

There is very little chance of anything going wrong with a music and movement session provided you use common sense. As with all activities involving people with profound and multiple disabilities, ensure that all electrical equipment used is to the appropriate British Standard. Move any heavy objects out of the way of participants. Ensure that the floor is not wet or slippery. If possible, check with the person's physiotherapist that the activity is appropriate for them and also seek advice from the physiotherapist and/or parent or carer regarding positioning, etc.

DRAMA AND MOVEMENT

The development of communication and body awareness through drama and movement experiences can begin with the individual's own body movements as the starting point. An increase in self-awareness may lead to an increase in awareness of others, so activities may begin by just finding out about ourselves and the space we occupy, for example shuffling along the floor, twirling on our bottoms or joining in with a partner.

Like music sessions, drama and movement require a 'warm-up' which cues people into the activities about to take place and prepares their muscles for further movement. Warming-up activities to music can start slowly with just fingers, hands, arms, shoulders and so on, gradually increasing the tempo and incorporating the whole body. An alternative could be to start with a vigorous piece of music and allow free expression. 'Follow me' involves sitting in a circle and following the actions of a chosen leader. This may include clapping, slapping the floor, stamping feet and so on.

People who have very limited movement will usually need someone to assist them to explore their surroundings. Gentle movement of arms, legs or whole bodies can be built up into a sequence, with or without music. For movement across the floor, a person with physical disabilities may be able to sit with their partner as previously illustrated, as long as they are properly supported. They can then feel the transfer of movement to their own body – shuffling, bouncing, rocking. Alternatively, they could be pulled along on a blanket or sheepskin (supplier provided at the end of this chapter) at varying speeds and spun round in the same way. If you are helping a person with limited movement, endeavour to present them with some opportunity of responding rather than always making them a passive partner.

Some ideas for specific activities are described below. Very stretchy long pieces of nylon fabric are shiny and see-through when pulled tightly across one or two people. Changing shapes can be observed, creating contours which respond to the body movements underneath. This activity could be set to music of varying tempo and atmosphere. The fabric could be slowly pulled over your partner to soft music, or shaken up and down like waves a few feet above those lying on the floor. Balloons may be bounced on top of the fabric, then the fabric removed to allow the balloons to float down on to the participants. If the fabric is strong enough and there are plenty of helpers, it may be possible to lift one person a few inches off the ground, with the fabric acting as a hammock. They can then be gently carried, swung or bounced.

Mime is an important vehicle for encouraging imaginative thought and one example of a drama activity would be the introduction of an imaginary box. The box contains several objects and each 'actor' in turn has to choose something from the box. Once chosen, the identity of the object is guessed by the rest of the group from the mime presented. Another activity which is good fun is the 'changing line'. A line is drawn on the floor or a piece of string laid out, then the 'actor' walks up to the line as her or himself. On crossing the line they then become a character, e.g. a teacher, window cleaner, etc., and the rest of the group has to guess their identity.

Any drama/movement activities can, with good planning, become the basis of a production/entertainment for others to enjoy, and it is well worth the initial effort to spark people's enthusiasm. Organizations such as SHAPE should be approached for help and advice in planning drama and dance activities. There are also commercially available packages which can be used as the basis for drama activities, e.g. Galaxies, Seaside, Funfair. For a fuller description see the chapter on Multisensory Environments.

DANCE THERAPY

Dance therapy provides a further way of assisting people to express themselves non-verbally through rhythm and movement. By observing how an individual dances, an experienced therapist can identify areas of tension which may be alleviated by more harmonious movement. Music and instruments are often used to encourage self-expression and the development of rhythm, mood and personal contact. While most arts activities focus upon the existing creativity of the participants, dance therapy directly addresses disorder, difficulty and areas of conflict, and seeks to bring about changes in emotions, physical functioning and behaviour. It is therefore necessary to obtain input from a qualified dance therapist if you are considering offering these experiences. The activities carried out in a dance therapy session may appear similar to those in a creative dance session, but they are carried out with different objectives in mind and for different reasons. Adaptation of dance therapy sessions for people with profound and multiple disabilities should use their movement, however minimal, as the starting point. The worker then facilitates a development of patterns of the individual's movements and extends their experiences of rhythm.

Wheelchair dancing

A majority of people with profound and multiple disabilities will spend some of their time in wheelchairs and will receive their main experience of movement in them. This experience may be enhanced through wheelchair dancing, in which an ambulant friend takes them through the movement of the dance. Although the title suggests that the participants, i.e. the dancers, are not independently mobile, there is no reason why ambulant people should not join in the dances as partners and/or in wheelchairs.

   Different folk dances lend themselves to adaptation for wheelchair users, and while 'free dances' are fun for some of the time it is advisable to structure the session. Folk dances from many regions within the British Isles and other countries may be used.

   One example is as follows (Figure 8.7):

1. Begin with eight 'couples' in 'longways set', partners facing.
2. Walk towards each other for the count of 4 and backwards away from each other for the count of 4.
3. Repeat the above action and the dancers should be in their original places.
4. Both lines then 'cast out', i.e. one line turns to the right, the other to the left, and the leaders move to the bottom of the 'set' with their respective lines following them. They then form an arch which individuals file through in turn.
5. Once under the arch participants should return to their respective lines and be facing each other again.
6. The sequence is then repeated until the end of the dance, with the 2nd, 3rd, 4th, etc. couples becoming leaders, 'casting out' as the lines move.

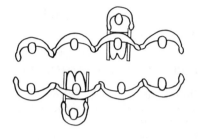

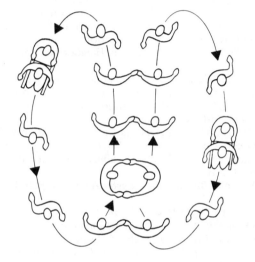

Figure 8.7 Longways set and casting out.

CONCLUSION

The activities described in this chapter provide a 'taster' to whet the appetite of anyone in the position of providing leisure activities for people with profound disabilities. Together with further reading and information from the bibliography/appendix they should provide a comprehensive list of creative arts activities which can be undertaken together by people both with and without disabilities. It is hoped that the description of activities has also demonstrated that you do not have to be an 'expert' or incur vast amounts of cost in order to widen the choice of activities you are already offering.

Acknowledgements

The author wishes to acknowledge the kind permission of Mencap

who have allowed some information from Lambe (1991) to be reproduced for this chapter.

REFERENCES AND FURTHER READING

Addison, R. (1989) *Bright Ideas – Music*, Scholastic Publications, Warwick.
Amery, H. and Civardi, A. (1975) *The Know-how Book of Print and Paint*, Usborne Publishing, London.
Arts Access Unit (1991) *Arts and Disability Directory*, Arts Access Unit, London.
Attenborough, R. (1985) *The Attenborough Report – Arts and Disabled People*, Carnegie UK Trust, Bedford Square Press, London.
Attenborough, R. (1988) *After Attenborough – Arts and Disabled People*, Carnegie UK Trust, Bedford Square Press, London.
Astell-Burt, C. (1981) *Puppetry for Mentally Handicapped People*, Souvenir Press, London.
Bailey, R. *Systematic Relaxation Pack*. This pack covers a systematic relaxation technique whereby each part of the body is worked on in turn. The pack contains a teacher's manual and audiotape. Available from Nottingham Rehab Ltd. (see address section).
Bartlett, N.L. (1989) *Children's Arts and Crafts*, Australian Women's Weekly.
Benjamin, F. (1986) *Floella's Fabulous Bright Ideas*, Methuen, London.
Chambers, J. and Hood, M. (1989) *Simply Artistic*, Belair Publications, Twickenham, London.
Fitzsimmons, J. (1990) *Bright Ideas – Easter Activities*, Scholastic Publications, Warwick.
Fulford, J. *et al.* (1990) *Bright Ideas – Drama*, Scholastic Publications, Warwick.
Gray, L. (1990) *Something Special – Seasonal and Festive Art and Craft for Children*, Belair Publications Ltd, Twickenham, London.
Hawkesworth, E. (1984) *Puppet Shows to Make*, Supreme Magic Co. Ltd, 64 High Street, Bideford, Devon.
Knill, M. and Knill, C. (1986) *Activity Programme for Body Awareness, Contact and Communication*, Learning Development Aids, Cambridge. Available from Winslow Press, Telford Road, Bicester, Oxon OX6 0TS (Tel: 0869 244733).
Know the Game series *Dancing, English Folk Dancing, Scottish Country Dancing, Sequence Dancing*, A.C. Black, Cambridge. NB. There is a whole series of music books from A.C. Black, Howard Road, Eaton Socon, Cambs., including folk and pop, songs from the Caribbean, songs for around the year. All books contain ideas for activities.
Lambe, L. (ed.) (1991) *Leisure for People with Profound and Multiple Disabilities*, Mencap, London.
Leavy, F. (1988) *Dance Movement Therapy*. Available from Dance Books Ltd, London.
Levete, G. (1982) *No Handicap to Dance*, Souvenir Press, London.
Levete, G. (1987) *The Creative Tree: Active Participation in the Arts for People who are Disadvantaged*, Michael Russell, Wiltshire.
Osband, G. (1986) *The Messy Book of Things to Make and Do*, Scholastic Publications, London.
Sherborne, V. (1991) *Developing Movement for Children*, Cambridge University Press, Cambridge.

Shreeves, R. (1987) *Children Dancing*, Ward Lock Educational, London.
Ward, M. (1982) *Music for Living*, BIMH, Worcester.

USEFUL ADDRESSES

British Association of Art Therapists, 13c Northwood Road, London N6 5TL.

The Arts Council, through the Arts Access Unit, offers advice, contacts and advocacy to people with disabilities, and other communities which experience difficulty in developing and promoting their art and achieving arts funding. The Unit produces a number of publications on arts and disability, produces an Arts and Disability Directory (available free).

Arts and Disability, Arts Council of Great Britain, 14 Great Peter Street, London SW1P 3NQ.
  Tel: 071 973 6557.
Arts Council of Northern Ireland, 181a Stranmillis Road, Belfast BT9 5DU.
  Tel: 0232 663591.
Welsh Arts Council, Holst House, 9 Museum Place, Cardiff CF1 3ND.
  Tel: 0222 394711.
Scottish Arts Council, 12 Manor Place, Edinburgh EH3 7DD.
  Tel: 031 226 6051.
Carnegie UK Trust, Comely Park House, New Row, Dunfermline, Fife KY12.
  Tel: 0383 721445.
Gina Levete, Flat 8, 114 Gloucester Terrace, London W2 6HP.
Puppet Centre Trust, c/o Battersea Arts Centre, Lavender Hill, London SW11 5TN.
  Tel: 071 228 5335.

Groups in the SHAPE network

SHAPE, 1 Thorpe Close, London W10 5XL.
  Tel: 071 960 9245.
Artlink Edinburgh and the Lothians, 13a Spippal Street, Edinburgh EH3 9DY.
  Tel: 031 229 3555.
Artlink for Lincolnshire and Humberside, Central Library, Albion Street, Hull HU1 3TF.
  Tel: 0492 224040.
Arts for Disabled People in Wales, Channel View, Jim Driscoll Way, Grangetown, Cardiff CF1 7NF.
  Tel: 0222 377885.
North West Disability Arts Forum, 2a Franceys Street, Liverpool L3 5YQ.
  Tel: 051 707 1733.
Artshare South West, Exeter and Devon Arts Centre, Bradninch Place, Gandy Street, Exeter EX4 3LS.
  Tel: 0392 218923.

Disability Arts Agency, The Yard, 6 Summerville Road, St. Andrews, Bristol B57 9AA.
  Tel: 0272 420721.
East Midlands SHAPE, 32 Park Row, Nottingham NG1 6GR.
  Tel: 0602 241700.
Equal Arts, Redheugh Studio, Cuthbert Street, Gateshead, Tyne and Wear NE8 2HT.
North West SHAPE, The Green Prefab, Back of Shawgrove School, Cavendish Road, West Didsbury, Manchester M20 89JR.
  Tel: 061 434 8666.
Disability Scotland, Committee on Arts for Scotland, Princess House, 5 Shandwick Place, Edinburgh EH2 4RG.
  Tel: 031 229 8632.
Artlink East, Ongar Educational Campus, Fyfield Road, Ongar, Essex CM5 0AU.
  Tel: 0277 364409.
SHAPE East, Eastern Arts, Cherry Hinton Hall, Cherry Hinton Road, Cambridge CB1 4DW.
  Tel: 0223 215355.
Artlink South, The Arts Connection Cumberland Centre, Reginald Road, Portsmouth PO4 9HN.
  Tel: 0705 828392.
ITHACA, Unit 1, St. John Fisher School, Sandy Lane West, Oxford OX4 5LD.
  Tel: 0865 714652.
South East Artability, St. James Centre, Quarry Road, Tunbridge Wells, Kent TN1 2ET.
  Tel: 0892 515478.
Artlink West Midlands, The Garage Arts and Media Centre, 1 Hatherton Street, Walsall WA1 1YB.
  Tel: 0922 616566.
Artlink West Yorkshire, 191 Belle Vue Road, Leeds L53 1HG.
  Tel: 0532 431005.

Suppliers of arts and craft materials

Branches of GALTS.
Branches of W.H. Smith.
Greater Manchester Play Resources Unit, Grumpy House, Vaughan Street, West Gorton, Manchester M12 5DU.
  (Suppliers of new art and craft materials at modest prices and cheap manufacturing waste products).
Nottingham Rehab Ltd, Ludlow Hill Road, West Bridgford, Nottingham NG2 6HD.
  Tel: 0602 452200.
Specialist Crafts, PO Box 247, Leicester LE1 9QS.
  Tel: 0533 510405
The Kite and Balloon Co., The Old Church, 160 Eardley Road, Streatham, London SW16 5TG.
  Tel: 081 679 8844.
  (Large selection of balloons, including giant balloons up to 6 ft in diameter which can be blown up with a vacuum cleaner).

Brusho available from:

Colourcraft Ltd, Unit H, Stanforth Works, Main Street, Hacaenthorpe, Sheffield, S12 4LD.
Tel: 0742 489107.

Slick-Writers and Easy Tie-Dye Fabric Markers available from:

Art Shops, Boots, W.H. Smith, but if unobtainable write to:

Inscribe, Bordon, Hants.

Sources of information on sound and music, movement, dance, aerobic exercise and popmobility

BBC Music Department, The Langham, Portland Place, London W1.
Tel: 071 580 44645.
Triple Earth Records, Dept. BX2, 4 Bedford Road, London W4 1JJ.
(Music from many countries – send large SAE for catalogue).
TUMI (Latin American Craft Centres), 8/9 New Bond Street Place, Bath, Avon BA1 1BH.
(Send SAE for information and music list).
Association of Professional Music Therapists in Great Britain, c/o Music Therapy Dept, Harperbury, Harper Lane, Shenley, Nr. Radlett, Herts WD7 7HQ.
Tel: 0923 854861.
British Society for Music Therapy, Guildhall School of Music and Drama, Barbican, London EC2Y 8DT. 071 628 2571.
National Music and Disability Information Service, Dartington College of Arts, Totnes, Devon TQ9 6EJ
Tel: 0803 866701.
Medipost Ltd, 100 Shaw Road, Oldham OL1 4AY.
Tel: 061 628 2571
(Suppliers of sheepskin bed fleece).
Playtrac, c/o Horizon Trust, Harperbury, Harper Lane, Shenley, Nr. Radlett, Herts WD7 7HQ.
Tel: 092 764861.
(Papers on practical music and drama activities available from them on request).
Disabled Living Foundation Advisory Service, 380–384 Harrow Road, London W9 2HU.
Tel: 071 289 6111.

Galaxies, Seaside, Funfair and other music and drama events available from:

Resources for Learning Difficulties, The Consortium, Jack Tizard School, Finlay Street, London SW6 6HB.
Tel: 071 736 8877

Shops/groups that specialize in dance

The Laban Centre for Movement and Dance, Laurie Grove, New Cross, London SE14 6NH.
Tel: 081 692 4070

Anglo American Book Company, Prior Chambers, Church Street, Weybridge, Surrey KT13 8DQ.
Tel: 0932 842485

Dance Books, 9 Cecil Court, London WC2N 4EZ.
Tel: 071 836 2314.
(Shop and mail order, also good selection of dance music on tape and CD and some videos).

JABADAO Dance Resource, 45 Elder Road, Bramley, Leeds LS13 4DB.
Tel: 0532 562287.
(Videotapes, reports, information on 'dance' projects and people with special needs. Also have a pattern for a 'parachute').

Organizations concerned with dance

English Folk and Dance Society, National Headquarters, Cecil Sharp House, 2 Regent's Park Road, London NW1 7AY.
Tel: 071 485 2206.

SESAME Institute UK (Drama and Dance in Therapy), Christchurch, 27 Blackfriars Road, London SE1 8NY.

National Association of Wheelchair Dance, Craig y Parc School, Pentyrch, Cardiff, S. Wales.
Tel: 0222 891029

RECIPES

Cornflour paste:
1 cup cornflour dissolved in a little cold water. Add 2 pints of boiling water and boil until thick. Away from the heat add 1 cup of soapflakes and beat well. Colour as desired (using food colour or non-toxic powder paint).

Starch paste:
Mix together ½ cup of soapflakes, ½ cup of cold water starch and one cup of cold water until the mixture has the consistency of mashed potatoes. Colour as desired.

Flour paste:
Mix equal quantities of flour and powder paint, then add cold water until the mixture is smooth and thick.

Leisure dough:
2 cups of plain flour; 1 cup of salt; 4 tablespoons of cream of tartar; 2 cups of water; colouring (food or powder paint); 2 tablespoons of oil

Mix first 3 ingredients together in a saucepan then add the rest. Cook over a low heat for about 5 minutes, stirring well. Any lumps should come out as it is kneaded. Cool before storing in an airtight container – it should keep for about 6 months.

Stretching dough: 1½ lbs of self-raising flour; ½ pint water; colouring (food or powder paint)

Mix all the ingredients together. This dough will only keep for 1–2 days, but gives a totally different consistency from the one above.

Dough which dries on exposure to air: 1 cup of cornflour; 2 cups baking soda; 1½ cups water

Mix all ingredients and cook over a medium heat until thickened. Knead well and make into desired shapes, e.g. jewellery, models, dishes. Decorate when dry. Enamel paints do not need varnishing but dry slowly. Acrylic paints dry quickly but need varnishing.

9

Holidays and outings

Loretto Lambe and Helen Mount

Holidays and outings make up a significant part of the total pattern of leisure which we all enjoy. Within society at large the amenities and resources that enable us so to enjoy our free time have taken on considerable social and economic significance. In the latter part of the 20th century tourism has become the largest single industry in the world, with the holiday trade forming a very large section of that industry. Most of us take at least one organized holiday per year, with many people taking two or more.

The first section of this chapter is concerned with organized holidays, and covers specialist holidays, package tours and adventure holidays. The second section looks at a range of activities and events, outings suitable for people with profound and multiple disabilities, the starting point for which might be the person's home, school, centre or holiday venue.

HOLIDAYS

People with profound and multiple disabilities have as much or more free time available as the rest of the population, but where holidays are concerned they do not always have the same options and choices. There are a number of reasons for this. In recent times travel by air, sea and rail has greatly improved, and it is now much easier for us to undertake what would once have been inconceivable journeys. However, these improvements in modes of travel have not always been matched with good access and facilities suitable for people with disabilities, although great strides are being made. The major transportation organizations are aware of the travel needs of people with disabilities, and a number of them will have a department or at least an officer designated to deal with travel and disability. Some produce regularly updated books or pamphlets detailing their facilities. For example, the Automobile Association publishes a *Guide for the Disabled*

Traveller; British Rail's leaflets, *British Rail and Disabled Passenger Travel Guide* and *Care Line Service*, which specifically deal with London Transport, are both updated annually and available free from any British Rail or London Transport station. In addition, BR operate a disabled person's railcard service. *Care in the Air* is a free booklet available from the Air Transport Users Committee. These are just a sample of the many publications that are now available. Full details of these and others and where to obtain them are given at the end of the chapter.

Many people with profound and multiple disabilities may find travel, particularly long journeys, uncomfortable and not much fun. Additionally, such a person will always need to travel with a family member, friend or companion to enable them to take a holiday. Cost is also a factor that must be considered. People with profound and multiple disabilities will typically not be in employment, and as they will need to have a friend or helper to accompany them the costs are inevitably doubled. Later in this chapter some ideas on sources of financial help are given. Last, but not least of course, the holiday venue will need to be accessible and have facilities for people with disabilities.

Bearing all these constraints in mind, it is refreshing to look at the range and variety of holiday options that are now available to people with profound disabilities. In a short chapter it is not possible to review or list all these options. However, what is feasible is to give a brief description of the different types of holidays that are on offer and some pointers as to where to go for further help and information.

The voluntary sector

Many of the voluntary agencies working in the field of disability run, organize or publish information on holidays for people with disabilities. Mencap, through its Holiday Services Department, arranges a programme of holidays without family members accompanying the person throughout the UK for children and adults with learning disabilities, whose needs are not normally catered for and who have profound or complex difficulties. These range from 'special care holidays' for people with profound and multiple disabilities, where a qualified nurse is always in attendance, to adventure and guest house holidays for people with a lesser degree of disability. Mencap Holiday Services produces a very comprehensive 2-yearly *Holiday Accommodation Guide* (Mencap, 1994–95), which gives the addresses of accommodation where people with learning disabilities are welcomed either unaccompanied, with their families, or in groups. The Guide is divided into four sections and lists establishments providing full catering, self-catering, holiday and activity centres, as well as specialist accommodation in England by county, followed by the Channel Isles, Northern Ireland, the Republic of Ireland, Scotland, Wales and Europe. In addition, there is a section on planning a successful holiday and a comprehensive list of useful addresses and publications list. Many Mencap local societies, of which there are now almost 600, also provide holiday services. You can obtain the address of your local Mencap society from the Mencap National Centre, or it should be listed in the telephone directory.

RADAR, the Royal Association for Disability and Rehabilitation, publishes two guides, *Holidays in the British Isles* and *Holidays and Travel Abroad*. The first provides details on holidays and accommodation in the British Isles; the second gives information on facilities in the UK and on over 100 countries, including air and sea transport information, insurance cover details and contact addresses. Both these guides are updated annually.

The Holiday Care Service, a national charity, provides free information and advice on holiday opportunities for people with disabilities. This service also runs the 'Holiday Helpers' scheme, which introduces volunteer helpers to people with disabilities or those who are elderly and need assistance to enable them to take an independent holiday.

Break, a registered charity in Norfolk, specializes in providing holidays and emergency and recuperative care for children and adults with learning disability and additional multiple disabilities. Holidays or breaks can be organized for individuals or groups, with and without accompanying parents or staff.

Enable, formerly The Scottish Society for the Mentally Handicapped (SSMH), through the Enable Holidays Section, provides a range of holidays for people with learning disabilities. 'The philosophy of Enable Holidays is to have a group of children, teenagers or adults, of mixed ability but similar age, holidaying together, sharing the fun and learning from each other' (Enable, 1994, p. 1). Enable does not organize holidays specifically for people with profound and multiple disabilities, but a number of people with this degree of disability do participate in Enable Holidays. Enable produces an annual Holiday Information Pack (Enable, 1994) which gives details on a range of holidays provided by the national organization as well as by local branches. The pack also includes information on possible sources of funding, agencies offering help and advice and a holiday guides and publications section.

There are many other voluntary organizations, both national and local, that provide holidays for people with disabilities or information on holiday opportunities. Contact your local Town Hall, local

Council for Voluntary Organizations, or the national headquarters of major charities for details of those in your area.

Specialist holiday centres and adventure holidays

Adventure or outdoor pursuits-type holidays are becoming increasingly popular and a number of centres throughout the country provide this type of holiday. Some of these centres are specifically designed for wheelchair access. Their activities range from abseiling, canoeing, sailing, orienteering, horse-riding and pony-cart driving, to exploring the countryside through nature trails and bird watching. Specialist equipment and protective clothing are to a British Standard and are usually supplied by the centre. All activities are carried out under strict supervision by qualified instructors. Recent years have seen many innovations in the development of equipment that enhances the safety and stability of participants in these types of leisure pursuits. Special note may be made of 'Eb's 'Arness', a body harness designed to avoid pain and pressure on the chest, ribcage and kidney areas (address of supplier at the end of the chapter).

Accommodation at these adventure holiday centres is suitable for all ages and is fully accessible. Some adventure/outdoor pursuits centres have separate chalets, suitable for small groups or families. Family members can choose whether they participate in the special activities organized by the centre or not. This type of holiday is particularly good for a family with a member with disabilities and children of different ages. A list of organizations providing adventure holidays is given at the end of the chapter. This list is not exhaustive: many other holiday and accommodation guides will also have details on adventure centre holidays. A word of caution: while we should be encouraging people with profound disabilities to participate in adventure and outdoor pursuits holidays, it cannot be stressed enough that the activities on offer often include sports that are deemed to be dangerous, and should only be engaged in under the supervision of qualified instructors and staff.

Narrowboat or barge holidays

A holiday on a narrowboat on a canal or inland waterway can be a relaxing or quite energetic way to spend your annual leave. Some companies and charitable trusts now operate narrowboats that have been converted for use by people with disabilities. The Bruce Charitable Trust, based in Berkshire, is a good example of an organization offering this type of holiday. Others are listed at the end of the chapter.

Skiing and winter sports holidays

Winter sports and skiing are now very popular holiday activities. There are numerous companies specializing in this type of holiday and there is no reason why people with profound and multiple disabilities should not at least consider these as a holiday option with family or friends. However, to participate fully in any winter sporting activities they will require the correct equipment. Specially designed or adapted equipment is available at many adventure or activity holiday centres. Such centres will also have qualified instructors and many will have dry ski slopes where beginners can learn to ski in a safe environment. There are also a number of clubs and associations concerned with winter sports for people with disabilities. The British Ski Club for the Disabled, the Uphill Ski Club and the English Ski Council will be able to give information on their own services, as well as providing information on skiing and winter sports for people with disabilities.

Package tour holidays

People with profound and multiple disabilities do not have to go on 'specialist' holidays. One of the most popular type of holidays for the general population is package tours offered through the high-street travel agencies. Tour operators are increasingly becoming more aware of the needs of people with disabilities. A few holiday companies offer holidays designed for people with disabilities, and many indicate access for people with disabilities as a matter of course in their descriptions of accommodation. However, it is advisable always to check beforehand exactly what the access and facilities consist of. Having a ramp, or one toilet with a 'disability sticker' is not what 'fully accessible' means. TV and radio holiday programmes usually now include details on facilities for people with disabilities in any holiday reviewed by them. The Broadcasting Support Services, an educational charity, runs helplines and provides follow-up services for viewers, including holiday and travel programmes. They published a booklet, *Disabled Traveller*, to accompany BBC1's 'Holiday 1994' programme. Copies are available free (see address at the end of the chapter.)

Assistance towards the cost of a holiday

A number of the holiday guides or information pamphlets produced by the voluntary organizations listed above give details of sources of funding towards the cost of a holiday for a person with disabilities. It is not always easy to obtain such funding, as the trusts listed usually have many calls on their finances. However, they are worth pursuing and the following information is taken from the Mencap Holiday Services information sheets *Assistance Towards the Cost of a Holiday* and *Funding for Mencap Holidays*.

Social Services Departments

Any person with disabilities, or their family, is entitled to approach their local social service department, either to participate in a holiday organized by the department or to receive financial assistance towards the cost of independent holiday arrangements. Some departments offer a basic grant to anyone who applies, until their funds run out. Others offer grants on a basis of assessed, rather than perceived, need. Additionally, if the person with disabilities is in receipt of income support and needs to meet the cost of a break away from home, it may be possible to obtain financial help under the heading of 'respite care'. This means that the cost of living away from home for a holiday is treated as the cost of living away from home in residential care. Since a holiday break is a respite break, this is acceptable. Rules and regulations are constantly changing, so discuss income support for respite care with a social worker, welfare rights worker or benefits agency. It is important to make it clear that you are talking about **respite** – talking about holidays may draw a blank!

Voluntary organizations and local groups

Many national organizations have local branches or groups, which will often respond sympathetically to requests for a grant towards the cost of a holiday for a person with disabilities. These include Mencap, the Spastics Society, Barnardo's, etc. In addition, local organizations such as Rotary Clubs, Round Table, Inner Wheel, etc. will also consider applications for financial assistance from people with disabilities within their locality. The addresses of the local branch of all these organizations should be in the telephone directory.

The Family Fund

The Family Fund will provide financial assistance towards the cost of a holiday for a person with severe or profound disabilities who is under the age of 16 years.

Family Welfare Association

The Association administers trust funds from which it is sometimes able to make a small grant, and will consider anyone who is in desperate need of a holiday. Applications must be made by a social worker.

The Prince's Trust

The Trust distributes £3 million each year through 57 local committees, to support projects put forward by others, including holiday projects. They focus on young people between the age of 14 and 25. Local committees should be listed in the telephone directory, or contact the head office for details on the committee in your area (address at the end of chapter).

Other grant-making trusts

There are many hundreds of grant-making trusts that support initiatives for people with disabilities. Some of these will give assistance towards holiday costs. There is no easy way to find out which do so. You will have to do some research and the best way to go about this is to go through *The Directory of Grant Making Trusts*, which should be available from your local library. Each entry in the Directory will give the individual trust's remit. A word of warning is in order here: if your request does not come within a trust's remit, then do not waste your time applying.

Planning and organization

A few final words about planning to ensure that the holiday is successful. We usually plan and organize our holidays well in advance. Although this will not guarantee that the holiday will run smoothly, good forward planning will at least help to ensure that when you arrive at the railway station or airport, there is a wheelchair available if required.

Many people with profound and multiple disabilities have additional medical problems and may require a range of medications. Check that there are sufficient supplies of medication for the duration of the holiday. Copies of prescriptions and medical cover and insurance documents should always be taken. It is also advisable to make sure that you have the address of the nearest local hospital in case of emergency, particularly if the holiday is abroad.

Finally, although in this chapter we have placed the emphasis on specialist holidays and resorts and facilities that are aware of the needs of people with disabilities, we should remind ourselves that every year many people with disabilities, including those with profound and multiple disabilities, participate in and enjoy the same types of holidays as the rest of the population. What we have tried to emphasize is that, with some forward planning, you will be able to alleviate possible holiday stresses and ensure a thoroughly enjoyable break for all involved.

OUTINGS

An outing, by definition, is something which takes place somewhere other than in a person's home, school or centre, or where they are staying for a time on holiday. As a leisure pursuit it is something which is planned and offers an element of choice, and the choices of outings available to most of us are usually only limited by a few obstacles. The first of these is our specific interest in particular events or activities. Some of us may choose to use our free time to go walking in the hills, others may prefer to go fishing, play tennis or listen to a concert. People who have profound disabilities invariably have more limited choices than the rest of us, and the majority spend most of their free time indoors engaged in passive situations such as watching television or listening to music (Hogg and Lambe, 1988; Prosser, 1992). Secondly, although we may be clear about our preferences, financial constraints may present a further obstacle. It will be seen in what follows that there are examples of a wide range of activities with respect to their cost. Some are indeed free, while savings can be made in the organization of others. Certainly the cost of transport, for example, is a consideration. It may be possible to use public transport so that you are not always dependent on getting access to a tail-lift vehicle or taxi, but that will obviously be affected by the amount of help required and the ease of access.

Organization and safety

As with planning a holiday, attention must be given to accessibility in relation to both travel and the amenity to which the outing is taking place. Different activities will raise differing issues of access, as well as of organization and safety. There are, however, some general considerations that need to be highlighted. The first and perhaps most obvious of these is that a person with profound disabilities will need at least one other adult (friend, helper or relative) to accompany them.

This is one of the most frequently voiced constraints preventing outings of any kind, although if you are planning an excursion it has to be given first consideration. Where the outing sets out from some form of statutory or voluntary provision, such as a school or resource centre, then additional support may be achieved through a number of sources, e.g. students on care courses, student nurses, teachers, nursery nurses and social workers. Appropriate contacts at relevant institutions of further and higher education are well worth pursuing. Local secondary schools may be able to supply assistance on a regular basis as a contribution to care schemes or part of personal and social education courses. Volunteers can sometimes be brought in from the local community through advertising or personal contact. Very few people will come knocking on your door, but there are those who would be interested in being involved if they are contacted in an appropriate manner. Kelly (1990) describes how a project with which he was involved achieved success in recruiting volunteers in this way. Parents are also an extremely valuable resource as volunteers if they can commit some time. They do not necessarily have to (or indeed want to) be involved in an outing with their own daughter or son, but can easily transfer their expertise in profound disability and apply it to another person or group.

Finally, a frequently untapped resource of volunteers, especially if you work in a school, resource centre or similar institution, is to consider asking people with learning difficulties to be volunteers. Williams (1990) emphasizes many benefits derived from involving such adults, including the development of self-esteem and self-advocacy skills. Above all, it alters the emphasis in our perception of people with learning difficulties from that of receivers to givers, creates a positive image of their skills and abilities, and enhances their value as members of the society in which they live.

Once you have established a network of good volunteers you will need to ensure that they are properly briefed on the outing so that they are clear what is expected of them. If they regularly come to help with other activities and form relationships with a person or people with profound disabilities, they will obviously require less guidance than someone new. If the planned outing is expected to take more than an hour or two, consideration must be given to the changing facilities available for those who need help with continence. Longer outings may also necessitate gaining access to refreshment facilities, and this also needs to be established at the planning stages. Whatever duration of outing you are planning it is advisable to make a list of everything you will need and check it with someone else in case you have forgotten something 'obvious'. It is also possible that the person with profound disabilities will have special feeding and/or dietary requirements, so special utensils and even food may have to go on your list. They will most certainly need assistance, so it is essential to identify appropriate helpers for those who have particular difficulties with feeding. In like manner, make sure that those in wheelchairs have help in adjusting their position from time to time to relieve any discomfort they may experience. Apparent lack of enjoyment of the outing may reflect extreme discomfort rather than anything specifically to do with the activity.

For these and other reasons it is essential to gain as much information as possible before the outing, rather than expect everything to fall into place when you arrive. Where appropriate, if you can establish a contact person at the venue who knows your approximate time of arrival, this usually facilitates more effective access.

The weather is something which is beyond the control of any of us, but it is important to be prepared for any eventuality and expect rain at any time! Waterproof clothing and covers for wheelchairs are permanent items on any list. Most of us are in a position to wipe rain off our faces or out of our eyes if we do not like it, and we can move around to get warm, or ask for a jumper if we feel cold. Be sensitive to the conditions you are likely to be confronted with and try to put yourself in the position of someone who has poor circulation, limited movement and who is unable to make a specific request. Conversely, it is equally important to ensure that there is adequate shade and cover if the weather is hot and sunny. Many people with profound disabilities have extremely sensitive skins, often compounded by their medication, which increases that sensitivity. They cannot escape from the sun, so do take every precaution and add high-filter suncreams (ensuring that there are no allergies) and sun hats to your list. Remember also that hands and feet can just as easily get badly burned and cause sunstroke as larger areas of exposed skin.

Equipment which enables people with disabilities to participate in leisure activities is continually being developed, and improved designs are appearing all the time. Again, organization requires that such equipment is available and properly prepared. For detailed reference to specialist equipment and suppliers, see the end of this chapter and Lambe (1991). Many people with disabilities have taken an active part in sporting events for a number of years, excelling and becoming champions in their chosen events. With suitable assistance, people with profound disabilities should also be given the opportunity to participate in and enjoy these same activities.

A final general point to consider when planning outings is to consider the care of those with medical needs, particularly those with epilepsy, in exactly the same way as described in the preceding section on holiday organization.

Where to go and what to do

Possibly the simplest and cheapest option for an outing is to go for a walk or ride in a wheelchair, taking advantage of facilities in the local community. This has the advantage of not requiring transport but will inevitably be limited by what is within walking distance of a person's home, day centre, college, school or holiday venue. Some suggestions are as follows:

- A neighbour's or friend's house for morning coffee, afternoon tea or any other social event;
- The local park. Wheelchairs are not, in most cases, designed for sociability, as the person in the wheelchair usually has their back to the one pushing. Conducting a conversation can therefore present difficulties and it is important to stop occasionally and talk about what you see, to offer the names of objects, and opportunities to touch different textures and experience different sounds, e.g. rustling leaves, crunching snow;
- A sports field, where the open space can be experienced or the development of an interest in a particular sport as a spectator can be encouraged;
- A church. Remember, this may not be something **you** would choose, but it may be that the silence at some times and the sound of the choir at others gives pleasure to other individuals;
- The shops. Shopping centres, malls and local shops also provide opportunities for outings if they are accessible, and offer venues for a short trip out, especially if you can sample the perfume or aftershave, or buy some new clothes;
- The library, where you can choose books, tapes and videos;
- The pub, a cafe, hotel or restaurant.

Moving further afield, some suggestions are offered for outings to indoor facilities, such as:

- Leisure centres
- Theatres and cinemas
- Concert halls, music halls and opera houses
- Museums and art galleries
- Libraries
- Horse-riding centres
- Stately homes

- Craft centres
- Auctions, antique fairs and flea markets
- Exhibitions, e.g. car shows, Ideal Homes
- Ballet and dance venues
- Ten-pin bowling
- Leisure classes at college
- Pubs and restaurants, etc., as on previous list
- Discos

and outdoor settings such as:

- Large parks/gardens/nature trails
- Walks along canals or river banks
- Water parks and water sports centres
- Large shopping centres or markets
- Zoos or farms
- Horse-riding centres
- Seaside resorts
- Seasonal venues, e.g. spring bulbs, autumn colour, sledging
- Car-boot sales
- Football, cricket and other sports stadiums
- Country parks and forests
- Garden centres
- Motor racing, horse-racing circuits
- Flower shows and festivals
- Funfairs
- Fishing

Although these lists are by no means exhaustive, they emphasize a range of activities that will be familiar to all of us, and many of which we ourselves enjoy. With respect to which activities are to be enjoyed, the fundamental questions to ask (as well as considering organizational aspects) are:

- Why have I chosen this particular outing?
- What do I think that the person/people will derive from this activity and why? How can I tell if the activity **is** enjoyed?
- Is it possible to extend the activities we tried and develop them by making a record of what we did, e.g. taking photographs, making videos or collecting mementos?
- Am I planning this with the interest of the person with profound disabilities in mind, or is it because it is easy to organize in the time I have available?

- Do I avoid or refuse to consider some options because they do not interest me?
- Do I positively select and repeat similar activities because they are what I like to do?

The last two options have a lot in common, and it is easy to be critical about why particular activities and outings are either frequently chosen or never offered. If real choices are to be offered, outings cannot be excluded because you would not consider them as options for yourself. Why not ask around and establish what other people do with their leisure time? Staff and volunteers are often willing to share their expertise in a leisure pursuit, and enthusiasm is often contagious.

Some sources of information and how to use what is on offer

Countryside Commission and Forestry Commission

For outings in the countryside, the country parks and national parks offer great potential. Information can be obtained from the Countryside Commission. For many years the Forestry Commission, too, has allowed access to their woodlands, which often have information centres containing exhibitions and detailed information on the local flora and fauna. It is possible to choose from a vast selection of pathways and woodland routes which present different challenges, depending on your requirements. It is, however, essential to consider the terrain for wheelchair users (not forgetting the helper who has to push). Few, if any, wheelchairs have suspension, and a walk through woodland on a bumpy earth or grass path could be not only uncomfortable but also painful for both the wheelchair user and their helper. This emphasizes the importance of good planning, and with a network of 120,000 miles of footpaths in England and Wales, there should be something within reasonable distance that is suitable for wheelchair users.

Tourist Information Centres

Tourist Information Centres are an excellent source of ideas for outings in your locality, and you can also obtain addresses of others which are further afield. You may then wish to build up a resource of your own to help with your planning and organization. If you work in a school, resource centre or similar facility and have responsibility for planning outings for anyone with profound and multiple disabilities, the setting up of an information resource may prove extremely valuable. This can be developed, expanded and evaluated as you try different venues and activities, and should be accessible to all members of staff, who can use it and add to it. To start, you could simply obtain a ring binder which is then available for filling with information leaflets offering a choice of ideas for outings. It is more useful if the resource develops to contain details which are relevant to the individuals or groups you have to plan for. Some kind of evaluation sheet is therefore extremely helpful. This would contain information on need for transport, time taken to reach the venue, whether it was easy to find, with a map of the location if it was not, suitable parking, accessibility of buildings and facilities, changing facilities, refreshment facilities, shelter suitable for different times of the year, age-appropriateness, helpfulness of staff and so on. Much of this information could be provided in the form of a simple checklist, but the addition of a brief paragraph highlighting the particular strengths and weaknesses of a venue would eventually produce a comprehensive resource for a variety of needs, save a lot of wasted time and, hopefully, help to prevent some unpleasant experiences. The addition of a few photographs will also provide accurate illustrations of suitable facilities at different venues. This information could be made available to parents via a newsletter and/or a duplicate set of photographs.

Local Authority Recreation Services

Local Authority Recreation Service Departments have an obligation to make provision for people with disabilities. Such departments will be responsible for local leisure centres, which offer potential for outings with a wide selection of indoor activities for everybody. It may be possible to use the swimming pool, for example, but access and suitability of changing facilities, access to the pool itself and water temperature are all fundamental points to establish before you arrive. When in doubt, make a preliminary visit yourself and do not depend on information from leisure staff, who are not usually aware of the specific needs of people with profound and multiple disabilities. Alternatively, you may choose to use other parts of the centre as spectators in a variety of sports. If you wish to be even more adventurous, you could investigate ways of promoting access so that a person with profound and multiple disabilities can be included. For example, the provision of a ramp may allow someone in a wheelchair to aim a ball at a target or, in the case of cricket, a batsman. You could consider making arrangements to use the Meldreth games (see Chapters 1 and 5 of this volume) in your local leisure centre, and if you own a set of the games you can take them with you and use them in a more appropriate setting. You could even try and put some pressure on your local Recreation Services Department to purchase a selection, or even one of the games, if you feel that there are groups who could make regular use of them. This is especially relevant for those local authorities who advertise equal opportunities for all.

Taking a long-term view

It should be accepted that some outings may be one-off events to a specific venue simply for enjoyment and fun. Others may have more long-term goals, and provide opportunities to develop skills and to learn about a chosen leisure activity. If, for example, we wish to learn how to play a particular sport, we will usually require assistance and advice from instructors with specialist knowledge. They will guide us towards appropriate choice of equipment and protective clothing, instruct us in the rules and demonstrate how we can develop our technique and ability.

The dignity of risk

Finally, it has to be recognized that some activities we engage in, especially sporting and outdoor pursuits, involve an element of risk. Risks should obviously be minimized for anyone taking part in any sport or potentially dangerous leisure activity, but some activities will involve more risk than others. Advice must be sought before planning an outing which involves, for example, strenuous physical exercise. The opportunity to take risks is, however, part of being able to make choices, and should not be denied to people who have profound and multiple disabilities.

REFERENCES AND USEFUL ADDRESSES

Holidays

Automobile Association *AA Guide for the Disabled Traveller*, The Automobile Association, London.
ATUC *Care in the Air*, Air Transport Users Committee, London.
British Rail *British Rail and Disabled Passenger Travel Guide*, British Rail, London.
Enable (1994) *On Holiday with Enable*, Enable, Glasgow.
Fitzherbert, L. and Forrester, S. (1991) *A Guide to the Major Trusts*, The Directory of Social Change, London.
London Regional Transport *Care Line Service*, London Regional Transport, London.
Mencap (1994–1995) *Holiday Accommodation Guide*, Mencap, London.

RADAR (1994) *Holidays in the British Isles 1994: A Guide for Disabled People*, Radar, London.
RADAR (1994) *Holidays and Travel Abroad 1994/95*, Radar, London.
Walsh, A. (1992) *Disabled Traveller*, Broadcasting Support Services, Luton.
Villemur, A. (ed) (1993) *The Directory of Grant Making Trusts*, Charities Aid Foundation, Tonbridge.

Useful addresses

Travel

Air Transport Users Committee, 2nd Floor, Kingsway House, 103 Kingsway, London WC2B 6QX.
The Automobile Association, Fanum House, Basingstoke, Hants RG21 2EA.
British Rail, PO Box XX, York YO1 1HT.
London Regional Transport, Unit for Disabled Passengers, 55 Broadway, London SW1H 0BD.

Voluntary organizations

BREAK, 20 Hooks Hill Road, Sheringham, Norfolk NR26 8NL.
Broadcasting Support Services, PO Box 7, London W3 6XJ.
Disability Scotland, Information Department, Princes House, 5 Shandwick Place, Edinburgh EH2 4RG.
Enable, The Scottish Society for the Mentally Handicapped, 6th Floor, 7 Buchanan Street, Glasgow G1 3HL.
Holiday Care Service, 2 Old Bank Chambers, Station Road, Horley, Surrey RH6 9HW.
Holiday Helpers, PO Box 20, Horley, Surrey RH6 9UY.
Mencap, National Centre, 123 Golden Lane, London EC1Y 0RT.
Mencap Holiday Services, 119 Drake Street, Rochdale, Lancs OL16 1PZ.
RADAR, 12 City Forum, 250 City Road, London EC1V 8AF.

Adventure Holiday Centres

Badaguish Centre, Aviemore, Inverness PH22 1QU.
Bendrigg Lodge, Old Hatton, Kendal, Cumbria LA8 0NR.
Calvert Adventure Centre, Little Crosthwaite, Underskiddaw, Keswick, Cumbria CA12 4QD.
Churchtown Outdoor Education Centre, Lanlivery, Bodmin, Cornwall PL30 5BH.
Kielder Adventure Centre, Low Cranecleue, Falstone, Hexham, Northumbria NE48 1BS.
The Stackpole Centre, Home Farm, Stackpole, Pembroke, Dyfed SA71 5DQ.

Equipment

Eb's 'Arness, 10a Grove Street, Oxford OS2 7JT.

Skiing and winter sports

British Ski Club for Disabled, Springmount, Berwick St John, Shaftesbury, Dorset SP7 0HQ.
English Ski Council, The Area Library Building, Queensway Mall, The Cornbow, Halesowen, West Midlands B63 4AJ.
National Handicapped Skiers Association, c/o The Harlow Ski School, Harlow Sports Centre, Hammersmith, Harlow, Essex CM20 3JF.
Uphill Ski Club, 12 Park Crescent, London W1N 4EQ.

Narrowboat holidays

British Waterways, Greycaine Road, Watford, Herts WD2 4JR.
The Bruce Charitable Trust, PO Box 13, Hungerford, Berkshire RG17 0RZ.
Inland Waterways Association, 114 Regents Park Road, London NW1 8UQ.
Peter Le Marchant Trust, Colston Bassett House, Colston Bassett, Nottingham NG12 3FE.

Financial assistance

Family Welfare Association, 501–505 Kingsland Road, Dalston, London E8 4AY.
The Family Fund, PO Box 50, York YO1 2ZX.
The Prince's Trust, 8 Bedford Row, London WC1R 4BBA.

Outings

Association of Swimming Therapy (1981) *Swimming for Those With Special Needs*, ASA, Loughborough.
Cotton, M. (ed) (1983) *Outdoor Adventure for Handicapped People*, Souvenir Press, London.
Croucher, N. (1981) *Outdoor Sports for Disabled People*, Woodhead Faulkner, Cambridge.
Hogg, J. and Lambe, L. (1988) *People with Profound Retardation and Multiple Handicaps Attending Schools or Social Education Centres – Final Report*, Mencap PIMD Section, Manchester.
Kelly, B. (1990) Facilitating volunteers, in *Innovations in Leisure for People with Mental Handicap*, (eds R. McConkey and P. McGinley), Lisieux Hall, Chorley.
Lambe, L. (ed.) (1991) *Leisure for People with Profound and Multiple Disabilities – A Resource Training Pack*, Mencap PIMD Section, Manchester.
Latto, K. and Norris, B. (1989) *Give us the Chance: Sport and Physical Recreation for People with a Mental Handicap*, Disabled Living Foundation, London.
McConkey, R. and McGinley, P. (eds) (1990) *Innovations in Leisure for People with a Mental Handicap*, Lisieux Hall, Chorley.
Prosser, H. (1992) *Evaluation of the Second Phase Workshop on Evolving Approaches to Leisure*, Mencap PRMH Report, Mencap, London.
Smedley, G. (1989) *A Guide to Canoeing with Disabled Persons*, BCU, Nottingham.

Williams, R. (1990) Shifting the emphasis: volunteering by people with a learning difficulty, in *Innovations in Leisure for People with a Mental Handicap*, (eds R. McConkey and P. McGinley), Lisieux Hall, Chorley.

Useful addresses/contacts

Association of Swimming Therapy (AST), 4 Oak Street, Shrewsbury, Shropshire SY3 7RH.

Amateur Swimming Association, Harold Fern House, Derby Square, Loughborough, Leics LE11 0AL.

British Disabled Water Ski Association, The Tony Edge Centre, Heron Lake, Wraybury, Nr. Staines, Middlesex TW19 6HW.

British Sports Association for the Disabled, 34 Osnaburgh Street, London NW1 3ND.

The Countryside Commission, John Dower House, Crescent Place, Cheltenham, Gloucs GL50 3RA.

The Countryside Commission of Scotland, Battleby, Redgorton, Perth PH1 3EW.

The Country Landowners Charitable Trust, Bohune Common House, Woodborough, Pewsey, Wilts SN9 6LY.

Forestry Commission, 231 Corstorphine Road, Edinburgh EH12 7AT.

The Mencap Profound Intellectual and Multiple Disabilities Section, Piper Hill School, 200 Yew Tree Lane, Northenden, Manchester M23 0FF.

The National Trust, 42 Queen Anne's Gate, London SW1H 9AS.

The National Trust of Scotland, 5 Charlotte Square, Edinburgh EH2 4DU.

Profound and Multiple Impairment Service (PAMIS), White Top Research Unit, Department of Social Work, University of Dundee, Dundee DD1 4HN, Scotland.

Riding for the Disabled Association (RDA), Avenue A, National Agricultural Centre, Kenilworth, Warwicks CV8 21Y.

RSBP, The Royal Society for the Protection of Birds, The Lodge, Sandy, Bedfordshire SG19 2DL.

UK Sports Association for the Physically and Mentally Handicapped, 30 Phillip Lane, Tottenham, London N15 4JB.

10

Play materials

Carol Ouvry and Suzie Mitchell

PLAY: A UNIVERSAL ACTIVITY

When we consider play materials within the provision of leisure for people with profound and multiple disabilities it is necessary to have an understanding of, or at least an opinion on, the role of play materials within the general population. To do this is only to reflect that people with profound and multiple disabilities are a part of the general population and that their leisure provision must be firmly placed within the context of that provided for society in general.

It is widely accepted that play is a universal activity and that children all over the world play. In more recent times it has become accepted that both adults and children play, and that play is therefore not wholly restricted to the childhood years. Indeed, play is recognized as being important for everyone's all-round development and wellbeing.

Many books have been written on the subject of play (Bruner, Jolly and Sylva, 1976; Einon, 1986; Moyles, 1989) which address both the definitions of play and the importance of play. Our task here is not to add to this but to accept that, since play is important for people with profound and multiple disabilities, so therefore are play materials. Moyles (1989) states that:

- Play must be accepted as a process, not necessarily with any outcome, but capable of one if the participant so desires.
- Play is necessary for children and adults.
- Play is not the obverse of work but a complementary activity: both are part of all our lives.
- Play is always structured by the environment, i.e. by the materials and context in which it takes place.

Moyles goes on to state her view that play also serves the function of being a potentially excellent learning medium, and one in which existing skills can be consolidated, practised and built upon. But above all, play is for pleasure. Garvey (1977) comments that play is enjoyable, even if, as Sheridan (1977) points out, this enjoyment is not necessarily obvious to others.

Although play is seen as a spontaneous and universal activity, like so many activities of value it often requires resources. Sheridan (1977) outlines four essential provisions for play: play space, play time, playthings and playfellows.

Play space is as important as the concept of 'personal space' and provides the person with a territory within which to feel safe and out of which to venture. Play time is seen as a peaceful and predictable time which is sufficient for the fulfilment of the play activity but not so long as to create boredom. She states that playthings must be appropriate for the person's age and stage of development and growth, and that there must not be too many or too few for fear of over or understimulation. Newson and Newson (1979) argue that a child's first plaything can be seen to be his or her primary care-giver. A child may, for instance, reach to grasp or touch its mother's face. At the earliest stages of play development a playfellow or playmate may be seen as plaything or as a form of play material. Playfellows are necessary at all stages of development to fulfil different roles within the play activity.

CATEGORIES OF PLAY

Play has been defined and redefined into many different categories, generally reflecting the individual skills and stage of development of the person who is doing the playing. In short, the type of play a person engages in varies with their needs and abilities. Whatever classification of play one uses, it is possible to see it in terms of a developmental continuum, paralleling human development and learning. If we take a relatively simple fourfold classification of active physical play, manipulative play, imaginative play and social play, it is possible to see each category as having its roots in very early development and moving through various stages to culminate in sophisticated activities carried out by skilled autonomous adults in society. Play materials required for each type and stage of play will change as the nature of the individual's play changes.

Active physical play may be seen to begin in the womb (Diagram Group, 1986) and to continue through childhood and into adulthood; it involves the large muscles and through it the child achieves physical control, coordination and balance, possibly leading towards skills in gymnastic or sporting activities. Manipulative play teaches control of the finer muscles, especially those in the hands. Beginning soon after birth as a baby learns to reach, grasp and hold, play may lead to such complex skills as drawing, writing and handicrafts such as embroidery or model-making. Imaginative and creative play helps the development of self-awareness and experiences of roles and situations beyond the child's immediate experience. It allows for the safe expression of emotions. Finally, within this particular classification of play, social play is seen as an essential part of social and emotional development, enabling the child to learn about sharing, turn-taking, cooperation and building satisfactory relationships with peers.

Play, then, at all levels and in each category, requires particular resources, be they playthings, playmates, play space or play time. What, then, makes it difficult for people with profound and multiple disabilities to play? Their disabilities are likely to restrict the opportunities for satisfying their needs for play because of the limitations they impose. Among such disabilities will be some or all of the following: learning disability, physical disability, sensory impairment and poor motivation, leading to a high degree of dependence on others for the satisfaction of personal needs, wishes and desires. When a person is affected by a combination of disabilities these are likely to create a complex barrier to interaction with the people and objects in that person's surroundings, i.e. the play materials necessary for satisfying play needs.

THE EFFECT OF DISABILITIES ON PLAY

How do such disabilities affect a person's ability to create and enjoy play opportunities for themselves? As we have seen, play is a spontaneous and universal activity. It is actively engaged in by the player and involves a wide variety of activities occurring in a developmental sequence, contributing to the person's continuing development and wellbeing. People with profound learning disabilities are likely to have a very limited range of strategies and skills for exploring and controlling their surroundings. It is this ability to explore and control which makes actions worthwhile, and helps to maintain interest in the activity.

If, in addition, a person's movements are seriously restricted or distorted so that planned actions cannot be successfully carried out, the interest, motivation, or even the ability to play may be considerably reduced. Add to this the fact that information from the senses – vision, hearing, touch, taste and smell – may be distorted or restricted, making it even more difficult for the person with profound and multiple disabilities to succeed in the actions and interactions they wish to undertake, then the barriers to playing successfully, enjoyably and creatively can seem unsurmountable. Therefore we must make playing as easy and satisfying as possible to prevent the player from becoming discouraged and giving up.

However, you only have to watch the interest, enjoyment and perseverance on the part of many people in this group to know that play is a fundamental need which can be enjoyed by all. The challenge is for those people who work with and care for this group of people to make play a positive experience, and to provide the environment, the materials and the context that make play possible, enjoyable and creative, however great the degree of disability.

Newson and Newson (1979) said: 'play comes first: toys merely follow', but perhaps in the case of people with profound and multiple disabilities suitable resources and conditions for play may have to be provided before the latent need, desire, interest and sheer effort required for play can be activated. The more complex a person's disability, the more individually designed their playthings may need to be, and the greater the attention that must be given to the context in which play is to happen in order to cater for their play needs. However, we must also not forget that play can happen anywhere, at any time, wherever and whenever the opportunity and state of mind for enjoyment arises. It is also important to bear in mind that conventional commercially produced toys are not essential to play, and that anything with which a person plays can be useful for that person.

A SUCCESSFUL PLAYTHING

What, then, are the characteristics of a successful toy or plaything? First, it must capture the player's interest and allow for the practice and integration of the person's current skills. Secondly, it must also allow for the development of new skills while providing a sense of pleasure and achievement.

With this in mind, what do we need in order to provide suitable play materials for a person with profound and multiple disabilities? First, we need to have a knowledge of the person – their abilities, disabilities, needs and motivations. Secondly, we should have an idea of what is wanted from the play in terms of allowing them to use the skills they already have and fostering new ones. Thirdly, it is also necessary to have some knowledge of the circumstances in which the person lives, be it in a rural or an urban environment, in a developed or a developing country, in a family home or in institutional care. With these aspects of the player and their world in mind, together with some imagination, we are in a position to find a suitable plaything for any one person, whatever their circumstances.

There are two essential resources necessary to make it possible for the person with profound and multiple disabilities to play. First, there is the contribution of an adult who can provide opportunities and encouragement either acting as a playmate, helping the person to play, taking part in the play situation, or simply being the provider of the play materials. Secondly, there are the tools for play, i.e. play materials, which are made up of anything with which a person plays. There is no such thing as a bad plaything unless it is dangerous. There is no plaything that is best for a particular person, but there are plenty of playthings that are irrelevant for a person at his or her particular stage of development.

The most important resource for the earliest stages of active play are other people, and playful interactions with adults are a baby's first experiences of play. The games can be very vigorous, and these experiences are likely to be particularly limited for people with physical disabilities. Movement games, such as those developed by Veronica Sherborne (Sherborne, 1990), can help to redress this by providing combined movement and interactive experiences for people of all ages. (The Sherborne Foundation will provide further information, see list of useful addresses.) The early active play of a child who is mobile relies more upon large equipment (either manufactured or natural) to use for climbing, swinging, rocking, jumping and riding around. There are now several firms who supply large equipment adapted to allow people of all ages with multiple disabilities to experience the excitement of these experiences.

COMMERCIALLY PRODUCED TOYS

The first things that usually come to mind when thinking about play and playthings are toys. The more severely disabled a child, or the older he or she is, the more difficult it is to find a suitable toy. For the very young child with profound and multiple disabilities there is a wide range of toys designed for babies which rattle, squeak, wobble or do other delightful things to interest the young child. They are relatively cheap, accessible and can fulfil the play needs of the small child well; they are appropriate in the way they work, their size, and the skills necessary to obtain results.

For the older child, the teenager, and adults who are at the very early stages of playing it is more difficult to find play equipment and materials which provide effects that are interesting and motivating, are an appropriate size and can be used successfully with a limited range of actions, whether this is because of the limitations resulting from a physical disability or because the person has only learned to use a few actions in exploring their surroundings. However, there is now a small but growing number of companies which design, produce or market toys and play equipment especially for people with special play needs. They are robust, often wooden in construction, and expensive. These playthings are usually of the 'reactive' type, i.e. they produce an effect with a very simple action from the player. These effects may be sounds – mechanical, musical or the human voice; visual effects, from moving parts, flashing or changing lights or reflective surfaces; tactile, including various forms of vibration and different textured surfaces; even aromas, activated by switch or some other action of the player. These playthings serve the needs of people who are at an early stage of development and can engage in exploratory and manipulative play (Figures 10.1 and 10.2).

Many of these toys are designed for tabletop or floor use, but some play equipment is very large and is designed to surround a child (such as a playring) or to be placed on a stand or wall-mounted for ease of positioning (such as a wall activity board), or used on the floor or table with the whole body or very large movements (such as play mats or cushions). Most of them are intended for use by one person at a time and equipment for games that involve more than one player at a

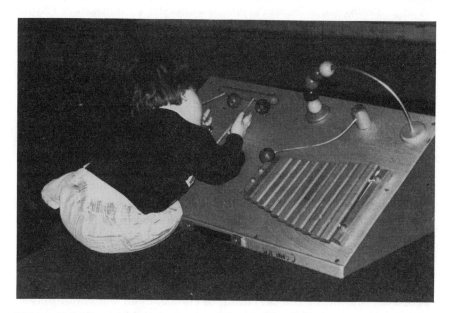

Figure 10.1 The sound and texture of the wooden balls on the activity centre appeal to this nursery-aged child, and encourage him to explore his surroundings.

Figure 10.2 The bells and mirrors on this reactive toy help this child to co-ordinate looking, listening and movement to provide a satisfying effect in spite of a degree of visual and hearing loss.

time is rare indeed. However, many playthings can be used in a cooperative way and 'rules' can be established by the people playing.

We must not forget the playthings which are common because of their universal appeal, such as balls. The range of balls available is vast: they can be large, small, hard, soft, light, heavy, coloured, patterned, plain, make a noise or not, contain bells, squeakers, have different tactile surfaces – the list of different properties is endless, and likewise their appeal.

Other commercially available, but not specialist, playthings might include executive toys, torches and lights from car accessory shops and a variety of things from novelty shops. One of the most universally popular playthings is a shiny survival blanket bought from a camping shop for a very small financial outlay.

It can be argued that, wherever possible, a commercially produced toy should be the plaything of choice, even if it is not played with in the manner intended by the designer. Although we would agree with this argument in general, it is fraught with difficulties when the player is an adult requiring playthings in the early developmental stages of play.

HIGH-TECH PLAYTHINGS

For the most severely disabled person, who may have a high degree of physical disability and sensory loss as well, playthings which are controlled by technology are useful. The area of technical toys is fast growing. It is not surprising that, in our ever more technical world, toys are becoming more and more technology-reliant. These can be of immense value for helping to motivate and enable a person with profound and multiple disabilities to play.

Elsewhere in this volume, Pronger describes the potential of the new technology for leisure activities for people with profound disabilities (Chapter 11). However, not all high-tech playthings make such demands on experience, finance and power resources. Many, such as mechanical toys, cassette players and other battery-operated items, are simple to operate. They can be easily converted to simple switch use which will enable anyone with even a minimal amount of controlled movement to play with them. The publication *Switch to Play* (NATLL/Play Matters, 1990) sets out all the necessary information for adapting and using such toys with switches. Nevertheless, it is important to recognize the value of simple or low-tech playthings which are either freely available or cheaply made, not requiring special equipment or a high degree of knowledge or skill.

NATURAL MATERIALS AS PLAYTHINGS

Before considering low-tech playthings, however, we should look at the play value of naturally occurring materials and items found around the home and in the environment. These will include sand, earth, water, vegetation, sticks, stones, cooking materials and domestic and gardening equipment. They cost us nothing, or relatively little, and are often in abundance in areas where commercially produced toys are most difficult to obtain. Exploration of such materials provides a wealth of experience which is not so readily available through manufactured and high-tech equipment. They encourage the use of touch and develop awareness of textures of all kinds, of shapes, the weight and strength of materials, and at the same time help to improve coordination and associated skills. They also provide a rich variety of forms to look at and many different sounds as they are used on different surfaces and in different ways. It can also be great fun collecting natural items on outings, such as twigs, leaves, fir cones, stones, etc. to use at home or school – or even better, perhaps, in their natural surroundings. Other natural playthings include the so-called 'free-play' materials which, although they may be bought to use as playthings, are nevertheless naturally occurring substances: sand, gravel, water, and clay, to mention just a few. There are many delights to be found in:

- splashing water;
- mixing sand or earth with water;
- burying hands and feet in sand or cocofibre;
- knocking down mounds of earth, sand or fibre;
- squeezing clay between fingers or toes;
- piling up twigs or leaves;
- rustling hands or feet through leaves;
- rolling stones or gravel in a tray;
- feeling fir cones with hands and fingers.

There are countless ways of using these materials (Figure 10.3).

Figure 10.3 Water is one of the most versatile of natural play materials and can provide a wealth of delightful experiences. Surrounded by water this young child is enjoying the effects of splashing while being safely supported by an adult.

There are also materials around the home which can be used as play materials, e.g. dry foodstuffs such as pasta shapes, flour, cereals and pulses. Add water to them and we change the feel of them entirely. Lastly there are all the items of equipment we use for cooking, cleaning and eating and drinking, which in themselves can provide many hours of satisfying play. The different sounds made by filling, emptying and banging them around can be most satisfying.

Most of these things are free or very inexpensive, are indestructible or easily replaced, and therefore allow great freedom in playing with them. However, we must always bear in mind the safety aspects, particularly of those things which are not normally used as playthings. Materials must be unbreakable if banged or thrown; non-toxic if eaten; too large to be put into the mouth if an obstruction would be caused if swallowed or inhaled; and not so sharp or prickly or rough as to cause injury. We must be vigilant, but not so protective that many delightful experiences are denied to those we are helping to play. It is vital that we realize the importance of allowing even people with the most profound and multiple disabilities to experience these aspects of life. It is very easy to protect them from the outside world and cocoon them so that they have little opportunity to learn about the ordinary things around them.

LOW-TECH PLAYTHINGS

In spite of all the play materials discussed above, there are some people whose play needs are not easily met by commercially made materials, high-tech equipment or even natural materials. For this group it may be necessary to create playthings specifically designed to provide for them the experience of satisfying play. This may sound daunting, but it need not be. These 'custom-made' materials are usually very simple in design and construction and can be referred to as 'low-tech', as opposed to 'high-tech' or commercially produced toys and playthings.

Over the years many people working in this field have made simple toys and playthings for disabled people of all ages for use in residential homes, hospitals, schools and their own homes, to be enjoyed with carers, teachers, nurses and their family and friends. All have been made to fill a gap in the commercial toy market, usually for a particular person and for little or no financial outlay. These low-tech playthings usually have in common certain features:

- They are easily made by anybody: no special skills are needed and their simplicity of design allows them to be adapted as the needs of the player change.

- They cost very little, being made from waste materials and odd-ments or items not specifically produced for use in play.
- They give the person a sense of pleasure and achievement, as they are designed to encourage them to use and develop the skills they already have.
- They produce an effect for little effort: this helps to motivate the player.
- Most have a multisensory appeal; this simply reflects the fact that they have been designed for people who may have difficulty in integrating sensory information or need help to make sense of residual vision or hearing.
- There is no right or wrong way to play with them; this assists the adult helper not to become anxious when the player follows a different path from that envisaged by the facilitator.
- They are made from locally obtained materials and are therefore likely to be acceptable to the culture in which they are conceived or made.
- Because they are made from materials which are freely available in the environment they are not age-specific, but can be made to be appropriate to any age.

Low-tech playthings are extremely versatile, as each one can be made with a particular person's play needs in mind (Figure 10.4).

What do we need to make such play materials?

- Knowledge of the person: their abilities, disabilities and what they particularly enjoy.
- Appropriate materials, i.e. natural materials, domestic or commercial waste materials, such as packaging, containers, etc., odd bits of fabric, ribbon or cord, elastic bands, thread, reusable parts of broken toys such as bells, interesting shapes, etc.
- Basic tools: scissors, craft knife, glue, string, tape, needle and thread.
- A little bit of imagination and a sense of fun.

The major disadvantage of low-tech playthings is that their value is often not appreciated. Both high-tech and low-tech playthings have advantages and disadvantages which make them more or less useful in a particular setting for a particular person. What, then, are the decisions that have to be made or the rules that we can use to choose between a high-tech or a low-tech plaything?

First, and most important, is the source of power required by high-tech playthings readily available and is there enough money available to buy, use and maintain the equipment? Secondly, are the

EMPTY PLASTIC BOTTLES   POTS   PANS   SPOONS

EMPTY PACKAGING FROM HOUSEHOLD GOODS

SCRAPS OF TUBING   PLASTICS + INDUSTRIAL WASTE

NATURAL MATERIALS   STONES VEGETATION WATER

Figure 10.4 Components for low-tech playthings (Mitchell, 1989).

advantages of high-tech really worth the outlay? In other words, never use high-tech if low-tech will do equally well. The status accorded to high-tech playthings can be seductive: think carefully. Thirdly, is the expertise to set up, operate, maintain and repair high-tech equipment readily available? Even if the answers to each of these questions is 'yes', low-tech playthings have advantages and qualities which cannot be provided by high-tech playthings, and these need to be considered when making a choice. First, they need no power source and are almost invariably extremely cheap to make, use and maintain. Secondly, low-tech playthings often offer similar or even better experiences than high-tech playthings: they can be truly multisensory. Thirdly, no expertise is required to 'operate' them, and only commitment, imagination and a few basic skills are necessary to create them. In addition, low-tech playthings can be tailor-made to individual needs and can be easily adapted or replaced as needs change. Because low-tech playthings are relatively cheap and easily made, the player can use them in the way that they wish without concern on the part of others that they are not being used in the 'right' way or that they will be damaged in the process. They are predominantly non-representational and therefore encourage a wider range of exploratory play. Finally, low-tech playthings can be made for any person of any age and, being made of ordinary everyday items, they relate to everyday life and to the culture in which they are made.

In conclusion, when choosing a plaything, whether high- or low-tech, the following questions will help to make your decision:

- What will the person find most interesting?
- Which will offer the most opportunity for the practice and integration of current skills?
- Which will encourage the development of new skills most effectively?
- Which will provide the greatest sense of pleasure and achievement to the player?

There are many sources of information and ideas for producing play materials and some of these can be found in the list of useful publications at the end of this chapter. However, for those who do not feel able to tackle the job of making play equipment themselves, there are sources of assistance available which may require some research but could pay dividends in terms of willing help to produce toys and equipment. They vary from area to area, and people and places to try might include some of the following:

- Local libraries;
- Adult education classes;
- Sheltered workshops;
- Adult training centres/social education centres;
- Volunteer bureaux;
- Retired craftworkers;
- Community service workers;
- Technology departments in schools.

DEVELOPMENTAL LEVEL AND AGE-APPROPRIATENESS

A major concern for many people is the need to provide play materials which are at the earliest developmental levels but which are also age and size-appropriate for older children and adults with profound and multiple disabilities.

The question of how age-appropriate play activities and materials ought to be for those who have reached adulthood has been debated for many years now, and it can generate strong feelings. The central dilemma is how do we provide activities and materials which are both age and stage-appropriate as people grow older and the gap between chronological age and developmental stage widens? Which of the two is the more important? In the interests of dignity, age-appropriate activities and equipment are necessary. In the interests of motivation, developmental progress and fulfilment, stage-appropriate activities and equipment are also necessary. How to dovetail these two elements is the problem, and an acceptance that at times one principle will have to be compromised in favour of the other is possibly the first hurdle to overcome.

In general, every effort must be made to ensure that what we offer a person, whether young or old, is as appropriate to their age as possible. There are some questions we can ask ourselves to guide our choice:

- Is there an obvious age group with which these play materials would ordinarily be associated?
- By how much does the age of the person playing differ from the age group for which the plaything was intended?
- How important is the function of the plaything to the person in their play?
- If the appearance of the plaything is inappropriate, can it be changed but the function retained?
- If not, is the function so important that it should still be used?
- Should playthings which are not age-appropriate be kept for a specific purpose, whether this is for use in a structured situation or to encourage spontaneous play without intervention?
- If the plaything is age-appropriate, can the person make use of it appropriately?
- If not, can the person use it in a way which is acceptable and dignified?

If we decide to use a plaything or activity for a specific purpose in spite of its being inappropriate to the person's age, we must make sure that it is used for this purpose alone and not accepted for general non-specific use, thereby putting the player's dignity in jeopardy.

There are, of course, good reasons for using many age-appropriate materials for older people other than personal dignity. Pop songs and traditional songs and music are more appropriate than nursery rhymes and children's songs, not only because they are appropriate to the person's age but because they are more likely to encounter them throughout adult life in the community, and they will therefore be more meaningful to the person listening to them.

Some equipment and activities are appropriate for all age groups, but need to be made both safe and accessible. The teenage boy in Figure 10.5 is enjoying his own reflection in a large, robust and safe tabletop mirror, which he can move to increase the interest of the reflection.

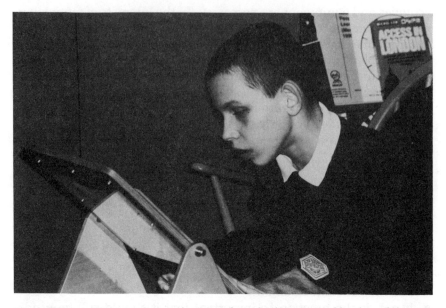

Figure 10.5 A tabletop mirror which is safe and robust is used by this adolescent boy. It is chosen in preference to a baby mirror as it is an appropriate size, relevant to both his age and his stage, caters for his particular interests and discourages his stereotyped waving around of hand-held objects.

Some of the best equipment for older age groups is the low-tech variety made from recycled bits and pieces already described. There is often no age association attached to the plaything itself because it is not a conventional toy and has therefore not acquired any age tag. It is likely to be constructed from items used by adults around the house or at work, e.g. soft drinks bottles, packaging for special items such as roller blinds, electrical goods, bales of material, toiletries, old buttons, cotton reels, etc. The functions will be appropriate to the early stages of playing, but the well-stocked 'home-made' playbox will also be irresistible to adults in all walks of life. This will ultimately show which of these toys fulfil the basic requirements of satisfying play materials (Figure 10.6).

The best play materials for any player are, of course, defined by that person's needs, abilities and personality. With careful thought, imagination and ingenuity the challenge of finding or producing a suitable plaything or range of play materials for anyone, whatever their disabilities, can be met.

Figure 10.6 This young adult is enjoying the sound made when he shakes a household container filled with buttons. It is safe, holds his interest, and he can use it independently.

REFERENCES AND FURTHER READING

Atkinson, P. (1991) *Switch to Play*, The National Association of Toy and Leisure Libraries/Play Matters, London.

Bruner, J.S., Jolly, A. and Sylva, K. (eds) (1976) *Play: Its Role in Development and Evolution*, Penguin, Harmondsworth.

Carlile, J. (1988) *Toys for Fun: a Book of Toys for Pre-school Children*, Macmillan, London.

Caston, D. (1993) *Easy to Make Toys for your Handicapped Child*, Souvenir Press, London.

Davis, S., Dawe, H., Hooper, J. and Reed, M. (1987) *Ready to Play*, The National Association of Toy and Leisure Libraries/Play Matters, London.

Dawe, H. (ed) (1989) *Play for All*, The National Association of Toy and Leisure Libraries/Play Matters and Lancashire Education Committee, London.

Diagram Group (1986) *Child Development: A Comprehensive Guide to Your Child's Growth and Ability*, Corgi Books, London.

Einon, D. (1986) *Creative Play: Play with a Purpose from Birth to Ten Years*, Penguin, Harmondsworth.

Fuller, C. (1991) *Tactile Books*, Resources for Learning Difficulties, London.

Garvey, C. (1977) *Play*, Fontana, London.

Hooper, J. (1991) *Toys and Play in Child Development*, The British Toy and Hobby Association and The National Association of Toy and Leisure Libraries/Play Matters, London.

Hooper, J. and Dawe, H. (1989) *Talk to Me*, The National Association of Toy and Leisure Libraries/Play Matters, London.

Jeffree, D., McConkey. R. and Hewson, S. (1977) *Let Me Play*, Souvenir Press, London.

Lear, R. (1977) *Play Helps*, Heinemann Medical, London.

Lear, R. (1990) *More Play Helps*, Heinemann Medical, London.

Lear, R. (1991) *Do it Yourself*, The National Association of Toy and Leisure Libraries/Play Matters, London.

Mitchell, S. (1989) Thinking about playthings for children with profound and multiple handicaps. Presentation to 16th World Congress on Rehabilitation, Japan, 5–9 Sept. 1988, pp. 38–40.

Mogford, K. (1981) *Mucky Play*, The National Association of Toy and Leisure Libraries/Play Matters, London.

Moyles, J. (1989) *Just Playing? The Role and Status of Play in Early Education*, Open University Press, Milton Keynes.

Newson, J. and Newson, E. (1979) *Toys and Playthings*, Penguin, Harmondsworth.

Ouvry, C. and Mitchell, S. (1990) *Make it Simple: Easy to Make Toys for Multiply Handicapped Children*, Resources for Learning Difficulties, London.

Riddick, B. (1982) *Toys and Play for the Handicapped Child*, Croom Helm, London.

Sherborne, V. (1990) *Developmental Movement for Children: Mainstream, Special Needs and Pre-school*, Cambridge University Press, Cambridge.

Sheridan, M. (1977) *Spontaneous Play in Early Childhood from Birth to Six Years*, NFER, Windsor.

USEFUL PUBLICATIONS PRODUCED BY THE NATIONAL ASSOCIATION OF TOY AND LEISURE LIBRARIES/PLAY MATTERS

Play Matters (1987) *Hear and Say: Toys for Children with Speech and Language Difficulties*

Play Matters and RNIB (1987) *Look and Touch: Play Activities and Toys for Children with Visual Impairment*

Play Matters (1990) *Special Needs Information Pack* (revised edition)

Play Matters (1987) *Special Needs Resource Pack for Adults*

Play Matters (1989) *Active Know How*

Play Matters Active Worksheets: Detailed instructions for making a wide range of toys and play materials for children and adults with disabilities. These worksheets are graded from the very simple to those which require knowledge and skill in woodwork, metalcraft and simple electrical circuits. Individual sheets are available for a small charge from Play Matters/ NTLA

Play Matters (1992) *Index of Suppliers of Special Needs Toys and Equipment*: This is a comprehensive list of catalogues of all firms which have produced play and learning materials which may be used with people who have a disability. The list is in categories, such as mainstream toy producer, specialist toy producer, high-tech toy producer, which makes it easy to use.

Hooper, J. (1991) *Toys and Play in Child Development*, The British Toy and Hobby Association and The National Association of Toy and Leisure Libraries/Play Matters, London.

PERIODICALS

Information Exchange, c/o Wendy McCracken, Oakes Green Royal School for the Deaf, Stanley Road, Cheadle Hulme, Cheadle, Cheshire SK8 6FR. Tel: 061 437 6744
This publication is written by and for those concerned with children and young people who have a sensory impairment and severe learning difficulties, and is always full of ideas for activities and materials to use.
PMLD-LINK, c/o Carol Ouvry, The Old Rectory, Hope Mansell, Ross-on-Wye, Herefordshire
This information newsletter is written by people working with children and adults who have profound and multiple learning difficulties and aims to provide a forum for discussion and exchange of news, views and information about activities and resources.
Eye Contact, published by RNIB Education and Leisure Division (see useful addresses).
This journal is published three times a year and is concerned with the needs of children with impaired vision and additional learning difficulties.
Focus, published by RNIB Information Service on Multiple Disability.
A newsletter for staff working with people with visual and learning disabilities.
Talking Sense, published by Sense, the National Deaf–Blind and Rubella Association.

USEFUL ADDRESSES

The National Association of Toy and Leisure Libraries/Play Matters, 68 Churchway, London NW1 1LT.
Tel: 071 387 9592.
This organization has a wide range of useful publications and advice leaflets, including information on the location of your local toy and/or leisure library.
British Toy and Hobby Association, 80 Camberwell Road, London SE5 0EG.
Tel: 071 701 7271.
Publishers of a catalogue of all toy manufacturers.
PLANET (Play Leisure Advice Network), Harperbury Hospital, Harper Lane, Radlett, Herts WD7 9HQ.
Tel: 0923 854861.
A resource centre with a display of toys and play materials of all kinds and a resource database with comprehensive information on suppliers, videos, books, etc.
Resources for Learning Difficulties, Jack Tizard School, Finlay Street, London SW6 6HB.
Tel: 071 736 8877.
This organization produces and markets teaching materials designed by practitioners.

Federation of Resource Centres, Greater Manchester Play Resource Centre, Unit 5, Vaughan Street, West Gorton, Manchester M12 5DU.
Tel: 061 223 9730
This organization can supply details of scrap banks throughout the country which offer manufacturers' offcuts and waste materials suitable for making equipment.

REMAP, National Organizer, J.J. Wright, Hazeldene, Ightham, Sevenoaks, Kent TN15 9AD.
Tel: 0732 883818
Local panels of professionals will help to solve problems of adapting or designing equipment for people with disabilities.

Royal National Institute for the Blind, 224 Great Portland Street, London W1A 4XX.
Tel: 071 388 1266.

Sense, The National Deaf–Blind and Rubella Association, 311 Grays Inn Road, London WC1X 8PT.
Tel: 071 278 1005.

Sherborne Foundation, c/o George and Cindi Hill, 1 The Vale, Pucklechurch, Avon BS17 3NW.
Tel: 0272 373647.
This organization promotes the work of Veronica Sherborne and provides information and training in using the approach.

Local Active Groups: addresses can be obtained from The National Association of Toy and Leisure Libraries/Play Matters (see above).

11

Microtechnology

Nick Pronger

In the early 1980s I was working with profoundly handicapped children in a special care unit at a hospital school, where we all felt there was a real need to develop new and exciting activities. Athough we used a number of battery-operated toys that the children enjoyed watching, they could not switch them on and off themselves. To enable them to play more constructively, a number of us started to find out how to make switches which our pupils could operate on their own. Our initial prediction was that only some of the children would develop an under-standing of the idea of switching, but as it turned out we were wrong. If we could find something a child really liked, and a switch they were capable of operating, then they would successfully learn the concept.

However, although we were interested in the academic side of the exercise it soon emerged that there were wider and more important aspects to what we were doing. Parents, delighted to see their children doing something that was stimulating and rewarding, added to the users' enjoyment with their increased attention. Brothers and sisters who wanted to play as well started interacting with their siblings in a more constructive way than before. Soon we found ourselves advising on the best sources of toys, showing people how to adapt them and how to make switches. Clearly, a whole new leisure interest had opened up for all the family. The ability to turn on and off radios and tape recorders meant that our pupils could do something that 'normal' teen-agers do in their own leisure time. It became clear that the application of a little technology could open up a range of new and exciting activities.

The step from using a switch with a toy to using the same switch with a computer is small, but the new opportunities opened up by the computer for education, and particularly leisure, are very extensive.

COMPUTERS ARRIVE ON THE SCENE

The age we live in is rightly called the age of technology. The microchip in particular has completely infiltrated our lives and can be found lurking in comparatively low-tech appliances such as washing machines and toasters. Our lifestyles are now greatly influenced by microchip products that were barely thought of 10 years ago, for example faxes, microwave ovens and wordprocessors. Against this background, attitudes towards work and leisure have changed.

The development of technology designed for those with special needs has rightly been led by education. As special education is a minor part of the whole education system, special schools benefited when a decision was taken centrally to introduce computers into all schools. Unfortunately, the training that should have come with them was rarely available, and it was some years before the new technology was widely used. However, the fact that computers were now available in the classroom gave interested teachers the opportunity to learn about computing and then to develop applications for their pupils. The result was the gradual development of special-needs technology applicable to both educational and leisure situations.

Why should you be interested in using technology for leisure? When considering the introduction of any new leisure activity the questions to be considered are the same:

- Is this activity seen as attractive by the participants?
- Does it add to their quality of life generally by opening up new opportunities for development of new interests, improved social interaction and utilization of potential abilities?
- Is it viable in terms of costs and expertise required?
- Is there a limiting factor in its future application?
- Is it fun?

The first four of these I can talk about in this chapter, the fifth you will have to find out for yourself.

HOW LEISURE RELATES TO EDUCATION

As you will have gathered from the introduction, my background is in education. I am involved in developing educational activities, primarily for schools but also for day centres and adult organizations. These must be enjoyable to be motivating. I consider it a great compliment if people choose to use materials I have developed for educational purposes in their leisure time. Clearly, one of my aims is to educate while the user thinks that they are playing.

It is perhaps worth considering here that one of the earliest require-ments for education is the ability and opportunity to play; thus much of the time in the nursery is spent in developing more intricate and complex play activities. Those who have a profound degree of disability do not have the same opportunities to do this, therefore any increased opportunity to enhance leisure activity presented by the computer is going to be beneficial educationally, no matter what age the user. If we can educate people to make constructive use of their leisure time, then they are going to benefit not only educationally but also in the social and emotional aspects of their lives. Thus educational and recreational activities are very closely interlinked.

WHERE TO START

As I have said, I started working with battery toys, tape recorders, radios and similar simple devices. Once connected to a switch we could play the 'on/off' game. I would show the user how to press the switch to turn things on and off; next I would say, 'whatever you do, don't press that switch'. I would then turn my back and pretend to be doing something else. They would then, of course, press the switch. I would then pretend to be very cross. This was a great joke and the children loved it. However, for many it was the first opportunity they had ever had to develop their sense of humour. Once the on/off concept is established, then it is only a small step to using the computer with switch-operated programs.

TERMINOLOGY

One of the problems with any new technology is that it comes prepackaged in its own jargon. Although I will try and keep this to a minimum, a basic understanding of the terminology and concepts is very useful.

Hardware and software

Fundamental to any discussion of computing is the difference between hardware and software, yet I know of people who have been successfully using computers for years who have difficulty with this concept. It is really very simple: a computer system is made up of two elements, the equipment itself, known as the hardware, and the instructions that tell the computer what to do, known as the software. Thus the computer keyboard, the monitor (computer screen), the disk drive and any related switches or input devices are all hardware. However, they are useless unless they do what we require of them. This only happens when sets of instructions, usually written on magnetic disks, are loaded into the system. These complex sets of instructions are called programs. Programs are collectively known as software.

As a producer of software I strongly consider that, no matter how technically good the hardware, it is the software that makes the system viable and easy to use. Without good software a computer system cannot be a success. Unfortunately, computer manufacturers pay little regard to this.

At this point it may be worth considering the strengths and weaknesses of particular types of computer. The world is divided into computer systems that are 'IBM-compatible' and the rest. The PCs (personal computers) are designed to work with software written for computers manufactured by IBM, the market leaders. But PCs are not necessarily made by IBM. These machines are designed primarily for use in running a business, although there is a variety of software suitable for other applications. However, the format does not lend itself easily to special-needs applications as it is difficult to obtain good graphics, sound and animation out of the basic PC machines. Of 'the rest', the leading educational machines are Apple 2 and Macintosh, Acorn, BBC, Archimedes and RM Nimbus. There is a range of software and special hardware available for these and the buyer should check this out for themselves. As there tends to be little compatibility between systems some careful planning and research before buying can save a lot of problems later.

Interfacing

Interfaces are places where two things meet. Thus where two pieces of equipment are connected, that is an 'interface'. However, the most important interface, and one that is often neglected, is the 'human interface'. This is where the user meets the computer. In most cases this would be at the keyboard, but there are other ways of interfacing people to computers that are more appropriate to their particular special needs. Whatever the method of 'human interfacing' used it should be the hardware that is moved to accommodate the user's requirements, and not the other way round. This may sound obvious, but I do see people forced to sit in uncomfortable positions because a table is too high or a monitor is at the wrong angle.

SWITCHES

The easiest way to enable someone to use a computer is through the use of the space bar on the keyboard. However, while this is often given as an operational option in programs there are a number of of problems. It is often hard to position the keyboard in a place where the user can easily access it. Keyboards tend to attract an overenthusiastic response from users, who bash every key in sight, often stopping the program in the process with the 'Break' or 'Escape' keys. However, the ultimate danger is that prolonged use of the space bar will break it, requiring the fitting of a whole new keyboard.

A more practical option is the use of single-switch input. This can be placed anywhere that the user finds comfortable. It can be as robust as required, and if it should come to grief it is easy and relatively cheap to replace. Therefore the introduction of a simple single switch is a good start to computing. The variety of switches available is enormous, making it certain that, given enough persistence, a suitable switch can be found for the user with the most profound disabilities.

The most commonly used switch has a simple action, staying on only for as long as the user holds it down. The pressure required will vary according to the switch type. If pressure is a problem there are electronic switches that require no pressure at all.

Switches are connected to the computer by means of an interface box. This is a box with a number of sockets that the switches plug into. The box itself plugs into the computer. The switch will then work the computer provided the computer is running a suitable switch-operated program.

For more complex programs a number of switches can be used, for example to move images round on the screen. An alternative method of doing this is a joystick. This will enable the user to move an image according to the direction in which they push the joystick. If the user were later to have access to a joystick wheelchair, the experience they will have gained playing games with this may prove useful.

TOUCH SCREENS

While switches offer a cheap and easy way of accessing the computer for people with severe disabilities, they do depend on the user understanding the cause and effect relationship. The user presses a switch on the table and something happens on the screen. Problems arise if the user is looking at the switch and completely misses the effect on the screen. Clearly, the nearer the switch is to the screen the more likely it is that the relationship will be established.

Touch-sensitive screens make the whole screen into a switch or an array of switches. These come in two forms. The first is like a frame that fits on to a particular model of monitor. It then detects touches on the screen via infrared beams. The second form, often called a 'touch window', resembles a clear piece of perspex that is attached to the monitor screen with velcro fixings. The physical pressure of touching the window activates it.

The attraction of touch inputs is that, given an appropriate program, the user can manipulate images on the screen by reaching out and touching them. The primary advantage of this is that the user tends to be looking the right way at the right time. This enables a quicker realization of the cause and effect principle. The main disadvantage of this type of equipment is that the user has to be physically able to reach and touch the screen. Careful positioning of the screen can help, but ultimately the user must have the movement control to direct his or her touch.

OTHER INPUTS

There are a number of other inputs available of a varying degree of usefulness to the user with profound disabilities. Two of the most commonly used are the overlay keyboard and sound-activated inputs. The overlay keyboard is a flat tablet on to which overlays are placed. These, in conjunction with the software, denote which part of the board is operating. At the simplest level the board could act as a single switch, but if required it could operate as a number of smaller switches. An example of this could be a simple program on animals. The overlay has a number of pictures of animals on it; when the overlay is located on the keyboard and the program is running, touching the picture of an animal will bring up a big picture of that animal on the screen.

There are a number of inputs triggered by sound. Some of these just act as switches when a sound of any sort is made. They can be coupled with any switch-operated software. Other devices, such as Micromike, only run with special software. However, these devices tend to be non-discriminating as to which sounds are responded to. As a consequence they can be triggered by background noise or by the user banging about in a way that may not be considered desirable.

SOFTWARE FOR LEISURE

Before discussing the specific types of software it may be worth considering the wider objectives of using the computer for leisure applications. For many people the computer is used either for 'serious' applications such as wordprocessing, databases or spreadsheets, or for 'non-serious' activities such as games. This school of thought tends to imply that playing games is a rather worthless and aimless pursuit. However, to limit the interpretation of events to what happens on the screen rather than the interaction between the user and the computer is to see less than half the situation. A VIP visiting a school where I was working took this attitude and made his disapproval of a child playing a 'Space Invaders' game rather clear. The pity was that he had not seen this child 6 months earlier as a sad, self-mutilating isolated individual. The introduction of the computer had given him the opportunity to build up self-esteem and had encouraged him to sit and concentrate for longer periods of time. He soon wanted to communicate with other children and adults about what was happening, how he was succeeding and what he wanted to do next. The use of computing technology gave the teacher the opportunity to introduce a number of activities as a reward for general cooperation. The hostel in which he lived, on seeing this transformation, was interested in acquiring similar equipment for him and other children to use in their leisure time: previously their main activity had been passively watching TV and videos. The lesson is clear: it is not what is happening on the screen that is important, it is what is happening to the user.

Types of software

There are three main categories of software suitable for people with profound disabilities. The first type is designed to establish the cause and effect relationship: the user presses a switch or a key to make something happen. Secondly, there are task-orientated programs designed to develop specific skills which can be used in other situations. Thirdly there are simplified 'games' programs. Although these look like 'real' games, they have enough flexibility in the options to enable people with a severe degree of disability to use them. A few suggestions of specific programs and sources of software are made in the reference section.

Cause and effect programs

A wide range of these programs is available, the simplest of which produce striking shapes and colours on the screen when a switch is pressed. There is often a facility for producing loud and intrusive noises as well. At this level a number of operating options can be introduced. The user can either press the switch briefly and then sit back and view the program running for a preset time, or be required to press and hold the switch to make the program run. In both cases there is a requirement to let go and re-press the switch periodically to keep the user active and interested. Simply physically relocating a switch so that more effort is required to reach it can introduce a greater degree of challenge to the use of any switch software. The ultimate goal at this level is to show that the user can make things happen.

For users who have better perceptual awareness there is a wealth of programs that build up pictures or patterns by pressing switches. The pictures are often made to animate with appropriate noises when they are completed. As well as being great fun these give an excellent opportunity for developing language and communication skills, and are often used by speech therapists and teachers.

Task-orientated software

The next step on from the simple causal programs above is to start to encourage a more active interaction between the user and the computer. In earlier programs the user has simply been pressing a switch when they felt like it to make things happen. Now we want them to wait for something to happen on the computer that tells them when it is appropriate to press the switch. The cues to press can be visual or auditory. At this stage it might be appropriate to introduce more complex inputs such as joysticks, so that the idea that a number of different responses can be made is developed. Programs at this level may give the opportunity for introducing very simple art activities, and manipulating colour and patterns. Also there are programs to enable the production and reproduction of sounds. The ability to manipulate a pointer on the screen developed through these activities can subsequently be used in conjunction with simple communication programs.

Games software

The problem with games software is that its use can lead to the experience of failure or defeat. While this is not in itself entirely undesirable, the challenge is to find games that can be made extremely easy to play at first, with the facility for gradually making them harder. The risk is that a person with profound disability may be reduced to a passive spectator rather than a participant. However, while the emphasis has so far been on participation, there is a place in computing, as in any sport, for active observation. It should be possible for an amicable turn-taking arrangement to be reached. Ideally, two people of widely different abilities should be able to play the same game by setting the relevant options so that they are both challenged.

Games give the opportunity for developing skills such as waiting, taking turns and anticipating events. They can also enable the user to be an active participant in pastimes that would otherwise be denied them because of their physical disabilities.

SELECTION OF SUITABLE SOFTWARE

The reader will have gathered that the initial restrictions on software selection are going to be determined by the type of computer system they are using and their own requirement for specialized inputs. Having overcome these, the next determinant of success is likely to be the flexibility of the options offered to adapt the software to the abilities of the user. If there is some doubt about suitability, contact the software vendor/producer before buying to see if there is the possibility of a 'try before you buy' or money-back arrangement should the programs not prove suitable. Most specialist suppliers will be sympathetic.

However, ultimately both the user and the carer must feel comfortable with the presentation and content of a program. The largest buyers of simple software are, of course, schools and this fact not surprisingly results in programs being produced for use by children. Therefore those working with adults often want to know how adult-appropriate a package is. This is such a common question that I feel it should be given some consideration here.

A few years ago this question might have been asked of computing generally. However, I am assuming that by now computer use is thought of as an acceptable adult activity. As to the software, the problem is quite complex. Apart from the fact that some images and sounds are definitely associated with childhood, e.g. teddy bears, toys, nursery rhymes and the like, culturally any simple bright image is deemed 'childish'. This raises two problems. The first is to do with the technology itself. Early computers had very limited memory capability, which meant they could only produce simple graphics. The result was that even an image that would not necessarily be seen as childish, e.g. a car, would look like a child's representation of a car. Thankfully, later generations of computer have a much greater graphic capability and can produce more realistic images.

However, there is a second reason to want simple bright images, i.e. they are easier for people with visual impairments to see. Clearly, the software producer has problems here. However, it is fortunate that graphics that are deemed adult are also rewarding for younger users. If these considerations are borne in mind from the beginning, a program can be equally rewarding for both groups. This can be additionally assisted by providing options to select types of presentations and tunes.

The decision as to which programs are used is probably going to be taken by the carer rather than the user. The danger here is that users will be denied the opportunity to decide for themselves. In my own experience if a program is presented openly to an adult as one written for children, but nonetheless interesting, even quite self-conscious adults will be happy to have a go. As with any activity it is variety that holds our interest, and to restrict choice artificially on rather contrived grounds is to risk losing scarce opportunities.

To summarize, the requirements for good software should be motivating graphics and sound, flexibility in type of input hardware used, and sufficient flexibility of options to enable the user to be challenged within the activity.

PRACTICAL CONSIDERATIONS

How should you go about choosing a computer system? As I have previously outlined, this is going to be largely determined by what you want to use the system for (software availability) and how you are going to use it (hardware compatibility). I do not feel it would be right to go into the merits of one system over another in detail in a publication like this, primarily because new products are continually being developed. I would, however, suggest to parents and other carers that there are probably local schools or adult day services using computers who may well be able to help and advise, and who may be able to provide an introduction to local suppliers. The system manufacturers or importers may also be able to provide lists of suppliers and at least one manufacturer has set up a special needs dealer network.

The cost of buying equipment is of course varied. As with any hobby or occupation it is probably best to buy good-quality equipment at the outset. Many computer systems are modular, that is, they can be built up gradually as the user requires extra disk drives and other upgrades. This means that it may not be necessary to start with a top of the range machine. As a rough guide, £1000 should purchase a good basic system plus specialized hardware and a selection of software to get the user started.

If cost is the primary consideration then a secondhand system may be a viable alternative. A relatively safe way of buying secondhand is through established dealers, who often take equipment in part exchange. They then service this and sell it with a short warranty. The disadvantage of older equipment is that it does not have the superb graphics and sound of the modern machines. However, this may be compensated for by a wider availability of software and secondhand or new hardware. One economy that it is tempting to make is to buy a system that will use the family TV or a spare TV, rather than a proper computer monitor. I would strongly advise against this: conflict might result over who is going to use the TV, and for what. It is often fiddly and inconvenient to convert from one to the other, and it would probably be better to do computing in a different part of the house anyway. The quality of picture is considerably better on a dedicated computer monitor. Indeed, if the user has poor eyesight it may be worth considering a higher-quality monitor from the outset, as it will greatly enhance the user's quality of interaction. Look carefully at trolleys and tables for ease of use. Arrange the system so that it can be set up and left out. If it is repeatedly plugged together and taken apart there is a good chance that it will become unreliable. It will be used more if it is constantly available anyway.

As with any hobby, buying the basics is just the start of the expenditure. Do make allowances from the outset for the specialized hardware and software needed to make the system viable. Also, budget for regular acquisition of new software (Christmas and birthdays are good excuses). While modern computer systems are very reliable if used properly, older systems may need periodic maintenance.

Hopefully, readers will now feel that computing is a viable and practical leisure activity. There may, however, be a lingering doubt over how the carer is going to get on with the complexities of the computer. I really feel that this is not a problem, given a willingness to learn. In the past, computer manuals were utterly unreadable, but this, I am pleased to say, has been changing. A combination of more powerful user-friendly computers and a realization among manufacturers that to succeed they must sell to a much wider market, have resulted in manuals and teaching materials that enable quick and easy access to their system. The user does not need to know anything about how the technology works to use it successfully, just as a driver does not need to know how a car works to drive it safely. Having said this, many people find they want to know more. Many schools and colleges now run courses on a variety of aspects of computing to satisfy this need. See the acquisition of the system as the end of the beginning, rather than the beginning of the end.

COMPUTING AS AN ENABLING TECHNOLOGY

If nothing else, I hope that the reader will go away feeling that computing has something to offer people with profound disabilities. Computing is often spoken of as an enabling technology: this is an idea that I wholeheartedly endorse. It enables people to enjoy new experiences and to take part in activities otherwise denied them. It enables people to experience success and the challenge of trying harder and doing better. It enables the sharing of experience and interest, resulting in an improved level of communication and understanding. But above all it opens up new opportunities, not only for the user with disabilities but for the whole family. I wish to end with an illustration of this. I was involved in lending a computer system to a family with a child with disabilities. The loan was a great success in unexpected ways: the local Scouts were interested and raised the money to buy the family their own system; the special school was supportive and lent software and hardware over school holidays; older brothers and sisters played more with the young person. However, the child's parents were also interested and experimented with wordprocessing when the children had gone to bed. Ultimately, his mother went to college to learn about computing and subsequently found a job as a computer operator. The lesson is clear: computing can seriously change your life. But above all it should be fun!

HELP AND INFORMATION

The purpose of this section is to give the reader a guide to sources of software, hardware, information and help. The first section lists suppliers and producers of hardware and software with particular experience in this field. The second section lists advisory organizations and their roles.

Software publishers and hardware suppliers

Acorn Computers
  Manufacture computers, including the BBC and Archimedes 32-bit machines. They have a helpful special-needs department.
  Acorn Computers, Acorn House, Vision Park, Histon, Cambridge CB4 4AE.
  Tel: 0223 245245.
AVP
  Publish a comprehensive special-needs software catalogue with special emphasis on PC software.
  AVP, School Hill Centre, Chepstow, Gwent NP6 5PH.
  Tel: 0291 625439.
Barnardo's
  Publish a suite of programs for the BBC called 'I can do it', specially geared towards those with profound learning difficulties.
  The Library, Barnardo's, Tanner Lane, Ilford, Essex IG6 1OG.
  Tel: 081 550 8822.

Brilliant Computing
A number of programs available for BBC, Acorn and IBM PCs using a wide range of inputs. Also supply switches, interfaces and touch screens.
Brilliant Computing, PO Box 142, Bradford BD9 5NF.
Tel: 0274 497617.

Daco Software
Supply a range of software and hardware, including voice-operated inputs.
Daco Software, 463 Warwick Road, Tysley, Birmingham.
Tel: 021 706 8933.

ESP
A specialist in creative music software, some of which is switch-operated.
ESP, Holly Tree Cottage, Strelley Village, Nottingham NG8 6PD.
Tel: 0602 295019.

Resource
Suppliers of touch windows and other alternative input keyboards.
Resource, 51 High Street, Kegworth, Derby DE74 2DA.

Mardis
Have some special software but also switches and communication aids.
Mardis, University of Lancaster, Department of Computing, Lancaster LA1 4YW.
Tel: 0524 65201.

NW SEMERC (Oldham)
Supply a wide range of special-needs software from a number of producers mainly supporting the Archimedes and BBC computers. They publish a comprehensive catalogue.
NW SEMERC, 1 Broadbent Road, Watersheddings, Oldham OL1 4LB.
Tel: 061 627 4469.

Microvitec
Manufacture touch screens for use with their own monitors.
Microvitec PLC, Futures Way, Bolling Road, Bradford BD4.
Tel: 0274 390011.

QED
A specialist supplier of switches and electronic devices, many suitable for use with computers.
QED, Ability House, 242 Gosport Road, Fareham, Hampshire PO16 0SS.
Tel: 0329 828444.

RCEVH
Fundamental software geared especially towards those with visual impairment.
RCEVH, School of Education, PO Box 363, Birmingham B15 2TT.
Tel: 021 414 6733.

TFH
Supply specialist toys, but also switches and computer programs.
TFH, 76 Barracks Road, Sandy Lane Industrial Estate, Stourport on Severn, Worcs DY13 9OB.
Tel: 0299 827820.

Widgit Software
A number of programs using various switch inputs. Especially geared towards younger children.
Widget Software, 102 Radford Road, Leamington Spa, Warwicks CV31 1LF.
Tel: 0926 885303.

Sources of help and advice

ACE Centres
Advise on the use of computers and microelectronic devices in education. They can assess the needs of individual young people and provide training to professionals. They also produce some specialist software.
ACE Centre, Ormerod School, Waynflete Road, Headington, Oxford OX3 8DD.
Tel: 0865 63508.
ACE Centre (Northern), 1 Broadbent Road, Watersheddings, Oldham OL1 4LB.
Tel: 061 627 1358.
CALL Centre
Aims to help people with disabilities to use new technology and techniques for communication and education.
CALL Centre, University of Edinburgh, 4 Buccleugh Place, Edinburgh EH8 9LW.
Tel: 031 650 4268.
CASE
Support the use of computers by clients with learning disabilities, especially interested in developing computer use by adults.
CASE, Psychology Department, Keele University, Keele, Staffordshire ST5 5BG.
Computability Centre
Supported by IBM, the centre seeks to provide information on all aspects of special-needs computing, especially geared towards PC use.
Computability Centre, PO Box 94, IBM UK, Warwick CV34 5WS.
Tel: 0926 312847.
NCET
Advisory body on use of technology in education.
NCET, Milburn Hill Road, Science Park, Coventry CV4 7JJ.
Tel: 0203 416994.
SEND
A special-needs database listing a wide range of available products.
SEND, Dowanhill, 74 Victoria Crescent Road, Glasgow G12 9JN.
Tel: 041 357 0340.
SNUG
Offers help and advice to special-needs computer users nationally. It has a number of local branches.
SNUG, 39 Eccleston Gardens, St Helens WA10 3BJ.
Tel: 0744 24608.

Spastics Society
Publishes a number of helpful guides on the use of computers by people with severe learning difficulties.
Spastics Society, Microtechnology Support Unit, c/o Meldreth Manor School, Meldreth, Hertfordshire SG8 6LG.
Tel: 0763 60771.

12

Aromatherapy

Helen Sanderson

INTRODUCTION

Aromatherapy is the use of essential oils, which are obtained from aromatic plants, to promote health and wellbeing. This ancient art has become increasingly popular and can be used as a leisure activity which enables people with profound and multiple impairments to experience relaxing and soothing touch, enhanced with fragrant oils.

Complementary therapies that involve touch, such as aromatherapy, represent a vast potential for enriching the experiences of people who have, in the past, often experienced isolation. The value and process of introducing appropriate touch into people's lives through aromatherapy massage is described in this chapter in the context of how it can be used as a leisure pursuit.

In addition to relaxation and enjoyment, the foundation of friendships is an important aspect of many leisure activities. Developing relationships, communication and interaction through touch can be achieved through interactive massage (Sanderson, Harrison and Price, 1991), which is also described in this chapter.

The accomplishment framework (O'Brien, 1990) identifies seven key areas that are important in the lives of people who have profound intellectual and multiple impairments; a lifestyle of a high quality involves selecting leisure activities that involve increasing and enhancing choice, community presence and participation, respect, competence, relationships, continuity and individuality. Throughout this chapter these will be considered in different ways, for example, acknowledging the importance of individual choice when selecting oils and discussing the value of visiting aromatherapists in the community.

Aromatherapy is experienced through the senses of touch and smell. Any introduction to this subject requires an examination of the importance of these senses in order to begin to appreciate the value and potential of aromatherapy.

THE SENSE OF SMELL

The sense of smell is a powerful and evocative sense which is often underused and understimulated. Astronauts suffered from olfactory deprivation during the initial long-term space flights as they had nothing except lemon-scented hand wipes to smell. These were soon saved for sniffing sessions and became valued items. During later flights astronauts carried bottled reproductions of familiar smells and scented items to prevent homesickness (Tisserand, 1988). In the animal kingdom the sense of smell provides information about territory, food and potential mates. The male silkworm, for example, is said to be able to detect a female by her aroma over a distance of 5 miles.

People are generally familiar with the terms used to describe someone who is unable to see or hear, yet the word which describes someone who is unable to smell – anosmic – is not widely known, although it is a condition which affects over two million people in the UK.

Research (Van Toller and Dodd, 1988) indicates that the sense of smell is powerful in creating moods and stimulating emotions. Smell memories are believed to last longer than visual memories. Many schools have developed activities and resources to encourage students to explore their sense of smell, recognizing that an improved awareness of this neglected sense can enhance a person's awareness of and pleasure received from their surroundings and activities.

THE SENSE OF TOUCH

Unlike the sense of smell, the importance of the sense of touch and the damaging effects that a lack of touch can have in people's lives has been the subject of a large amount of research (Montagu, 1986). This has illustrated how children fail to thrive without it, and the psyche can be damaged if appropriate and caring touch is missing from a person's life. We need to receive and give touch throughout our lives, as this reassurance and warmth enhances self-esteem and is essential throughout our existence. Hugs of friendship conveying warmth, understanding or empathy reassure us of the feelings of others towards us and touch transcends the restrictions imposed by language and disabilities.

The pleasure of touching and being touched is not often available to people who have profound intellectual and multiple impairments, and as a consequence they may seek their tactile stimulation in other, less appropriate and damaging, ways, through rocking or self-abuse (Hogg, Sebba and Lambe, 1990). An aromatherapy massage can introduce age-appropriate and valuable touch into a person's life which can help them feel nourished and valued. It can have a powerfully relaxing effect, as the body is soothed and scented through the combination of diluted essential oils with caring touch which has brought healing and restoration to people for many centuries.

AN ANCIENT ART

The popularity of aromatherapy has significantly increased over the last decade, and many people, including people who have disabilities, have begun to visit aromatherapists and use essential oils in their homes. Aromatherapists have been asked to visit day centres and hospitals to treat people there, and many people who provide services for people with disabilities have sought training in aromatherapy and use it to soothe and relax the people they support.

Although aromatherapy has only recently become popular, the principles on which it is based have ancient origins. The earliest recorded use of aromatic plants for medicinal purposes dates back to the Egyptian times. The Romans and Greeks discovered the benefits of essential oils as they were used during bathing and for scented massages. The Greek physician Marestheus recognized that flowers had either refreshing or relaxing properties (Tisserand, 1988).

In 17th century England pomanders made of cloves and oranges were used in an attempt to ward off plagues, and strewing herbs were used on the floors of houses for the same purpose. In the 19th century chemists began to create synthetic drugs, and gradually the use of herbs and aromatic plants for medicinal purposes became less common. However, it is a French chemist, Gattefosse, who is known as the 'father' of aromatherapy. He first used the term 'aromatherapie' in 1928 in the first book on the subject. He had become interested in the therapeutic potential of essential oils through an accident which occurred in his own laboratory. A small explosion burned his hand severely and he immediately put his hand into the nearest liquid available, which happened to be essential oil of lavender. The speed with which his hand healed, with minimal scarring, suggested that the essential oil of lavender could be used to promote healing. His research in this field was supplemented by Valnet, who used essential oils during the first world war when he worked as a surgeon in the field hospitals. The contributions of these two men laid the foundations for modern aromatherapy.

The practice of aromatherapy has developed in many ways since the initial work of Gattefosse and Valnet. In England, essential oils are used by aromatherapists in massage, baths, compresses, vaporizers and lotions. In France, where most aromatherapists are medically trained doctors, essential oils may also be injected or taken internally. Aromatherapy is a complementary practice based on a holistic view of people which takes into account all aspects of the person's mental and physical health in order to promote health and general wellbeing. In the context of this chapter we shall be looking at the most popular way of using aromatherapy, which is to help people to relax.

ESSENTIAL OILS

Essential oils are volatile essences derived from different parts of fragrant plants: from the flowers, seeds, fruit, leaves, wood or the whole of the plant itself. Different methods are used to extract the essential oil. The flowers of the lavender plant become the essential oil of lavender through a process of steam distillation, and the fruit of an orange becomes essential oil of orange after the peel is squeezed and expressed. Each essential oil has therapeutic properties, which may include antiseptic, antifungal or anti-inflammatory actions in addition to their relaxing, uplifting, invigorating or balancing effects.

Popular essential oils

There are over 50 different essential oils available; some of the most popular, which are used to help people to relax, include lavender, chamomile, geranium and sandalwood. Essential oil of **lavender** is generally considered to be the most popular and versatile, and has a sweet, familiar aroma. Another popular oil is essential oil of **chamomile**, which is soothing and calming. **Geranium** essential oil is uplifting and relaxing and has a fresh, floral scent. Essential oil of **sandalwood** has an exotic and oriental fragrance which has been used in perfume for thousands of years.

Using essential oils

There are three main ways in which essential oils can be used: diluted in a carrier oil to make an aromatherapy massage oil; diluted in water in the bath or footspa; or vaporized into the air through the use of a burner. These methods are commonly used and are simple ways in which aromatherapy can be used in the home.

Aromatherapy massage oils

An aromatherapy massage can be completely relaxing, both mentally and physically. The essential oils are absorbed into the bloodstream, where they have an effect on the organs of the body, and the person will also be soothed by the delicate fragrance (Tisserand, 1988). To make an aromatherapy massage oil, essential oils are diluted into a carrier oil. This is an unscented vegetable oil, grapeseed and sweet almond oils being the most popular.

Mixing or blending oils is not difficult and there are a few principles which should be followed. The general principle to observe when making up a massage oil is to use two drops of essential oils for each 5 ml or teaspoon of carrier oil. To blend 25 ml of an aromatherapy massage oil, take a clean glass bottle similar to those available at pharmacies, and fill it with grapeseed oil. To this then add up to 10 drops of essential oil. Two or three different essential oils can be used together to make up the 10 drops. Shake the bottle and label it with the date and the essential oils which have been used. This aromatherapy massage oil will last for a few weeks; however, to make a massage oil which will last for a couple of months, add 5% of wheatgerm oil, a carrier oil with preservative properties, to this mixture.

Aromatherapy baths

Another way of using essential oils is in the bath. An aromatherapy bath can be wonderfully relaxing and is simple to create. Once the bath has been run, between four and six drops of a relaxing essential oil can be added. Again, two or three different essential oils can be used to make a maximum of six drops in total. The water should then be agitated and the person encouraged to stay in the water for 10–15 minutes. The benefits of the essential oils will be experienced through their aroma, and some of the oil will also be absorbed into the blood-stream (Valnet, 1980). Essential oils can also be added to footbaths (again, using four to six drops) to refresh and relax the feet.

Where people have difficulties sleeping, a few drops of one of the essential oils with sedative properties, which include lavender and chamomile, may be useful.

Aromatherapy burners

The third way of using essential oils to help people to relax is to scent the room with a relaxing fragrance. The traditional way of doing this is to use an aromatherapy burner. These may be ceramic or brass, and have a saucer on the top into which about a tablespoon of water is placed. Up to 12 drops of essential oil (either one oil or a combination of two or three) are then added to the water and the nightlight underneath it is lit, diffusing the aroma around the room. Electric diffusers are also available which, although more expensive, avoid the use of a naked flame. Another way to scent the room is to use a vaporizing ring, which fits snugly onto the lightbulb of a standard lamp. Vaporizing rings are either metallic or ceramic and essential oils are placed directly into the ring before it is placed on the lamp and switched on.

Using essential oils safely

In general essential oils are safe to use. There are a few contra-indications for some conditions and it is recommended that, when planning to use aromatherapy, a check is made in a book on the subject. If you are in any doubt, seek the advice of an aromatherapist. Where people are receiving specialized treatment it is important to contact the general practitioner before using aromatherapy with them.

Essential oils are usually used in a diluted form as they are extremely concentrated and could irritate the skin if applied directly to it. They should not be taken by mouth. If someone accidentally gets any essential oil or massage oil in the eye or eye area, wash thoroughly with cold clean water for 5 minutes. If after 15 minutes the stinging has not subsided, seek medical attention.

USING AROMATHERAPY WITH PEOPLE WHO HAVE PROFOUND INTELLECTUAL AND MULTIPLE IMPAIRMENTS

As stated earlier, the most popular way of using aromatherapy is to soothe and relax. The ways in which essential oils can be used to do this, in massage, baths and burners, have been described briefly and we will now consider in more detail how aromatherapy can be used with people with profound intellectual and multiple impairments. We will also examine the use of interactive massage, where massage can be used as a participative, rather than a passive, activity.

Visiting an aromatherapist

Most people who are interested in aromatherapy either visit an aromatherapist or buy one of the many books on the subject and a few essential oils and begin to use them at home. These are the two most valued and usual ways of enabling a person with profound intellectual and multiple impairments to experience aromatherapy. Aromatherapists practise from their own homes, natural health clinics or beauty salons. An aromatherapy treatment usually lasts about an hour, although the first session may take longer as the therapist will need to find out about the person's health and lifestyle in order to choose the most appropriate oils to use. Once the oils have been selected, the therapist may massage the person's back, legs, arms, stomach, face, hands and feet, depending upon which areas of the body the person needs massaging. If the person has very tense shoulders, the therapist may spend most of the session on the back or shoulders. Some people may need a gradual introduction into massage and for the first few sessions the aromatherapist may just massage hands, feet, face or back, depending on what the person is comfortable with.

When considering enabling a person with profound intellectual and multiple impairments to visit an aromatherapist, it is important to ensure that the person is qualified and insured, and that the premises are accessible. There are two societies which keep a register of qualified aromatherapists in the area. These are the International Society of Professional Aromatherapists and the International Federation of Aromatherapists. Aromatherapy training schools can also provide a list of local aromatherapists.

Aromatherapy at home

Aromatherapy can be very beneficial when used with the person in their home to help them to relax. Enabling the person to choose their own favourite soothing essential oil is an important part of using aromatherapy with people who have profound intellectual and multiple impairments. Such people have limited opportunities to make meaningful choices and exert a level of autonomy in their lives. Any opportunity to enable a person to make an informed choice should be encouraged, and when using aromatherapy an emphasis should be placed on helping the person to choose which essential oil they prefer, when and where the massage should take place, which parts of the body they would like to be massaged and, most importantly, whether they want a massage at all. One way of achieving this is to present the person with two or three different relaxing essential oils to smell, either directly from the bottle or by putting a few drops of each oil on to a smelling strip, tissue or piece of cotton wool. It is sometimes difficult to identify which oil the person prefers, and there are different assessments and techniques which can help support workers in identifying the responses the person makes when they enjoy an activity, object or fragrance. One such assessment is the Affective Communication assessment (Coupe *et al.*, 1985), which involves presenting the person with a range of objects or activities and recording on a tick chart the responses the person makes. In consultation with other support workers, it should then be possible to identify how that person responds when they enjoy or dislike an activity. This can be used to identify favourite fragrances.

Once the person has identified a favourite relaxing fragrance, this essential oil can be used to create a relaxing bath, a soothing aromatherapy massage oil or to delicately scent a room to create a restful ambience.

After a difficult day, a room scented with a relaxing essential oil in which to unwind could be followed by a calming footspa session where the same relaxing oil is used. After the person has had their feet massaged by the vibration of the water and soothed by the relaxing aroma, a foot massage using an aromatherapy massage oil will complete the restful experience.

Preparation for massage

There are many different ways of using massage, from a one-to-one basis to working with a small group, massaging each other's hands for a few minutes or up to an hour. Whichever way it is used, there are some basic principles to consider which will help to ensure that the person is able to relax and receive optimum benefit from the aromatherapy massage. These involve preparing the person who is giving the massage, i.e. the practitioner, the person who is receiving the massage, and the environment where the massage will take place.

Preparing the practitioner

There are many books available on aromatherapy in general and literature is also available on how it can be used with people who have learning disabilities. In addition to reading about the subject, a training course will give experience and practice in massage. Some professional organizations recommend a certain length of course to their members to allow them to use aromatherapy in a hospital or community setting.

Before beginning an aromatherapy massage it is important to ensure that any jewellery is removed and nails are short. It is equally important to be able to concentrate and focus on the person who is receiving the massage. It is easier to establish this focusing, which is also

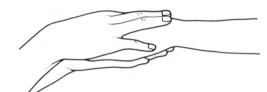

Beginning a hand massage
  Take the individual's hand
  in your own and sandwich
  it gently in yours so that
  as much as possible is
  covered. Remain in this
  position for 30-60 seconds.

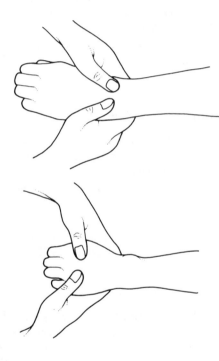

Wrist circles
  Use your thumbs to circle
  around the two small
  wristbones. The rest of your
  fingers are positioned under
  the person's hand to support
  it.

Thumb circles on the
back of the hand
  Keeping your fingers in the
  same position, move the
  thumbs down from the
  wrists and move them in
  small circles over the back
  of the hand.

Finger massage
  Supporting the person's
  hand in your left hand,
  enclose the fingers of your
  right hand around the
  person's little finger.
  Gently twist and pull the
  finger using a corkscrew
  motion as you slide your
  hand off the tip. Do this for
  each finger and the thumb.

Thumb circles on the
palm of the hand
  Hold the hand with both of
  your hands, with your
  fingers at the back and your
  thumbs resting on the palm.
  Make small circles with the
  thumbs over all the palm area.

Ending a hand massage
  End the massage with the
  'sandwich' with which you
  began it, and after you have
  repeated the movements on
  the other hand, explain to the
  person that you have
  finished the massage.

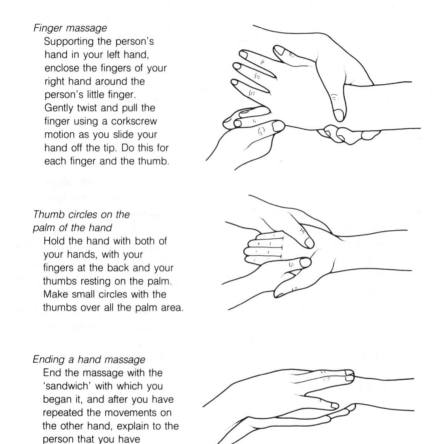

Figure 12.1 Aromatherapy hand massage (from *Mencap PRMH Project: Leisure Resource Training Pack*, (ed. L. Lambe), Mencap 1991, with permission).

known as 'centring', if the practitioner is aware of her posture and breathing, and concentrates on the person she is about to massage.

Preparing the area

The fundamental requirement of a room is that it is warm and draught-free. Furnishings should be selected which offer warmth, colour and texture, together with pleasing aroma and gentle sounds. Choice of ways of receiving aromatherapy can be enhanced by providing a variety of shapes and sizes of cushions, plinths, easy chairs or hammocks. An environment which is aesthetically pleasing will promote positive feelings and is more likely to generate interest and provide pleasure.

Preparing the individual

The issues of choice have been considered and another important aspect of giving an aromatherapy massage to someone who has profound intellectual and multiple impairments is to communicate that the practitioner would like to give a massage. The way in which this is done depends on the abilities of the person. If the person is able to sign, try signing 'M' for massage on their hand. Another alternative is to rub some masssage oil or make a circling movement with the flats of your fingers on the back of the person's hand, to communicate your intention. For people who have dual sensory impairment, giving an object of reference of a particular essential oil or lotion, such as peppermint foot lotion, to smell, can become a familiar sign that they can associate with massage. In these ways each person can learn to recognize the sign and be given the opportunity to choose whether they would like massage at that time or not.

HAND MASSAGE

A hand massage is a useful way to introduce a person to massage as hands are easily accessible and simple to massage. Figure 12.1 shows some basic massage strokes which can be adapted for most people.

OTHER USES OF AROMATHERAPY

It has been described how aromatherapy can be used to assist people with profound intellectual and multiple impairments to relax. However, compromises often have to be made where resources are not available to allow people to visit a local aromatherapist, and essential oils can be used to help people to relax in a day centre or club, perhaps as part of a relaxation session. Drama activities such as atmospherics can provide further leisure opportunities incorporating the use of essential oils.

Relaxation sessions

Identifying tension and being able to relax and release it forms part of many stress management and health awareness courses. Relaxation sessions can take place in various quiet environments, or sensory environments where fibreoptic lights and other equipment can help to create a soothing atmosphere. Vaporizing relaxing essential oils and using them in massage or footspas can help people to release tension, quieten and relax.

Atmospherics

Atmospherics is an activity which can be used at a club or leisure centre for relaxation, or at a drama session where essential oils are used to help to create the ambience required. Devised by Sheena Laurent, atmospherics is a group activity which takes place in a relaxing 'sanctuary'. Laurent (*Information Exchange* 1992, Edition 36) suggests that such an environment can be created with light and colour, using non-geometric forms which refract and diffuse the light. Relaxing essential oils form an important part of this as they are used to help to create this relaxing environment. Participants are encouraged to lie on the floor, mats and pillows are provided and appropriate relaxing music is played. The room is usually in semi-darkness, with 8–10 people lying on the floor. When the group is settled, large semi-transparent silks are drawn sensitively over the heads and bodies of the group in rotation. These silks are heavily impregnated with soothing and relaxing essential oils and are gently placed on the individual in order that the aroma can be inhaled. This can be effective and non-intrusive, allowing the enabler to make contact with a large number of people. The silks are semitransparent and therefore do not block out the sense of sight, even temporarily, which could cause the experience to be threatening. This innovative way of using essential oils demonstrates how versatile the use of aroma can be in the area of relaxation and leisure.

INTERACTIVE MASSAGE

Developing relationships and becoming involved in activities with other people is an important aspect of most leisure activities. The ways of using aromatherapy which have been described so far have concentrated on relaxation, where the person is a passive recipient of the experience. Aromatherapy can also be interactive, a shared experience with shared active involvement, from which a trusting relationship can be built. This provides a good basis from which to share other activities or learn other skills. Interactive massage (Sanderson, Harrison and Price, 1991) is based on the work of McInnes and Treffrey (1982), who identified an eight-stage sequence through which they believe people who have multiple impairments progress when introduced to any new activity. This sequence is as follows:

- Resists
- Tolerates
- Cooperates passively
- Enjoys
- Responds cooperatively
- Leads
- Imitates
- Initiates.

Initially, according to this sequence, a person may be resistant to the new activity. In an interactive hand massage, this suggests that the person may pull their hands away. McInnes and Treffrey suggest that you do not give up at this stage but continue, as the next stage in the sequence is toleration and the person may learn to tolerate this touch. In interactive hand massage this would involve trying very gently to stroke the person's hands fleetingly over a number of sessions until their toleration for this touch increases.

Further states of the sequence are passive cooperation, which leads to enjoyment. Using hand massage as an example, this would indicate that the length of time that the person could tolerate the touch would increase until they begin to cooperate passively. This would involve allowing the practitioner to turn the hand over, so that the other side can also be stroked without pulling away. If this continues over a number of sessions signs of enjoyment should soon be evident. At this stage the person begins to move from being a passive recipient of the massage to becoming more actively involved. The next stage of the sequence is 'cooperates actively', which may mean the person turning their own hands over when appropriate to be massaged on the other side.

From cooperating actively the sequence moves to leading, imitating and finally initiating the activity. At these stages the person who is being massaged may offer their hands in turn to be massaged, make stroking movements themselves, or try to massage another person's hands, and finally may reach the stage where they are able to give the bottle of massage oil to a person to indicate that they would like a massage, or communicate this in some other way.

If the person who receives the massage does not make any movements at all, then the practitioner moves the limbs or turns the hands over to massage the other side. In interactive massage the emphasis is not on an enjoyable, passive experience, but on interacting and involving the person with profound intellectual and multiple impairments. In practice this means waiting to see whether the person moves their own hand when one side has been massaged, and stopping to see whether the person makes any responses to any particular movement. Interactive massage therefore is a way of extending a relaxing passive aromatherapy massage into a shared, reciprocal activity.

CONCLUSION

Aromatherapy is a valuable, relaxing leisure activity and healing therapy where the therapeutic properties of essential oils bring additional benefits to the soothing touch of massage. Touching is contact and communication, providing a channel through which people can reach each other. Touch enables us to share and exchange, and is an enriching experience from which to establish trust, warmth, security and develop relationships. This chapter has described how, by introducing touch through aromatherapy, a wonderfully relaxing leisure activity can be experienced upon which a relationship between the giver and receiver can deepen and develop. However, aromatherapy is a shared activity and, like many leisure pursuits, it does not have to be a passive experience. Interactive massage enables aromatherapy to be used in an active and reciprocal way.

REFERENCES

Coupe, J. *et al.* (1985) *The Affective Communication Assessment*, Education Department, Manchester.

Hogg, J., Sebba, J. and Lambe, L. (1990) *Profound Retardation and Multiple Impairment. Volume 3, Medical and Physical Care and Management*, Chapman & Hall, London.

McInnes, J. and Treffrey, J. (1982) *Deaf–Blind Children: A Developmental Guide*, Open University Press, Milton Keynes.

Montagu, A. (1986) *Touching – the Human Significance of the Skin*, Harper and Row, New York.

O'Brien, J. (1990) *Design For Accomplishment*, Responsive Systems Associates, Georgia.

Sanderson, H., Harrison, J. and Price, S. (1991) *Aromatherapy and Massage for People who have Learning Difficulties*, Hands On Publishing, Birmingham.
Tisserand, R. (1988) *Aromatherapy for Everyone*, Penguin Books, London.
Valnet, J. (1980) *The Practice of Aromatherapy*, C.W. Daniel Co. Ltd., Saffron Walden.
Van Toller, S. and Dodd, G. (1988) *Perfumery: the Psychology and Biology of Fragrance*, Chapman & Hall, London.

ADDRESSES

For oils, contact:

Hermitage Oils, East Morton, Keighley BD20 5UQ

For details of training schools contact:

The International Society of Professional Aromatherapists, Hinckley and District Hospital and Health Centre, The Annex, Mount Rd, Hinckley, Leics LE10 1AG.
The International Federation of Aromatherapists, Department of Continuing Education, The Royal Mason Hospital, Ravens Court Park, London W6 6TN.

For training in aromatherapy with people who have learning difficulties contact:

Hands On Training, 62 Cobden Street, Wollaston, Stourbridge, West Midlands DY8 3RT.

Part Three

Leisure Training for Parents, Carers and Volunteers

13

Leisure workshops for parents and carers

Loretto Lambe and Helen Mount

INTRODUCTION

The organization of meaningful leisure-time activities for people with profound and multiple disabilities has always been a major concern of their parents and carers. Where to buy suitable equipment and toys, how to use them, what games and activities could be adapted to allow participation, whom to turn to for advice and help: these and many other similar questions were raised by families in meetings held in the early stages of the Mencap Profound Retardation and Multiple Handicap (PRMH) Project (since April 1992, Mencap Profound Intellectual and Multiple Disabilities (PIMD) Section). As an initial response to these concerns, the Project organized a 3-day exhibition of toys and equipment at a school in Manchester. Suppliers and manufacturers of specialist equipment in the UK participated in the exhibition, and families and relevant professionals were invited. An information sheet giving details of a large number of manufacturers and suppliers of toys and equipment was drawn up as a result of the exhibition. This is updated regularly and copies are available from the Mencap PIMD Section (see address at the end of this chapter). Following on from this, the Project organized a number of leisure schemes for children and adults with profound disabilities during holiday periods. Feedback from these schemes on the activities organized was passed on to parents and carers. However, it became clear that this was not enough, and that there was a real need to provide advice and assistance on leisure activities for families in a more formal and organized way. A further impetus to develop training, in the form of workshops on leisure provision for the parents and carers of people with profound and multiple disabilities, arose from findings on leisure needs in the Mencap PRMH Project's national survey

(Hogg and Lambe, 1988). In this, questions were asked about both existing patterns of leisure and the needs parents had for more information. A full description of these data will be found in Hogg and Lambe (1988) and Lambe and Hogg (1990). The principal findings, however, were that most families devoted a considerable amount of time to leisure provision for their daughter or son during the week, and an even greater proportion of time at weekends and during holidays. For all families, relatively passive pursuits such as watching TV and listening to music predominated. Families clearly indicated that they would welcome more information and advice on leisure provision. Although the demand for this information was not equal to other major areas such as assistance with communication or dealing with behavioural difficulties, the need was persistently indicated throughout the survey returns.

The above findings are clearly consistent with a wider view of the principles underlying leisure provision for people with profound and multiple disabilities. Several guiding principles of this philosophy may be noted. The first of these recognizes that leisure is essential for any individual's intellectual, physical, emotional and social development. Secondly, everyone, regardless of disability, is entitled to take part in the leisure activities of their choice. This principle emphasizes the right of people with disabilities to use the same community facilities that are available to the rest of us, and also addresses issues of access. It also recognizes that most individuals with profound and multiple disabilities may need to be taught how to engage in such activities before they can themselves spontaneously explore. Thirdly, it identifies the parent or carer as the fundamental resource who can best facilitate access to leisure pursuits. Fourthly, it draws attention to the need to consider activities appropriate to the age of a person with profound and multiple disabilities, while accepting that they are also developmentally appropriate.

ORGANIZATION OF WORKSHOPS

The leisure workshops discussed here were undertaken as part of a programme of 14 workshops covering a variety of topics run by the Mencap PRMH Project. All workshops have been evaluated employing an approach described by Lambe and Sebba (1988). Most, including the two workshops on leisure, were held during the long summer holidays when the Project ran leisure schemes for people with profound and multiple disabilities. Thus it was possible for sons and daughters to enjoy the leisure scheme while their parents or carers spent 3 days on the workshop. Similar leisure schemes were established for siblings without disabilities, in order to further ensure that parents could attend. Transport to and from the workshops and lunch was provided free, and no charge was made for attendance. Finance for the workshops was provided by a variety of charitable trusts.

Each workshop was run for 3 days, from 9.30 a.m. to 3.00 p.m., each spread across the 3 weeks of the summer leisure scheme, in July–August 1989 and 1990. Thirteen parents and eight professionals attended the two workshops. The second workshop underwent some revision in the light of the evaluation of the first undertaken by Prosser (1990). For illustrative purposes we describe here the timetable of this second workshop:

Day 1: **Using our leisure time.**

9.30 a.m.	Welcome and coffee
10.00 a.m.	Introduction to course
	What is leisure?
10.45 a.m.	Commercially available equipment – demonstration
11.30 a.m.	Practical session using equipment
12 noon	LUNCH
1.00 p.m.	Building resource banks – practical session
2.15 p.m.	Small group discussion
	Topic: Last two sessions
2.45 p.m.	Feedback from discussion groups
3.00 p.m.	TEA – depart

Day 2: **Arts and crafts and the use of microtechnology**

9.30 a.m.	Coffee
10.00 a.m.	Arts and crafts – demonstration of specific activities
10.45 a.m.	Practical session: arts and crafts
11.40 a.m.	Review of last session – questions and answers
12 noon	LUNCH
1.00 p.m.	Aromatherapy and massage – talk and demonstration
2.15 p.m.	Practical session: aromatherapy involving daughters and sons
3.00 p.m.	TEA – depart

Day 3: **Stimulating environments**

9.30 a.m.	Coffee
9.45 a.m.	Talk and video presentation on adapted games, snoezelen, dance and drama

10.15 a.m.	Practical session involving sons and daughters
11.00 a.m.	Creating multisensory environments: using commercial and 'home-made' materials
	DIY snoezelen
	creating a sensory garden
12 noon	LUNCH
1.00 p.m.	Using microtechnology
1.30 p.m.	Practical session: microtechnology
2.00 p.m.	Assessing community resources: slide presentation
	information exchange
2.50 p.m.	Evaluation
3.00 p.m.	TEA – depart

In addition, participants received an information pack (i.e. the 'participants' handbook') on leisure. This provided a full description of the organization of the workshop and extensive details of the materials and resources dealt with on the course.

AIMS OF WORKSHOPS

Several aims and objectives were established, which should be achieved by the participants by the end of the workshop. They would be able to:

• Comment on the features that distinguish leisure from other aspects of their son's/daughter's/client's life, making specific reference to activities that differ from education, training, therapy and care. They would also involve sons/daughters/clients in decision-making when planning leisure activities by noting preferences/choices.

• Identify one or more commercially available sensory stimulating object suitable for their son/daughter/client which they had not previously considered using.

• Demonstrate how to make one or more objects appropriate for their son's/daughter's/client's leisure activities.

• Describe three or more leisure activities which people with profound and multiple disabilities could take part in, and describe one or more activities for their son/daughter/client not reported in the pre-workshop interview.

• Set up one or more microtechnological devices unaided and be able to demonstrate the use of such a device. Related to this, they would also demonstrate how prompting is used to engage their son/daughter/client in using the device and be able to describe how to access such devices, i.e. from whom they can be borrowed, where they can be used, etc.

- Describe how visual and tactile stimulation can be an enjoyable experience for people with profound and multiple disabilities; and how environments employing such sensory stimulation can be set up and a game can be adapted so that someone with profound and multiple disabilities is then able to participate.
- Identify any special community facilities available to all Manchester residents (in the case of the workshops run in Manchester, this included obtaining resident's passes, which allowed much cheaper access to leisure facilities for Manchester residents); six community facilities generally suitable for people with profound and multiple disabilities; two facilities suitable for their son/daughter/client which they were not aware of at the pre-workshops interview.

CONTENT OF LEISURE WORKSHOPS

The content of the 3-day workshop was established in three ways. First, the evaluator conducted pre-workshop interviews with all the participants, which identified existing leisure pursuits engaged in by their son/daughter or client. These interviews (Prosser, 1990, 1992) confirmed the results from Hogg and Lambe's (1988) survey noted above, particularly with respect to the high prevalence of watching TV and listening to music. The interviews also identified areas of leisure/play in which parents and carers would like more advice and ideas. Secondly, it was necessary that the content should reflect the principles outlined earlier. Thirdly, and most importantly, the format and content of the workshop was designed specifically to meet parents' and carers' needs. The organizers had a long experience of working with people with profound and multiple disabilities and their parents and carers. They were fully aware of the problems faced by families, the restrictions that the caring tasks place on their time, the abilities of the daughters and sons who would be the focus of the workshop and the fact that families, in the main, were not used to attending courses or seminars. As mentioned earlier, these workshops on leisure were part of a series of workshops for parents and carers organized by the Mencap PRMH project. A tried and tested formula had been developed and, apart from the specific content related to the workshop topic, very few changes were made to the model. Sessions had to be short, interesting and practical. Everything presented in the workshop would be complemented with written back-up material, which would be contained in the participants' handbook. Additionally, estimated costs of equipment and materials would be provided, as would further sources of help, advice and, wherever possible, details of locally based leisure initiatives and services. The content of each session in the programme was planned against these three criteria. We will now describe in more detail the programme for the 3 days.

Day 1

On the first day there was an introduction to the workshop and a session discussing what we understand by leisure, emphasizing the issues highlighted in Chapters 1 and 2 of this book. During the second half of the morning, there was a demonstration of commercially available equipment specifically designed for people with profound and multiple disabilities. After the demonstration participants were encouraged to use the equipment and consider ways in which they might introduce it to their son/daughter/client, and what leisure purposes it might serve for people with profound and multiple disabilities in general.

After using the equipment they felt was most interesting, the participants were split into two groups and asked to discuss the advantages and disadvantages of using such equipment. They then came together as a group to report their findings. Some of the main points raised were that the equipment was often expensive, sometimes costing over £100. After investing what, for some parents/carers, was a considerable amount of money, the interest value had to be considered and some of the equipment did not rate very highly. Some participants commented that their son/daughter/client had a very limited concentration span so they lost interest within a few minutes. Also related to this point was the likelihood that continual use of the same piece of equipment was inevitably going to result in declining responsiveness. The issue of choice was again discussed at this point, as it became obvious that many of the people with profound and multiple disabilities were often presented with a particular activity and were not given the opportunity to indicate their preference for it.

Some of the large wooden activity centres were cited as being cumbersome and difficult to store in an average household, alongside all the other essential equipment such as wheelchairs and standing frames. However, participants did see a use for such equipment in a school or day service setting. In contrast, most participants had not previously considered purchasing a footspa, such as the one demonstrated, for their son/daughter/client. After trying it out, many considered that it would be a suitable present for either Christmas or birthday, especially as their son/daughter/client had poor circulation. Other items of equipment demonstrated were also seen as potential

Christmas or birthday presents, and the comment made by several parents was that it had been really helpful to see such a variety of equipment displayed, as it was often difficult to know what to buy for someone with profound and multiple disabilities. There is a considerable amount to choose from, and many of the toys demonstrated were not produced as 'specialist' equipment in that they are available as playthings for the majority of children. There has been little if any consideration given to equipment for adults with profound and multiple disabilities. However, very gradually, manufacturers and designers are becoming aware of the need to address this issue. Though much still remains to be done in order to redress the balance, they are beginning to work together and are also consulting with parents and professionals to ensure that their specialist knowledge is noted.

It was suggested that one way of overcoming the difficulty of purchasing an expensive piece of equipment and then finding it to be inappropriate for a variety of reasons, was to make use of toy or leisure libraries. The item could be borrowed, tried out and evaluated before any greater commitment to expense was made. The National Association of Toy and Leisure Libraries/Play Matters runs a large number of Toy and Leisure Libraries throughout the country. These cater for both children and adults, and the NATLL is aware of the needs of people with profound and multiple disabilities. It is worth contacting your local leisure library, and if they do not have items suitable for people with profound disabilities draw attention to this: every effort will be made to obtain relevant equipment. (The address of the head office of NATLL is given at the end of the chapter.)

The afternoon session illustrated several ways in which less conventional materials could provide ideas for leisure activities. There was a discussion about how we learn to explore our surroundings using our senses, and how people with profound and multiple disabilities need additional stimulation to help them discover and play. A variety of modestly priced materials were then displayed and suggestions were offered as to how they might be used. The issue of access was raised, as many people with profound and multiple disabilities have difficulty in holding an object or in moving towards it to explore it if, for example, it rolls out of reach. It was suggested that there are different ways of overcoming this and one way would be to use a simple wooden frame, like a small but stable goalpost on to which appropriate attention-gaining articles could be added. This method has the advantage of presenting a person with profound and multiple disabilities with several choices of objects to explore, even if this may only be a move or change of gaze. A discussion followed regarding the type and range of objects that might be used and how interest could be maintained by ensuring a regular change of objects. A suggested alternative to providing a random selection of objects made from different materials was to take a thematic approach and, for example, provide all wooden objects, all soft objects, all furry objects, all sound-producing or musical objects, and so on.

Bright, shiny materials such as tinsel, baubles (especially the faceted type) and a foil survival blanket were all shown to the participants. When used in a darkened room in conjunction with torches which had differing light intensities and even coloured lenses, a variety of visually interesting patterns was observed.

Other senses were identified in turn, and it was suggested that participants may wish to develop 'sensory' resource banks as a store of potential leisure activities for their son/daughter/client. It was also emphasized that activities that combined two or more of the senses could also be developed. Music/sound makers suspended from the frame previously mentioned could combine touch with sound. It could also add sight to other senses stimulated if the instrument had metal bells which caught the light as they were moved. A selection of scented fabric-coated sachets could combine touch with smell. This theme was developed further to consider other activities which may involve the participation of a helper or friend for the person with profound and multiple disabilities. For example, aromatherapy and massage combine the senses of smell and touch; cookery can involve all the senses.

Listening to music as a leisure pursuit was considered next. Compilation tapes that demonstrated the huge diversity of styles and types of music were played, and included classical, jazz, folk, country, pop, etc. The range and type illustrating each of these musical genres was also explored, for example instrumental as contrasted with vocal, differing rhythms, harmonies and types of tune. Participants were given the opportunity to comment on the different styles and to consider how they could be used to offer choices to their daughter/son/client. The cost of purchasing such a diversity of music was addressed by suggesting that if the person with profound and multiple disabilities joined their local library, it would be possible for them to borrow tapes and compact discs as appropriate, for a modest fee. This would have the additional advantage of offering further opportunity in this leisure pursuit. It was also suggested that if the choice of music was not acceptable to the rest of the family (or group), one way of overcoming this would be to use a personal stereo. One parent particularly welcomed this suggestion, as she had recently discovered that her son loved classical music and opera, while her own preference was for 'heavy metal' and pop.

Participants were then encouraged to design and make something from the materials provided which they thought their son/daughter/client might enjoy using, producing a selection of musical instruments, sound-makers and glove puppets.

Day 2

The morning session of the second day focused on a demonstration of, and participation in, a selection of art and craft activities. The issue of access was addressed initially within a theme of applying colour to a surface. It was shown that paint brushes and pens could be adapted for people who have difficulty in holding anything by the use of special grips and straps. Much of the content of this session is described in detail in Chapter 8. Once the various techniques had been demonstrated participants were invited to use the materials themselves, after which they brought their sons and daughters in to the session to see how they responded to the activities on offer.

The afternoon session was devoted to aromatherapy and massage as a leisure activity. General techniques of massage and aromatherapy were described and demonstrated, including hand and foot massage. The uses and benefits of a selection of essential oils were also discussed. Participants then chose a partner and gave each other a hand massage. The final part of the session involved the participation of the daughters and sons, who were given massages by their parents, and everyone took away an aromatherapy massage oil of their choice. The content of this type of session is discussed in much greater detail in Chapter 12.

Day 3

The final morning examined a further range of activities that people with profound and multiple disabilities could enjoy as leisure activities. Dance, movement and drama, sports and games, together with multisensory environments, were all discussed, and these were illustrated by supporting videos. One multisensory drama event was then experienced by all participants and their daughters/sons who were there. This was 'Galaxy', a space adventure which consists of a taped story interspersed with songs and music, and accompanying slides of the sights likely to be seen on the journey.

After this session, some commercially available multisensory equipment was demonstrated. Participants were shown bubble tubes, fibreoptic light tails, special projectors that had an accompanying selection of rotating wheels and cassettes, and a bubble machine. They were then given the opportunity to try these out for themselves.

It was recognized that much of this equipment is very expensive and could possibly have a limited interest value if it was available all the time. Participants were therefore shown much more modestly priced alternatives that involved the use of a variety of Christmas decorations, Christmas tree lights, foil survival blankets and fine white netting. Suggestions were also offered regarding how this material could be used to produce a restful environment or, alternatively, how a different use of colour could provide stimulation. Both commercially available and home-made multisensory environments are described more fully in Chapter 4. The final part of the morning session was devoted to the creation of a multisensory garden, a topic covered here in Chapter 7.

In the afternoon of the final day, the use of microtechnology as a leisure activity for people with profound and multiple disabilities was discussed. A wide range of computer programs and switches that had been specially developed to enable individuals with profound and multiple disabilities to operate them were demonstrated. Everyday battery-operated toys and other equipment were also shown, and it was emphasized that these can be easily adapted for individuals with limited motor control by the introduction of a suitable switch. A large part of this session was devoted to allowing the participants plenty of time to try out the various items demonstrated. Some participants brought their daughters and sons into the session and presented them with a selection of switches in order to establish which would be the most appropriate for their use. A full account of this area appears in Chapter 11.

The final part of the afternoon was devoted to a slide presentation illustrating a variety of venues that were accessible in and around the locality of the workshop. Suggestions included swimming pools, parks, gardens, museums and art galleries, among many others. For further discussion of ideas for outings see Chapter 9. Further information on all of the activities discussed in the content of this workshop can be found in the relevant chapters in this book, and in the resource sections at the end of each chapter.

Throughout the 3 days of the course, participants were also given the opportunity to observe other leisure activities not presented on the workshop. These were activities organized as part of the leisure scheme run in conjunction with the workshop (Lambe and Barrett, 1987). They include wheelchair dancing, music and movement, horse-riding and pony-trap driving, etc. Although most of these particular activities could not be organized in the home, parents welcomed the opportunity to observe their daughter or son engaging in such a variety of pleasurable activities. The horse-riding and pony-trap driving were of particular interest to a number of families, and for one mother the latter was one answer to her quest to identify leisure activities in which all her children could engage equally. This parent had four young children, two non-disabled and two with profound and multiple disabilities. She was constantly looking for ways in which they could play together without the activity being exclusively linked to the presence or absence of disability. The Shetland pony and small cart used on the leisure scheme would be ideal for her younger son with disabilities and her non-disabled daughter, and the adapted trap, which accommodates a wheelchair and also a child or adult and a driver, would be suitable for her two older sons. This type of equipment is available at most of the Riding for the Disabled Association's (RDA) centres (address at the end of this chapter).

EVALUATION OF THE WORKSHOPS

Both workshops were evaluated by Prosser (1990, 1992). A pre-workshop interview was carried out which established existing leisure opportunities and reviewed what areas would be of particular relevance in the workshop. During the workshop all sessions were evaluated using a content evaluation protocol, while at the end of the workshop post-course perceptions and future plans were established through an interview. Here participants also indicated the three best and three worst aspects of the workshop, and made suggestions for further improvements. A post-workshop interview, in the home, was also undertaken to establish the impact of the workshop on family leisure provision.

Pre-workshop interviews indicated that only a limited number of leisure options were pursued, and the difficulties of introducing new activities and accessing them were noted. Participants were motivated to attend the workshop in the hope that they would be given guidance on these problems.

During the workshop ratings of the individual sessions were consistently positive, with the exception of the microtechnology session. Despite increased 'hands-on' involvement, the new technology still presented difficulties for some, but not all, participants. The aromatherapy and massage sessions gained the highest rating, and its impact was confirmed by the number of participants who were found on follow-up to have introduced such activities into their home. The participants' handbooks were well received, and contact with other parents and carers, as in all workshops, especially valued.

A variety of 'best' aspects was noted. These included the resourcefulness of the arts and crafts sessions, the relaxed, informal and friendly presentations, the focus on age-appropriateness, the interactive nature of the workshop and the opportunity to meet other parents and carers. All respondents mentioned the aromatherapy session as one of the best aspects, though most sessions were mentioned by at least one participant. Most respondents noted 'none' for the 'three worst aspects', the only exception being a participant who found the noise of traffic on the adjacent main road disturbing. Many participants did comment that they felt the time available was too short, or that a further day would have been welcomed; these, however, cannot be seen as really 'worst aspects'. The only suggestion for improvements related to the situation of a single parent who would have preferred six half-days to the three full-day format.

With regard to proposed changes in leisure provision, participants were able to offer specific and general suggestions as to aspects of leisure the workshop had stimulated them to consider. Not surprisingly, in view of the above comments, aromatherapy figured large in these proposals, but so did the less well received use of computers. The follow-up home interview indicated that all partici-pants had successfully introduced new leisure activities for their son or daughter. As noted, massage and aromatherapy were introduced, as were aspects of sensory gardening. A parent who before the workshop had expressed difficulty in making varied provision, noted that she had tried out a lot of the ideas from the workshop. She had bought a footspa for her daughter, which was well received, and had improved the circulation in her feet. She had combined aromatherapy and massage using several scents and oils. Her daughter's bedroom was to be redecorated incorporating visual stimulation, lullaby light toys, etc. It is also interesting to note that a staff member from an adult training centre had replicated the workshop the following summer, while a teacher had organized fund-raising to purchase appropriate switches and computers.

Only a few restrictions to applying the lessons of the workshop were reported. For example, one participant, a teacher, felt that the suggested material, while appropriate for her individual child, would be too vulnerable to damage in a classroom setting. With respect to organizational aspects of the workshop, both the transport to and from the venue and the leisure scheme for sons and daughters were very well received.

Prosser (1992, p. 27) comments on the workshop: 'The evaluation suggests that the workshop in its present form was very well received by all who attended and certainly gave participants inspiration for trying out new leisure activities with their daughter, son or client. As suggested by the evaluation of the pilot workshop on evolving approaches to leisure held the previous year, participants benefited from the extended practical session which allowed them 'hands-on' experience with the microtechnology equipment ... very positive comments establish that workshops of this nature provide parents and carers with valuable information and advice which they would otherwise have difficulty in accessing. It is clear that this workshop on leisure presented participants with a great variety of novel and exciting suggestions for leisure pursuits. This is reflected in the change in participants' practice, noted on the follow-up evaluation, when all participants reported that they had successfully introduced at least one new leisure activity to their daughter, son or client which had been received with enthusiasm.

LESSONS LEARNED

These workshops on leisure clearly indicated to the organizers that parents and carers do want to learn more about this important area of their daughters' or sons' lives. Participants did benefit from attending the workshops and, as the evaluation showed, ideas and techniques developed over the 3 days were put into practice. It is important when organizing any training initiative related to profound and multiple disabilities to ensure that parents and carers are included. They are the people with the responsibility for full-time caring, but quite often are forgotten or overlooked by professionals. Initially we did not think that parents would want to spend 3 full days discussing and trying out leisure activities but, as noted above, participants cited the lack of time as one of the worst aspects of the workshop. It is also important to note that leisure activities do not always have to involve purchasing costly equipment, and that, given the correct help and advice, parents can and do organize very full, imaginative and varied leisure-time activities for their daughter or son with profound disabilities.

REFERENCES

Hogg, J. and Lambe, L. (1988) *Sons and Daughters with Profound Retardation and Multiple Handicaps Attending Schools and Social Education Centre: Final Report; Mencap PRMH Project Report 6*, Mencap, London.
Lambe, L. and Barrett, S. (1987) *Summer Playscheme for Children with Profound and Multiple Handicaps: A Report of a Pilot Scheme*, Mencap, London.
Lambe, L. and Hogg, J. (1990) Developing leisure initiatives for people with profound and multiple handicaps, in *Creative Arts and Mental Disability*, (ed. S. Segal), AB Academic, Bicester, pp. 67–78.
Lambe, L. and Sebba, J. (1988) The development and evaluation of workshops for parents and carers of people with profound and multiple impairments. *European Journal of Special Education*, **4**, 257–66.

Prosser, H. (1990) *Evaluation of the Pilot Workshop on Evolving Approaches to Leisure: Mencap PRMH Report 15*, Mencap, London.
Prosser, H. (1992) *Evaluation of the Second Phase Workshop on Evolving Approaches to Leisure: Mencap PRMH Report 19*, Mencap, London.

ADDRESSES

National Association of Toy and Leisure Libraries/Play Matters, 68 Churchway, London NW1 1LT.
   Tel: 071 387 9592.
Developed from existing toy libraries and has information on toys and equipment for people with disabilities.
Profound Intellectual and Multiple Disabilities Section (Mencap), Piper Hill School, 200 Yew Tree Road, Northenden, Manchester M23 0FF.
   Tel: 061 998 4161.
Riding for the Disabled Association (RDA), Avenue 'R', National Agricultural Centre, Kenilworth, Warwickshire CV8 2LY.
   Tel: 0203 696510.

14

The development of a leisure resource training pack for those working with people with profound and multiple disabilities

Loretto Lambe

INTRODUCTION

The impetus to develop the Mencap Profound Retardation and Multiple Handicap Project (PRMH) Leisure Resource Training Pack came from both the expressed needs of parents and carers, described more fully in Chapter 2, and the growing awareness in the National Federation of Gateway Clubs that Gateway was not as yet providing adequately for club members and potential club members with profound and multiple disabilities. In addition, the Hester Adrian Research Centre at Manchester University was at the same time involved in looking at such provision on a Europe-wide basis (see Chapter 3). Although the workshops for parents and carers described in Chapter 13 gave a very direct 'hands-on' means of disseminating information on leisure, it was clear that a distance learning approach would make such material available to a much wider audience. Representatives of these three groups came together and formed a working party to plan a leisure resource pack. The specific aim in developing the pack was to provide a distance learning resource that would be of particular relevance to parents, carers and volunteers working in the field of leisure and profound disability, although as we shall see, its use in a workshop context has also proved highly successful. It should be added in anticipation, however, that it is clear from its subsequent use that a wide range of professionals working in this field have also found the pack useful, and that its scope has proved to be much wider than at first anticipated. Nevertheless, while we have welcomed this wider use, the real target audience has always been the many individuals and organizations who are looking for ways of developing provision in this field, often with virtually no experience.

DEVELOPMENT OF THE PACK

The PRMH Project, Gateway and the HARC working party, supported by a variety of professionals working in the field, spent 3 years researching material and activities that would contribute to high-quality leisure provision for people with profound and multiple disabilities. It soon became apparent, however, that knowledge of leisure *per se* would have to be complemented by information on other aspects of caring for people with multiple disabilities, and the total situation in which specific activities were to be enjoyed. Thus background information on how to understand the person for whom leisure provision was being made and appreciate their strengths had to be provided. How to cope with the person's disabilities and their consequences had to be covered if the person was to be dealt with in a sensitive and dignified manner. It also had to be acknowledged that leisure would not be provided in a vacuum, and that an understanding of how to organize leisure and draw upon the wider resources available in society was crucial. In addition, although the pack was designed for use by an individual, it clearly had potential to provide the basis for workshops such as those described in Chapter 13, particularly in training volunteers working in leisure services (a development to which we return later in this chapter). The final pack, therefore, far from being just a list of activities, is in reality a comprehensive attempt to place the person with profound and multiple disabilities in a much wider context. Indeed, the evolution of such a view of the pack was one reason why its development took so long.

With this enlarged view of the pack's function, a principal challenge to the working party was how to organize and present the material in a way that was both intelligible and attractive. With such a burgeoning mass of information it became clear that the pack should be carefully broken down into well defined sections or modules. Thus an individual topic, such as how to go about understanding the individual for whom leisure provision was being made, was to constitute one module, while the actual leisure activities would make up another. However, the material covered in the latter case was extensive and a further subdivision had to be made into separate books.

DESIGN OF THE PACK

From the point of view of the designers who undertook the development and production of the pack, this division into modules and books was paramount; they decided that the modules should be clearly differentiated in the pack, and physically separated from each other. Similarly, the module concerned with leisure was also to be broken down into constituent books.

This approach led to the production of 11 distinctive books, brought together in a specially designed pack. The books were complemented by a videotape illustrating some of the activities, to which we will return later. Supplementary information in the form of relevant leaflets was also incorporated. The overall appearance of the pack may be seen

Figure 14.1 The Leisure Resource Training Pack.

in Figure 14.1. Each module is colour-coded, though all have a common appearance in terms of layout.

The sequence of books and their modular organization follows a logical order, beginning with a guide to the pack, as follows, which orientates the user to the contents:

- Introduction
- For whom is the pack?
- Some definitions
- Aims and objectives
- How is the pack organized?
- Starting to use the pack

This notes the scope of the pack with respect to a variety of users, including individual parents/carers/professionals, people with profound and multiple disabilities, those working in club settings and indeed ... 'anyone interested in leisure'.

Module A, 'Getting Started', is concerned with gaining knowledge of the individual and the situation, and is designed to give confidence to those providing leisure opportunities for people with profound and multiple disabilities. The module emphasizes the importance of gaining sufficient knowledge about the individuals for whom leisure provision is being made, and reminds readers that the basis for their relationship is ultimately going to be their own interactions with the person based on their own impressions and observations.

Section 1
Knowledge of the person
- Introduction
- Establishing interests and needs
- Strengths in development
- Sensory strengths
- Physical strengths
- Health

Section 2
Knowledge of the situation
- Introduction
- Physical management
- Hygiene
- Feeding
- Toileting
- Communication
- Management of difficult behaviours
- Management of epilepsy
- Transport
- Information resource index

The material covered was provided by a number of professionals specializing in this area of disability, including physiotherapists and psychologists. Supplementary reading is also included for those who may want to take their knowledge further.

The main component of the pack, Module B, is divided into six books, the contents of which are as follows:

Book 1: Having an effect on the world
- Introduction
- Using microtechnology
- Non-computer-based activities
- Information resource index

Book 2: Outdoor activities
- Introduction
- Winter sports
- Abseiling and rock climbing
- Water sports and activities
- Horse-riding and driving
- Exploring the countryside
- Information resource index

Book 3: Sports, games and their adaptations
- Introduction
- Principles of adapting sports/games
- Specific adapted games
- The Meldreth series
- Cooperative games
- Parachute activities
- Table games
- Information resource index

Book 4: Experiencing the world: Creative arts
- Introduction
- Adapted arts and crafts
- Sound and music
- Movement
- Dance
- Aerobic exercise and popmobility
- Information resource index

Book 5: Experiencing the world: Therapies and oriental arts
- Introduction
- Aromatherapy and massage
- Yoga
- T'ai chi
- Beauty therapy and make-up
- Information resource index

Book 6: Experiencing the world: Sensory environments
- Introduction
- Creating a sensory garden
- Sensory cooking
- Multisensory environments
- Information resource index

The books describe a whole range of activities which might be developed or adapted for use by individuals with profound and multiple disabilities. The emphasis of this module is on adaptation, the aim being to adapt and/or modify activities in which more able individuals will also want to participate, rather than attempting to establish a set of special activities. It will be noted that these activities are also the main concern of Chapters 4–12 of this book.

Each of the six books forming this module is organized around seven major areas. First, the activities themselves are described and, as throughout the pack, an emphasis is placed on trying to determine people's choice of an activity by observing their response to that activity. As noted in Chapter 2, people with profound and multiple disabilities often cannot 'tell' us directly whether they are enjoying an activity or getting something from it. Only by understanding them and their responses can we ensure that what we offer is as welcome as our own choice of a leisure activity would be. Secondly, the equipment that is required is described and the information necessary to locate it noted. Thirdly, the way in which we go about preparing for and organizing the activity under review is described. Fourthly, where an activity can be enjoyed is considered. In some cases this will obviously be in a person's home or service setting, but with some more specialized activities the person will have to go to a specific place, e.g. for skiing or sailing. Fifthly, safety issues are considered. While it is acknowledged that there is an element of risk in some activities, and this should not be denied to people with profound and multiple disabilities, those assisting with leisure activities have to act responsibly in making the provision. Faulty ropework in abseiling or dangerous wiring on a switching device does not enhance what has been called 'the dignity of risk'. Sixthly, throughout the pack community facilities where people with profound disabilities can enjoy leisure are identified, and the opportunities for integrated leisure considered. Finally, for each activity, an information resource index is provided which covers helpful addresses, equipment, books, etc.

We noted above that, although the intention was that the pack should be used by individuals, it could also provide the basis for a training course, and a description of how this may be undertaken is given in Module C which includes:

- Introduction
- Aims of workshop
- Programme and content
- Organization and administration

In the following section we briefly describe one such initiative.

Module D deals with monitoring and assessment of progress in introducing a leisure programme for an individual. It contains forms for completion that establish what is known about the person, potential activities, and their response to the leisure programme. While this module is an optional extra, and many will choose to become involved in leisure provision for people with profound and multiple disabilities without using it, as we shall see, it can provide a valuable tool to facilitate communication and might provide the basis for small-scale projects by staff or students with a special interest in this area. Xeroxing of the forms is permitted, so there is no fear of breaking copyright.

The sequence of books concludes with a comprehensive Resource Directory listing further reading, useful addresses, training initiatives and a very wide range of references and resources.

This index is supplemented by pamphlets describing the PRMH Project and Gateway, as well as the management of seizures and ensuring safe sport for people with Down's syndrome. A video tape illustrates a variety of the activities described in Module B. Here the intention is to show what is feasible, with activities ranging from multisensory environments through to abseiling and horse-riding. The video tape does not attempt to teach the details of these activities, but to show to those unfamiliar with leisure activities for people with profound and multiple disabilities what can be achieved, a function which preliminary feedback indicates it successfully achieves.

EVALUATING A PACK-BASED WORKSHOP

Following two abortive efforts in England, the Newtownards Gateway Club in Northern Ireland was identified as a receptive venue to conduct a pack-based workshop for volunteers in the field of leisure provision for people with learning disability. A report of this initiative has been edited by Mount (1993). The club is for adults with learning disabilities, and has 30–40 members. Volunteers join the club as associate members and are referred to as such. The age range in the club is from 16 years to 70 years. The club has its own purpose-built well-equipped premises. Leisure activities in the club are planned democratically, with committee meetings held to discuss which leisure activities are to be planned in the coming weeks. Members with learning disabilities serve on the committee, representing the interests of the other members. The range of leisure activities is wide, and on an ordinary club night might include snooker, table-tennis, pool, drawing and painting, cookery, doing jigsaws or just socializing. For those who enjoy dancing, a disco is held for 30 minutes each night. In the summer there is the opportunity to play a variety of outdoor sports. The Newtownards Club also has good contacts with community groups, including sporting links.

The club was clearly forward-looking and enthusiastic to extend its provision to a wider range of people, including those with profound and multiple disabilities. This enthusiasm began with the club leaders, and extended to both members and associates. Prior to the workshop the club's leaders and members had identified a group of young people with profound and multiple disabilities for whom involvement in the club was welcomed by them and their parents, and a principal aim of the workshop was to facilitate their integration into the club.

Following a period of detailed negotiation by the author, a workshop was held in Northern Ireland. It ran for 2 days, the first in a local hotel, the second in the club. The detailed programme appears on pp. 6–7 of Module C, 'Planning a pack-based workshop', of the Leisure Resource Pack. The timetable is described below (Mount, 1993, 20–21).

Day 1

9.30 a.m.	Welcome and coffee
10.00 a.m.	Introduction
10.15 a.m.	What is leisure?
	Whom are we talking about?
	How do we cope?
10.45 a.m.	General management of the person with profound and multiple disabilities
11.45 a.m.	Specific leisure activities
12.30 p.m.	LUNCH
1.30 p.m.	Introduction
1.40 p.m.	Accessing community resources
2.00 p.m.	Small-group practical sessions

Session 1:	Session 2:
Arts and crafts,	Aromatherapy &
painting/printing	massage

Sessions 1 & 2 ran simultaneously for 45 minutes each, then participants changed over

2.45–	TEA/COFFEE
3.15 p.m.	
3.15 p.m.	Sessions 1 & 2 changed over
4.00 p.m.	Session 3: (whole group)
	Building resource banks
	Arts & crafts: sensory environments
	Making/adapting materials
5.00 p.m.	Feedback from groups
	EVENING MEAL (whole group)

Day 2

Small-group practical sessions

10.00 a.m.	Session 4:

Session 4:	Session 5
Adapted games: the	Micros/switches
Meldreth series	

Sessions 4 & 5 ran simultaneously for approximately 20 minutes each, then groups changed over

10.45 a.m.	Session 6:
	Parachute games
	Wheelchair dancing
11.15 a.m.	Session 7:
	Optikinetics, light stimulation
12.30 p.m.	Parents and sons/daughters arrive
	Welcome
12.45 p.m.	LUNCH
2.00 p.m.	Practical sessions involving prospective new members and their parents
	Multisensory stimulation
	Aromatherapy
	Music session
	Music and movement
	Parachute games
	Computer games
3.00 p.m.	COFFEE/TEA
3.30 p.m.	Where do we go from here?
4.00 p.m.	Evaluation
	DEPART

The specific practical activities which made up the main part of the workshop incorporated the adapted leisure activities that make up Module B of the pack, although Modules A and D were also employed. Several of the pack's authors participated in the workshop, demonstrating activities in which they had special expertise and encouraging participants to join in. Fourteen associates took part in the workshop, of whom five had been involved with the club for over 14 years, with an average of 9 and a range of 1–22 years. Of particular significance was the involvement of the club leader and two assistant leaders, none of whom had experience of people with profound and multiple disabilities. During the second day the prospective new members who had been identified joined the workshop, accompanied by their parents. Although five had been identified, only four individuals were able to attend: the fifth was too ill, and although she did join the club for a short time, sadly she died some months later. The four new members who did attend were all young women between 23 and 37 years, with profound learning disabilities and physical impairments, and all used a wheelchair. Each lived at home with her family and attended the local Adult Training Centre. None attended any form of organized out-of-home leisure activity. During the afternoon the new members and their families were introduced to a range of leisure activities about which the volunteers had learned during the morning sessions. Aromatherapy/relaxation therapy, the use of microtechnological equipment and multisensory stimulation devices were all employed. The whole group participated in parachute games and wheelchair dancing. Discussion with parents about future involvement in the club then took place.

There were clearly, then, two outcomes of this initiative that were of central interest: first, the effectiveness of the workshop on leisure, in its own right, including responses to the leisure pack material; secondly, the extent to which the collaboration between those putting on the workshop and the Newtownards Club led to successful integration of the new members into the club setting. A thorough evaluation was undertaken and is reported by Prosser (1993). The evaluation procedure was in three parts. First, a pre-workshop evaluation was conducted in February 1990. This entailed the evaluator visiting Northern Ireland prior to the workshop. She met with and interviewed club leaders, associates and members some weeks before the workshop was held. Questions included knowledge of leisure and learning disability generally, knowledge of profound and multiple disability and of the specific topics to be dealt with on the workshop, e.g. what did they know about the use of microtechnology as a leisure activity?

During the course of the workshop participants' views on each of the sessions were evaluated with respect to their helpfulness. Immediately after the workshop, the participants' post-course perceptions and future plans were explored. Specifically, the evaluator set out to establish what leisure activities they intended to begin in the club as a result of their workshop experiences, as well as their judgements about the success or otherwise of the workshop itself. Six months later, a post-workshop interview was conducted in the club to consider the longer-term impact of the workshop and the degree of success in integrating the new members into its activities. The kinds of activities that had been introduced were noted, as were special successes or difficulties. Of particular interest were responses to the question: 'To what extent do the other club members integrate with the new club members?', and the exploration of how existing members had responded to their new peers.

The pre-workshop interviews clearly indicated the expectations of the participants. Specifically, they were anticipating learning about new approaches to leisure that would enable them to involve a wider range of people with disabilities in their club. More generally, their interest in leisure led them to hope for a wider appreciation of leisure activities as a result of the workshop. During the course of the workshop all sessions received positive ratings. The most highly rated were those involving practical sessions in which participants could join, such as parachute games, wheelchair dancing, aromatherapy, adapted games, the multisensory stimulation demonstration and the arts and crafts activities. Their expectation was that these particular sessions would have wider application in the club. Indeed, when asked what they found best about the workshop, it was interactive activities that had convinced them that leisure provision in the club setting for people with profound disability was feasible. In terms of information received, the participants were also enthusiastic, believing that they had been equipped to meet this particular challenge. A further important element that they valued was the cost-effectiveness of many of the activities, i.e. simple ideas with great potential that would not make serious demands on the club's funds. Negative comments were limited to organizational aspects and time constraints. Several of the participants would have liked to spend more time on particular activities and to learn more about the general management of people with profound disabilities. None, however, suggested any major difficulties that could be seen as suggesting that the workshop was anything less than highly successful. Indeed, for all participants expectations had been exceeded.

As part of this evaluation, information was collected specifically on the response to the Module A pack material on knowledge of the situation and the person, and Module D, i.e. coordinating resources, which was concerned with developing a leisure action plan. Module A was well received, with workshop participants typically commenting on its clarity and high information content. While noting some minor suggestions, this part of the evaluation indicated that no substantial revisions of the module were needed. Module D, however, required considerable simplification in the light of participants' comments, and the version in the published pack reflects this. Nevertheless, the value of documenting such activities is vividly seen in the way in which the forms provided in this module were used to illustrate the progress of one new member over the first few months. The following summarizes the programme as presented in these forms for one new member, C:

'Week 1:   Painting, bowling and dancing involving all the club. She wasn't interested in any activity tonight. No eye contact; no verbal or non-verbal cues.

Week 2:   Music video and bowling. This week she seemed more interested in looking at us, and she smiled quite a lot and laughed at a few helpers. Her eye contact was good and she appeared generally more relaxed and happier.

Week 3:   Cookery and painting. She appeared lethargic and

Week 4:
Week 5:
Week 6:

> sleepy, probably due to the fact that she had a minor seizure prior to coming to the club. No response this evening was noted.
>
> Galaxies; music and light stimulation. This evening S. and G. (two other new members) were not directly involved in C's programme.
>
> No signs of pleasure or dislike, although it appears she does not like loud music.
>
> Bowling; feather collage pictures; parachute games. As C. lacks voluntary movement she needs guidance when doing these activities. Some eye contact was noted when she looked at picture but this was momentary.

These careful and observant notes highlight several useful points. First, following the workshop, associates were able to provide a varied range of activities. Secondly, C. was clearly integrated into the activities other club members were enjoying: fears of a separate group developing were not realized. Thirdly, the associates were very acute in observing C.'s changing moods and interactions. Progress was not smooth and each week had to be taken in its own right and something new learnt.'

The value of such notes cannot be overemphasized in relation to communication between different people making provision for the same individual. Whether in a single setting, e.g. the club, or between settings, e.g. club and day service, they would help to ensure both consistency and variety in provision.

C. was, of course, one of the five new members who joined the club following the workshop, although for the reason given above, only four were considered in the evaluation. Observations some months later showed that they were fully integrated in the club, and that many of the activities dealt with at the workshop were incorporated into the evening's programme. These included ten-pin bowling, bowls, parachute games, wheelchair dancing, arts and crafts sessions, baking, Galaxies and microtechnology. Indeed, few of these activities were limited to the new members, and established club members were also often involved.

Prosser (personal communication) describes the response to new members as follows:

> 'Over the weeks the club's leaders and associates became aware of a number of ways in which the new members [with profound and multiple disabilities] were showing their pleasure at being involved in the club and participating in new activities. They noted an increase in smiling and laughing among new members and, in

general, they seemed to become more relaxed as the project continued. Two members were able to express their pleasure verbally and would tell volunteers whether they liked a particular activity or not. Volunteers registered new members' enjoyment also through eye contact, a sense of excitement, singing in the case of one individual and by their continued return to the club. Indeed, during the informal evening session, the driver of their transport reported that he too had noticed a change in individuals' behaviour since they had been attending the club. He was aware of a sense of excitement and anticipation on the nights he drove the new members to the club. He was also the driver for the transport that took these young people to and from their day services, knew them quite well, and was able to assess their responses.'

There was some concern in the first weeks of the new members' attendance that they would not be well received by the longer-term club members. Indeed, a few members did show apprehension, and even resentment at first. However, these responses were transitory and full integration was rapidly effected.

CONCLUSION

Evaluation of the usefulness of the leisure resource pack will be, of course, an ongoing activity. The Newtownards experience, however, clearly demonstrates that it provides an invaluable basis for conducting a workshop with volunteers. The material proved both informative and enjoyable. Both this and the introduction of new members in the context of the workshop clearly facilitated their integration into the club. Nevertheless, such a success was dependent in a significant way on the openness and motivation of both the club leaders and the associates. They wanted this initiative to work in a way which has not always proved the case when other clubs have been approached. However, their success and that of the club members indicates that there is no bar to involving people with profound and multiple disabilities in such club-based activities, any more than there is to extending their leisure experiences to the wider community. It is anticipated that the Mencap PRMH Project Leisure Resource Pack will continue to facilitate these and other models of leisure provision for people with profound and multiple disabilities.

Funding for the development of this work came from a number of grants awarded to the Mencap PRMH Project and the National Federation of Gateway Clubs. Grants were received from Burmah Oil,

Seabourne Express, Mencap/Gateway in Northern Ireland and the Stanley Thomas Johnson Foundation (Switzerland).

The pack was designed by Buxton, Wall, McPeake, Manchester.
The PRMH Project Leisure Resource Pack is available from the Mencap Profound Intellectual and Multiple Impairment Section, Piper Hill School, 200 Yew Tree Road, Northenden, Manchester M22 0FF, price £49.50 inc. p&p.

REFERENCES

Lambe, L. (1991) *Leisure for People with Profound and Multiple Disabilities: A Leisure Resource Pack*, Mencap, London.
Mount, H. (ed.) (1993) *Planning Leisure and Recreation for People with Profound and Multiple Disabilities*, Mencap, London.
Prosser, H. (1993) Evaluation of the training initiative at the Newton Gateway Club, in *Planning Leisure and Recreation for People with Profound and Multiple Disabilities*, (ed. H. Mount), Mencap, London, pp. 17–27.

Author index

Clarke, J. 4, *27*
Cole, D.A. 20, 21, *27*
Coles, E. 17, *29*
Coles, P. 7, *27*
Collacott, R.A. 13, *27*
Conneally, S. 63, *64*
Cotton, M. 14, *27, 176*
Coupe, J. 219, *225*
Crisp, A.G. 7, *27*
Critcher, L. 4, *27*
Croucher, N. *176*

Davis, S. *193*
Dawe, H. *193, 194*
Dayvault, K.A. 16, *31*
Deakin, D. 7, *32*
Deem, R. 15, *28*
De Kock, U. 17, 21, *27, 30*
Denziloe, J. 11, *28*
Dewson, M.R. 15, 16, *28*
Dines, A. 12, *28*
Dodd, G. 213, *226*
Douglas, J. 10, *28*
Duncan, P. 14, *28*

Einon, D. 178, *193*
Emerson, E. 42, *47*
Evans, G. 17, *26*
Evans, P. 3, 22, *28*

Fain, G.S. 3, *28*
Favell, J.E. 16, 18, 19, *31*
Felce, D. 17, 21, *27, 30*
Firth, H. 21, 22, *28*
Fitzherbert, L. *174*
Fitzsimmons, J. *154*
Flint, K. 124, *128*
Forrester, S. *174*
Fowler, M. 16, *33*
Frank, S. 20, *28*
Fulford, J. *154*
Fuller, C. 11, *28, 193*

Garrett, B. 23, 25, *28*
Garvey, C. 179, *193*
Gillard, N. 19, *26*
Golding, R. 3, *28*
Goldsmith, L. 3, *28*
Goode, D. 45, *47*
Graham, G. 10, *32*
Gray, L. *154*
Green, C.W. 15, *28*

Green, E. 36, *47*
Green, K. 18, *30*
Guess, D. 43, *47*

Hagedorn, R. 14, *28*
Haggar, L.E 8, *28*, 70, 78, 81, 82, *83*
Hamre-Nietupski, S. 16, 18, *28, 30*
Harchik, A.E. 46, *47*
Harris, J. 23, *28*
Harrison, J. 14, *31*, 212, 224, *226*
Harrison, J.A. 12, *28*
Hautala, R.M. 12, *27*
Hawkesworth, E. 137, *154*
Hebron, S. 36, *47*
Heddell, F. 10, *28*
Heeley, J. 4, *28*
Hegarty, J.R. 10, *28*
Hempshill, N.J. 21, *32*
Hesaltine, P. *96*
Hessayon, D.G. 117, *128*
Hewson, S. *194*
Hogg, J. 3, 4, *28*, 29, 37, 41, *41*, 167, *176*, 213, 225, 253, *256*
Hood, M. *154*
Hooper, J. *193, 194, 195*
Hope, M. 10, *29*
Hopkinson, P. 39, *47*
Horner, J. 9, *29*
Horner, R.D. 16, 18, *29*
Hulsegge, J. 7, 8, *29*, 67, 68, 70, 77, 78, 79, 80, 81, *83*
Hunter, D. 18, *27*
Hutchison, P. 19, *29*
Hutchison, R. 8, *29*
Hutchison, R.B. 8, *28*, 70, 78, 81, 82, *83*

Jackson, R. 90, 94, *96*
Jeffree, D.M. 3, *27, 194*
Jenkins, J. 17, *30, 83*
Jennings, S. 8, *29*
Johnston, R. 21, *26*
Jolly, A. 178, *193*
Jones, A.A. 17, *29*

Kalev, N. *96*
Kelly, B. 168, *176*
Kewin, J. 80, *83*
Knight, L. 13, *26*
Knill, C. 34, *154*
Knill, M. 34, *154*

Subject index